Bicycling For Dummies®

How much should you spend on your bike?

Ultimately, that's really between you and your accountant, but if you want to get the most bang for your bicycle dollar, try the two-bucks-a-ride rule. Got your pencil and paper ready?

1. **Figure out how often you're going to ride the bike.**

   Will you ride about twice a week through the spring, summer, and fall? That rounds out to about 50 times a year. Are you more of a once-a-weeker? Figure on 25 times a year. Will you ride four days a week or maybe a little more? That's about 120 times a year.

2. **Multiply your yearly figure by five. (Any quality bike should last you a lot more than five years.)**

3. **Multiply that five-year's-worth of rides figure by two bucks a ride.**

This formula puts a once-a-weeker on a $250 bike, a twice-a-weeker on a $500 bike, and an almost-every-day rider on a $1,000 bike.

What size bike should you get?

Before you go shopping, do the following:

1. **Stand with your back to the wall wearing the same kind of shoes and shorts you wear when you ride.**

2. **Take a book and put it between your legs as if it were a bicycle saddle, making sure that the edge is flush against the wall.**

3. **Reach behind and mark a spot on the at the top of the book.**

4. **Measure the distance between the floor and the mark and write it down.**

This is your inseam measurement, and you use this measurement to choose what size bike frame will fit best for you. Here's how you choose your frame size:

- If you're looking for a **road bike**, subtract **10** inches from your inseam measurement.
- If you're buying a **mountain bike**, subtract **12** inches from your inseam measurement.
- For a **hybrid bike**, subtract **11** inches from your inseam.

So if your inseam is 32 inches and you're shopping for a mountain bike, you should be trying out bikes with a frame size of around 20 inches.

These guidelines should at least get you within a ballpark range for choosing the right frame size. For much more information on this topic, see Chapter 3.

...For Dummies®: Bestselling Book Series for Beginners

Bicycling For Dummies®

Gear you shouldn't be without on your rides

Always have these items when you ride:

- **Sunglasses:** They keep debris out of your eyes.
- **Sunscreen:** You don't want skin cancer, do ya?
- **A dollar in change:** You may need to call someone to pick you up.
- **Money for a cab:** You never know when you're going to need to take a cab ride home.
- **An ATM or credit card:** It's always good to have a way to cover unexpected expense.
- **Your contact info:** Bring a piece of paper with your name, address, and phone number on it. It should also have your health insurance number and the name of the hospital where you'd like to be taken in an emergency.

Tools you need to carry with you

Here's a list of basic tools that'll pack up small and fit neatly into a saddlebag.

- **Hex (Allen) wrenches:** A 5 mm and a 6 mm. These are the ones that adjust your seat binder bolt and your stem.
- **A chain rivet tool:** This tool is optional for road riders, but mountain bikers had better bring one.
- **A frame pump:** Not only should you carry it, but you should also use it every once in a while so that you'll know it's working when you need it.
- **A spare tube:** Make sure it's folded properly, with the valve in the center so it can't rip or puncture the tube.
- **Three lightweight tire levers:** They should be small and light enough to fit in your saddlebag but big enough to do the job.

The IDG Books Worldwide logo is a registered trademark under exclusive license to IDG Books Worldwide, Inc., from International Data Group, Inc. The ...For Dummies logo is a trademark, and For Dummies and ...For Dummies are registered trademarks of IDG Books Worldwide, Inc. All other trademarks are the property of their respective owners.

Copyright © 1999 IDG Books Worldwide, Inc. All rights reserved.

Cheat Sheet $2.95 value. Item 5149-3.

For more information about IDG Books, call 1-800-762-2974.

...For Dummies®: Bestselling Book Series for Beginners

Praise for Bicycling For Dummies

"*Bicycling For Dummies* is the perfect antidote to esoteric bike shop snobs. It's a thorough, easily understood, and frequently hilarious book that will make you want to ride."

— Rob Story, Editor-at-Large, *Bike* magazine

"*Bicycling For Dummies* is a humorous, non-technical, straightforward introduction to all aspects of cycling. A kind of survival guide, if you will. I've been racing for 11 years and even I learned something after reading this book!"

— Alison Dunlap, Professional Mountain Biker, 1996 Olympic Team Member

"Allen St. John does a terrific job of covering just about every conceivable aspect of this increasingly complex sport for people who love to ride but hate wading through techno-jargon. In a humorous and user-friendly way, the book answers cycling's three big questions: how to buy a bike, how to fix it, and how to have fun while you're riding."

— Lucy Danziger, Editor-in-Chief, *Condé Nast Women's Sports & Fitness* magazine

"The section on riding with kids is straightforward, realistic, and — most important — helpful."

— Josh Lerman, Articles Editor, *Parenting* magazine

"*Bicycling For Dummies* gives every person on our planet a reason to dust off the cobwebs, pump up the tires, and go for a ride. When you're out pedaling, you smell the blossoms blooming, feel your heart pumping, and remind yourself that life is good. Whether it's for a casual ride to Starbucks or a more serious workout, this book will help you to get rolling. It's the most cost-effective therapy I know."

— Shari Kain, member of the Polo Sport World Cup Mountain Bike Team

"The quickest way to advance beyond bicycling dummy status is to buy and read Allen St. John's book. The mountain biking sections are right on target — solid information delivered concisely, yet lightly. Every off-road ride should be a memorable adventure. St. John provides a backbone of history, techniques, and environmental common sense to help you make it so."

— Tim Blumenthal, Executive Director, International Mountain Bicycling Association

"From a novice rider to an experienced racer, this book has something to offer everyone. Very informative and fun to read."

— Steve Morrissey, Operations and Equipment Manager, USA Cycling Inc.

BICYCLING
FOR
DUMMIES®

by Allen St. John

IDG Books Worldwide, Inc.
An International Data Group Company

Foster City, CA ◆ Chicago, IL ◆ Indianapolis, IN ◆ New York, NY

Bicycling For Dummies ®

Published by
IDG Books Worldwide, Inc.
An International Data Group Company
919 E. Hillsdale Blvd.
Suite 400
Foster City, CA 94404
www.idgbooks.com (IDG Books Worldwide Web site)
www.dummies.com (Dummies Press Web site)

Library of Congress Catalog Card No.: 99-62289

ISBN: 0-7645-5149-3

Printed in the United States of America

10 9 8 7 6 5 4 3 2 1

1B/RU/QU/ZZ/IN

Distributed in the United States by IDG Books Worldwide, Inc.

Distributed by CDG Books Canada Inc. for Canada; by Transworld Publishers Limited in the United Kingdom; by IDG Norge Books for Norway; by IDG Sweden Books for Sweden; by Woodslane Pty. Ltd. for Australia; by Woodslane (NZ) Ltd. for New Zealand; by TransQuest Publishers Pte Ltd. for Singapore, Malaysia, Thailand, Indonesia, and Hong Kong; by ICG Muse, Inc. for Japan; by Norma Comunicaciones S.A. for Colombia; by Intersoft for South Africa; by Le Monde en Tique for France; by International Thomson Publishing for Germany, Austria and Switzerland; by Distribuidora Cuspide for Argentina; by Livraria Cultura for Brazil; by Ediciones ZETA S.C.R. Ltda. for Peru; by WS Computer Publishing Corporation, Inc., for the Philippines; by Contemporanea de Ediciones for Venezuela; by Express Computer Distributors for the Caribbean and West Indies; by Micronesia Media Distributor, Inc. for Micronesia; by Grupo Editorial Norma S.A. for Guatemala; by Chips Computadoras S.A. de C.V. for Mexico; by Editorial Norma de Panama S.A. for Panama; by American Bookshops for Finland. Authorized Sales Agent: Anthony Rudkin Associates for the Middle East and North Africa.

For general information on IDG Books Worldwide's books in the U.S., please call our Consumer Customer Service department at 800-762-2974. For reseller information, including discounts and premium sales, please call our Reseller Customer Service department at 800-434-3422.

For information on where to purchase IDG Books Worldwide's books outside the U.S., please contact our International Sales department at 317-596-5530 or fax 317-596-5692.

For consumer information on foreign language translations, please contact our Customer Service department at 1-800-434-3422, fax 317-596-5692, or e-mail rights@idgbooks.com.

For information on licensing foreign or domestic rights, please phone +1-650-655-3109.

For sales inquiries and special prices for bulk quantities, please contact our Sales department at 650-655-3200 or write to the address above.

For information on using IDG Books Worldwide's books in the classroom or for ordering examination copies, please contact our Educational Sales department at 800-434-2086 or fax 317-596-5499.

For press review copies, author interviews, or other publicity information, please contact our Public Relations department at 650-655-3000 or fax 650-655-3299.

For authorization to photocopy items for corporate, personal, or educational use, please contact Copyright Clearance Center, 222 Rosewood Drive, Danvers, MA 01923, or fax 978-750-4470.

is a registered trademark or trademark under exclusive license
to IDG Books Worldwide, Inc. from International Data Group, Inc.
in the United States and/or other countries.

About the Author

Allen St. John is a contributing editor at *Bike* magazine and has written about road cycling, mountain biking, and other active sports for a wide variety of publications, including *The New York Times, Men's Journal, Los Angeles Magazine,* and *Condé Nast Women's Sports & Fitness*, where he also worked as senior editor. He is an avid road cyclist and mountain biker, having raced and ridden throughout the United States and in Europe.

Allen is also a contributing editor and columnist at *Skiing,* the winner of the North American Ski Journalist's Assocation's Harold Hirsch Award for excellence in magazine writing, and the author of the upcoming *Skiing For Dummies.* He also contributed to the hardcover book and CD-ROM of *Tim McCarver's The Way Baseball Works* and is the author of *Major League Baseball's American and National League Pocket Almanacs.* An experienced journalist, he's covered everything from a presidential campaign to a World Series locker room.

Allen lives in Upper Montclair, New Jersey, with his wife Sally, son Ethan, and Alison the Brown Dog.

ABOUT IDG BOOKS WORLDWIDE

Welcome to the world of IDG Books Worldwide.

IDG Books Worldwide, Inc., is a subsidiary of International Data Group, the world's largest publisher of computer-related information and the leading global provider of information services on information technology. IDG was founded more than 30 years ago by Patrick J. McGovern and now employs more than 9,000 people worldwide. IDG publishes more than 290 computer publications in over 75 countries. More than 90 million people read one or more IDG publications each month.

Launched in 1990, IDG Books Worldwide is today the #1 publisher of best-selling computer books in the United States. We are proud to have received eight awards from the Computer Press Association in recognition of editorial excellence and three from Computer Currents' First Annual Readers' Choice Awards. Our best-selling *...For Dummies*® series has more than 50 million copies in print with translations in 31 languages. IDG Books Worldwide, through a joint venture with IDG's Hi-Tech Beijing, became the first U.S. publisher to publish a computer book in the People's Republic of China. In record time, IDG Books Worldwide has become the first choice for millions of readers around the world who want to learn how to better manage their businesses.

Our mission is simple: Every one of our books is designed to bring extra value and skill-building instructions to the reader. Our books are written by experts who understand and care about our readers. The knowledge base of our editorial staff comes from years of experience in publishing, education, and journalism — experience we use to produce books to carry us into the new millennium. In short, we care about books, so we attract the best people. We devote special attention to details such as audience, interior design, use of icons, and illustrations. And because we use an efficient process of authoring, editing, and desktop publishing our books electronically, we can spend more time ensuring superior content and less time on the technicalities of making books.

You can count on our commitment to deliver high-quality books at competitive prices on topics you want to read about. At IDG Books Worldwide, we continue in the IDG tradition of delivering quality for more than 30 years. You'll find no better book on a subject than one from IDG Books Worldwide.

John Kilcullen
Chairman and CEO
IDG Books Worldwide, Inc.

Steven Berkowitz
President and Publisher
IDG Books Worldwide, Inc.

Eighth Annual Computer Press Awards ➤ 1992

Ninth Annual Computer Press Awards ➤ 1993

Tenth Annual Computer Press Awards ➤ 1994

Eleventh Annual Computer Press Awards ➤ 1995

IDG is the world's leading IT media, research and exposition company. Founded in 1964, IDG had 1997 revenues of $2.05 billion and has more than 9,000 employees worldwide. IDG offers the widest range of media options that reach IT buyers in 75 countries representing 95% of worldwide IT spending. IDG's diverse product and services portfolio spans six key areas including print publishing, online publishing, expositions and conferences, market research, education and training, and global marketing services. More than 90 million people read one or more of IDG's 290 magazines and newspapers, including IDG's leading global brands — Computerworld, PC World, Network World, Macworld and the Channel World family of publications. IDG Books Worldwide is one of the fastest-growing computer book publishers in the world, with more than 700 titles in 36 languages. The "...For Dummies®" series alone has more than 50 million copies in print. IDG offers online users the largest network of technology-specific Web sites around the world through IDG.net (http://www.idg.net), which comprises more than 225 targeted Web sites in 55 countries worldwide. International Data Corporation (IDC) is the world's largest provider of information technology data, analysis and consulting, with research centers in over 41 countries and more than 400 research analysts worldwide. IDG World Expo is a leading producer of more than 168 globally branded conferences and expositions in 35 countries including E3 (Electronic Entertainment Expo), Macworld Expo, ComNet, Windows World Expo, ICE (Internet Commerce Expo), Agenda, DEMO, and Spotlight. IDG's training subsidiary, ExecuTrain, is the world's largest computer training company, with more than 230 locations worldwide and 785 training courses. IDG Marketing Services helps industry-leading IT companies build international brand recognition by developing global integrated marketing programs via IDG's print, online and exposition products worldwide. Further information about the company can be found at www.idg.com.   1/24/99

Dedication

In loving memory of my dad, who taught me how to ride a bike; my mom, who made a furry green seat cover for that first bike out of one of my sister's old coats; and my sister Mary, whose always open door (and well-stocked pantry) served as the destination for some of my best rides.

Author's Acknowledgments

Most bicycles are built for one, but a bicycle book is definitely a group effort. I'd like to thank Stacy Collins at IDG Books, who dreamed up the idea for *Bicycling For Dummies* and helped guide that idea into this book. I'm grateful to my agent Mark Reiter of International Management Group for his sage advice and savvy deal-making. Thanks too to my editor Tim Gallan, who helped transform my often-empty e-mails into a real, live book, and to Kathleen Dobie who provided smart, sensitive copy editing, and even added a few jokes along the way, as well as all the rest of the folks at IDG, without whom this book wouldn't have happened. I'd also like to thank the good people at Precision Graphics for providing the illustrations that are worth more than a thousand words. And finally a few words about my technical editor, Keith Mills. He was a senior editor at *Bicycle Guide* when it was the best bike magazine on the planet, and is flat out one of the best writers I know. He helped make this book smarter, more accurate, and just plain better than I could have made it alone, and for that I can't thank him enough.

There were of course many folks in the bicycle world who provided me with valuable insight as I researched this book. Hats off to Steve Johnson, Steve Morrissey, Alison Dunlap, Leigh Donovan, Cindy Whitehead, Shari Kain, Tim Blumenthal, and many others for their expert advice. For providing product information and images, I'd like to thank Tom Armstrong at Cannondale, Lori Ipsen at Specialized, Nate Tobekson at Trek, Steve Boehmke at Shimano, Terry Mann at Raleigh, and Mike Jeraci of Stanwood and Partners. And thanks to Ben Serotta for building my favorite bike.

I'd also like to thank the editors who keep giving me assignments, thus keeping me from having to get a real job: Mark Sani and Rob Story at *Bike;* Lucy Danziger and Dana White at *Condé Nast Women's Sports Fitness;* Jim Kaminsky at *Maxim's;* Terry McDonnel and Jeff Csatari at *Men's Journal;* Rick Kahl and Helen Olsson at *Skiing;* Kyle Creighton at *The New York Times Magazine;* Jack Schwartz at *The New York Times;* Michael Anderson at *The New York Times Book Review;* and Miles Seligman at *the Village Voice.* Finally, I'd like to mention two of my teachers: Robert Linn, who introduced me to the works of that great cyclist, Henry Adams, and my great and good friend Allen Barra, who taught me how to make a living in this business we have chosen.

But most of all, I have to thank my family, without whom this book would be, well, blank. I don't grope for words often, but that's what I'm doing when faced with trying to explain the infinite wonderfulness of my wife and the CFO of the Allen St. John Publishing Empire. Sally Catherine Waack-St. John is everything a guy could want in an advisor, a confidante, a partner, a best friend, and much, much more than that. As for my son Ethan, during the months I wrestled with this book, he would run up to me every time I emerged from my office, and smiling his sweetest two-year-old smile he'd say, "Daddy back!" as he shoved me toward my computer. If it weren't for you, Boy-o, I'd still be working on Chapter 4.

Publisher's Acknowledgements

We're proud of this book; please register your comments throught our IDG books Worldwide Online Registration Form located at `http://my2cents.dummies.com`.

Some of the people who helped bring this book to market include the following:

Acquisitions and Editorial

Senior Project Editor: Tim Gallan

Aquisitions Editor: Stacy Collins

Copy Editors: Kathleen Dobie, Stephanie Koutek

Technical Editor: Keith Mills

Editorial Manager: Leah P. Cameron

Aquisitions Coordinator: Lisa Roule

Editorial Coordinator: Maureen F. Kelly

Editorial Assistant: Beth Parlon

Production

Project Coordinator: Karen York

Layout and Graphics: Linda Boyer, Angela F. Hunckler, Anna Rohrer, Brent Savage, Janet Seib, Michael A. Sullivan, Brian Torwelle

Illustrators: Precision Graphics

Proofreaders: Christine Berman, Kelli Botta, Rachel Garvey, Nancy Price, Rebecca Senninger, Janet M. Withers

Indexer: Liz Cunningham

General and Administrative

IDG Books Worldwide, Inc: John Kilcullen, CEO; Steven Berkowitz, President and Publisher

IDG Books Technology Publishing: Brenda McLaughlin, Senior Vice President and Group Pubisher

Dummies Technology Press and Dummies Editorial: Diane Graves Steele, Vice President and Associate Publisher, Mary Bednarek, Director of Acquisitions and Product Development; Kristin A. Cocks, Editorial Director

Dummies Trade Press: Kathleen A. Welton, Vice President and Publisher; Kevin Thornton, Acquisitions Manager

IDG Books Production for Dummies Press: Michael R. Britton, Vice President of Production and Creative Services; Cindy L. Phipps, Manager of Project Coordination, Production Proofreading, and Indexing, Kathie S. Schutte, Supervisor of Page Layout; Shelley Lea, Supervisor of Graphics and Design; Debbie J. Gates, Production Systems Specialist; Robert Springer, Supervisor of Proofreading, Debbie Stailey, Special Projects Coordinator; Tony Augsburger, Supervisor of Reprints and Bluelines

Dummies Packaging and Book Design: Patty Page, Manager, Promotions Marketing

◆

The publisher would like to give special thanks to Patrick J. McGovern, without whom this book would not have been possible

◆

Contents at a Glance

· ·

Introduction *1*

Part I: Buying a Bike: A Consumer's Guide *5*

Chapter 1: The Anatomy of a Bicycle 7

Chapter 2: Just My Type 17

Chapter 3: Having a Fit 39

Chapter 4: Shop Smart: Buying the Right Bike for You 49

Chapter 5: Gearing Up: The Right Accessories for Your Bike 57

Part II: Techniques and Safety *69*

Chapter 6: Getting Ready to Ride 71

Chapter 7: Riding Right: The Fine Art of Turning the Pedals 81

Chapter 8: You're Saaaafe: Dealing with Road Hazards 95

Chapter 9: Fitness: The Final Frontier 111

Chapter 10: Getting Serious: The Easy Way to Train 125

Part III: The Fix Is In *139*

Chapter 11: The Tools of the Trade 141

Chapter 12: Gearing Up: Demystifying the Drivetrain 153

Chapter 13: These Are the Brakes: How to Stop Right and Roll Better 163

Chapter 14: Roadside Repair Guide 173

Part IV: Having Fun with Your Bike *187*

Chapter 15: Riding with Kids 189

Chapter 16: Joining In: The Joys of Social Cycling 203

Chapter 17: Happy Trails: The Many Faces of Mountain Biking 213

Chapter 18: Riding Off-Road: A Mountain Biking Primer 223

Chapter 19: Hitting the Road: The Wonderful World of Bike Touring 235

Chapter 20: To There and Back: Making Your Bike a Second Car 245

Chapter 21: Life in the Fast Lane: Bicycle Racing 255

Part V: The Part of Tens 265

Chapter 22: The Ten Best Bike Web Sites 267

Chapter 23: Ten Places You Ought to Ride at Least Once 271

Chapter 24: The Ten Most Extreme Things to Do on a Bike 275

Chapter 25: The Ten Best Mountain Bike Slang Terms 279

Chapter 26: Top Ten Bike Movies 281

Appendix A: Glossary 285

Appendix B: Bicycling Clubs and Resources 293

Index 317

Book Registration Information . . . . .Back of Book

Cartoons at a Glance

By Rich Tennant

"There's reflectors and blinking lights, but if you really want to feel safe in traffic, I suggest mounting these signs on your back fender."

page 265

"Listen, thanks. I'll return them as soon as I get the wheels fixed."

page 139

page 5

page 187

"I don't know if the deluxe helmet is safer or not. It keeps tipping him over."

page 69

Fax: 978-546-7747 • E-mail: the5wave@tiac.net

Table of Contents

....

Introduction *1*

Part 1: Buying a Bike: A Consumer's Guide *5*

Chapter 1: The Anatomy of a Bicycle **7**

The Bones of the Bike: The Frame 7
Material Gains: What Bikes Are Made Of .9
    Steel 9
    Aluminum 10
    Composites 10
    Titanium 10
    Weld done: How bikes are built 11
    Buy smart 11
The Soul of the Bike: The Wheels 12
    Rim shots 12
    Well spoken 13
    Tired out 13
The Brains of the Bike: The Drivetrain .14

Chapter 2: Just My Type **17**

Quiz Time: My Bike, Myself 17
Components: A Primer 19
The Mountain Bike 22
    Where it came from 23
    What it's used for 23
    The mountain bike frame 24
    Mountain bike wheels 26
    Mountain bike components 27
The Road Bike 27
    Where it came from 28
    What it does 28
    The road bike frame 29
    Road bike wheels 30
    Road bike components 30
Hybrids 30
    How it started 31
    What it does 31
    The hybrid frame 31
    Hybrid wheels 32

Hybrid components 32
The City Bike 33
How it started 33
What it does 33
The city bike frame 34
The wheels 35
Components 36
From the Wide World of Bikes 36
Tandems 36
Recumbent bicycles 37
BMX bikes 37
Electric bikes 37

Chapter 3: Having a Fit . . . . **.39**
Sizing Yourself Up 39
Getting Framed 40
Trying It On 42
The Great Size Swindle 43
A Weighty Proposition 44
Points of Contact 44
Handlebars 44
Saddles 46
Pedals 46

Chapter 4: Shop Smart: Buying the Right Bike for You . . . . **.49**
Bike Budgeting: The Two-Bucks-a-Ride Rule 49
What's in a Name: Brand Shopping for Your Bike 50
The Price/Weight Equation: Less is More, More or Less 51
This, That, or the Other: How to Compare Bikes 52
Where to Buy Your Bike 53
When to Buy Your Bike 54
Buy during the off season 54
Don't buy on weekends .54
The Test Ride: The 15-Minute Moment of Truth 55

Chapter 5: Gearing Up: The Right Accessories for Your Bike . . . . **.57**
A Helmet: The Accessory You Can't Live Without 57
Buying the Right Brain Bucket 58
Let There Be Lights 60
Lights that help you be seen 60
Lights that help you see .60
Rack 'Em Up: Making Your Bike a Beast of Burden 61
I'm Coming: Horns, Bells, and
Other Warning Devices 61
The Lock Mess 62
Keeping Tabs: The Cycle Computer Story 63

Fender Bending 64
Mirror, Mirror On 64
Water, Water Everywhere 64
Cool Threads 65
    Jerseys 65
    Shorts 66
    Gloves 67
    Foul weather gear 67
    Cycling shoes 67

Part II: Techniques and Safety 69

Chapter 6: Getting Ready to Ride 71

Going In for a Fitting 72
    Setting the seat height 72
    Saddling up 73
    Passing the bars 74
Dressing for Success 77
    It's cool to dress warmly .77
    See and be seen 78
Other Important Things You Shouldn't Forget 78
    Sunglasses 78
    Sunscreen 79
    Money for a cab 79
    Change for a phone call 79
    An ATM or credit card 79
    Your phone number 79

Chapter 7: Riding Right: The Fine Art of Turning the Pedals 81

Getting Underway 82
The Three Secrets of Proper Pedaling 83
    Position your foot 83
    Choose the right gear 84
    Pedal in circles 85
Your Turn 87
Them's the Brakes 88
    Always use both brakes 89
    Use the front brake more .89
    Leave 'em unlocked 89
"Look Ma, No Hands" 90
Wrist Management 91
To Hill and Back 91
    Shift 92
    Spin 93
    Stand 93
    Psyche yourself up 93
The Down Side: A Few Words about Descending 94

Chapter 8: You're Saaaafe: Dealing with Road Hazards **95**

A Pre-Ride Checklist 96
    Wheelie important 96
    Give it a brake 96
    Pressure situation 96
    Bar associations 97
    The frame thing 97
Cars Are Cars 97
    Be decisive 98
    Be alert 98
    Be prepared 98
    Be a vehicle 98
Traffic School 99
    The route of the problem 100
    Your turn signals 101
    The lefty 101
    The case for common courtesy 102
    The hidden dangers of stationary cars 103
    A few words about trucks 104
    Slippery when wet 104
No Dogs Eating Bicycles 106
    Watch for dogs 106
    See Spot run 107
    See Dick walk 107
The Path to Enlightenment 107
    Who to watch out for 108
    Bike path survival strategies 109

Chapter 9: Fitness: The Final Frontier **111**

Bicycling: The Perfect Exercise? .112
    Weight watch: Ride on, slim down 113
    The best medicine 114
My Food, My Self 114
    Before the ride 114
    During the ride 115
    After the ride 116
The Hydration Quotient 116
The Big Hurt: Injuries and Their Prevention 117
    Overuse injuries 118
    Acute injuries 121
    Treating injuries 122
Cycling and Impotence 122

Chapter 10: Getting Serious: The Easy Way to Train **125**

The Fitness Yardstick 126
Maxing Out 128

The Building Blocks of Better Riding 128
    Endurance 128
    Power 129
    Speed 129
The Three Kinds of Rides 129
    Long, steady distance 129
    Power intervals 130
    Speed intervals 131
Building a Workout Plan 132
    Charting your progress 134
    In recovery 134
    Overtraining 135
The Off Season 135
    A stationary bike 136
    A training stand 136
    Rollers 137
    A studio cycling bike 138

Part III: The Fix Is In *139*

Chapter 11: The Tools of the Trade **141**

The Basic Tool Chest 142
    A set of good screwdrivers 143
    A set of metric hex wrenches 143
    A set of metric open-end wrenches 144
    A metric socket set 144
    A pair of pliers 144
    A pump 144
    A set of three tire levers 145
    A tire patch kit 145
    A chain rivet remover 145
    A pair of cable cutters 145
    Grease and chain lube 146
    More cool tools 146
The Take-It-With-You Tool Kit 146
Cable Guidance 148
    Straight 149
    Well groomed 149
    And lubricated 149
Tool Rules 150
    Be observant 150
    Be realistic 150
    Be orderly 150
    Be neat 151
    Be methodical 151
    But not too methodical 151

Chapter 12: Gearing Up: Demystifying the Drivetrain **153**

How Do Your Gears Work? 154
Fixing the Rear Derailleur 155
    Adjusting cable tension 155
    Adjusting limit screws 156
Fixing the Front Derailleur 157
Don't Touch That 158
    Indexed shift levers 158
    Freewheels and freehubs 158
    Internally geared hubs 159
Chain, Chain, Chain 159
    Cleaning the chain 159
    Lubricating the chain 159
    Replacing your chain 160
Getting Your Bearings 160
In Search of Strange Noises 161

**Chapter 13: These Are the Brakes: How to Stop Right
and Roll Better** **163**

Brakes: An Overview 164
Troubleshooting Your Brakes 164
    The rims 165
    The pads 165
    The levers and cables 166
Fixing Common Brake Problems 166
    Adjusting pads that are too far from the rims 166
    Tightening the brake cable 167
    Installing and lubricating a cable 167
    Installing new pads 168
Your Tires 169
    Blown out of proportion: The real deal behind tire pressure . . .169
    Patching a tube 170
Be True: Dewobbling Your Wheels 171

Chapter 14: Roadside Repair Guide **173**

Removing and Replacing Your Wheels 173
    Removing the front wheel 174
    Replacing the front wheel 174
    Removing the rear wheel 175
    Replacing the rear wheel 176
The Top Five Roadside Problems and How to Fix Them 177
    A flat 177
    A broken spoke 180
    A thrown or broken chain 182
    A bent rear derailleur 183
    A tacoed wheel 184

Part IV: Having Fun with Your Bike *187*

Chapter 15: Riding with Kids **189**

Kids as Passengers 190
    Check it over 190
    Dress them right 190
    Keep them safe 191
    Keep them occupied 191
Trailers and Tandems 191
Buying a Kid's Bike 192
    Bike bonding 194
    The responsibility game 194
    Training wheels 194
Teaching Your Child to Ride 195
    Making learning fun 195
    Finding a place to start 196
    Holding on 197
    Breaking it down 198
Kids and Safety 199
    A child's eye view of the road 199
Riding with Your Kids 200

Chapter 16: Joining In: The Joys of Social Cycling **203**

Partnering Up 203
    The pros 204
    The cons 204
    The cure 204
    Getting hooked up 204
Club Rides 205
    The pros 205
    The cons 205
    The cure 206
    Getting hooked up 206
Charity Rides 206
    The pros 207
    The cons 207
    The cure 207
    Getting hooked up 207
Bicycling Vacations 208
    The pros 208
    The cons 208
    The cure 208
    Getting hooked up 209
Riding in a Group 209
    Following the rules 210
    The fine art of riding in a paceline 211
    Mountain biking in groups 211

Chapter 17: Happy Trails: The Many Faces of Mountain Biking . . .213

In the Beginning. 214
The Wheres and Hows 214
    Cross-country 215
    Cross-country racing 215
    Downhill 216
    Backcountry 217
Fit for the Trail 218
Trail Access 218
    IMBA's Rules of the Trail 219
    Trail maintenance 220
    Sensitive when wet 221

Chapter 18: Riding Off-Road: A Mountain Biking Primer 223

Be a Human Shock Absorber 224
    Your arms as springs 224
    Your legs as springs 224
The Eyes Have It 225
Practice, Practice, Practice 226
Uphill Battles: A Quick Guide to Climbing .227
    Seated climbing 227
    Out-of-the-saddle climbing 228
    Getting back on 229
Downhill Fast: The Fine Art of Descending 229
Water Crossings 230
Overcoming Obstacles 231
A Guide to Trail Safety 232
    Do leave early 232
    Don't ride alone 232
    Do carry tools 233
    Don't cut off your options 233
    Do leave word 233
    Do take emergency supplies 233
    Don't panic 233
    Don't zone out 234

**Chapter 19: Hitting the Road: The Wonderful World of
Bike Touring 235**

Preparing for Your Tour 236
    Be clear 236
    Be realistic 236
    Be flexible 237
    Be prepared: Your route 238
    Be prepared: Your gear 238
Buying Bags 239

Touring Together 240
    Equal ability 241
    Similar attitude 241
    A sense of humor 241
Packing 241
    Wardrobe 241
    Miscellaneous equipment 242
    Stuff for the campers 242
    Trial packing 243
Riding a Loaded Bike 243
On the Road 244
    Start early 244
    Pace yourself 244
    Treat yourself right 244

**Chapter 20: To There and Back: Making Your Bike
a Second Car** . . . . **.245**

Walking vs. Riding vs. Driving 246
Taking the Plunge 246
    Make a resolution 246
    Keep your bike handy 247
    Don't rush 247
    Keep it simple 248
    Reward yourself 248
Getting to Work: Commuting on Your Bike 248
    Dressing for success 249
    The sweat factor 250
    Parking 101 251
    When the rack walks away 252

Chapter 21: Life in the Fast Lane: Bicycle Racing . . . . **.255**

Road Racing 256
    Single-day races 256
    Stage racing 257
    Criteriums 258
Track Racing 258
    Sprint racing 258
    Pursuit racing 261
    Keirin 261
    Six-day races 261
Mountain Bike Racing 261
    Cross-country 262
    Downhill 262
    Dual slalom 263
    24-hour races 263
    Iditabike 263

Part V: The Part of Tens 265

Chapter 22: The Ten Best Bike Web Sites .267

Chapter 23: Ten Places You Ought to Ride at Least Once 271

Chapter 24: The Ten Most Extreme Things to Do on a Bike 275

Chapter 25: The Ten Best Mountain Bike Slang Terms 279

Chapter 26: Top Ten Bike Movies 281

Appendix A: Glossary 285

Appendix B: Bicycling Clubs and Resources 293

Index 317

Book Registration Information . . . . .Back of Book

Introduction

· ·

When I see an adult on a bicycle, I do not despair for the future of the human race.

— H.G. Wells

Approach a physicist and he'll be happy to provide you a long-winded dissertation on why the bicycle is an engineering marvel, one of the most ingenious and efficient machines ever designed. But if you want to really understand why a bike is 25 pounds of magic, you simply have to see the look on a nine-year-old's face as she whizzes down the street.

Hopping on the saddle yourself may just be the quickest way to recapture a little of that pre-adolescent delight. Turning the pedals is a perfect little act of defiance, a way to move under your own power just a little faster than Mother Nature ever intended. And there's something about the pace of a bicycle. Fast enough that you can cover a lot of ground but slow enough that you still get to smell the roses along the way. Whether it's cruising along a winding country road, pedaling slowly along a bike path, or exploring the forest on a wooded trail, a bike is a human-powered passport to the world. That's why more than 50 million Americans ride every year.

And if you haven't been on a bike for a while, I've got some great news: Bicycling is even more fun than you remember. Bikes of all kinds are lighter, more comfortable, and more user-friendly. Mountain bikes have opened up a whole world of new places and ways to ride. Even accessories, from helmets to lights to child carriers, have improved. But the simple thrill of balancing atop two spinning wheels hasn't changed a bit. And that's the best news of all.

Why You Need This Book

In the past few years, there's been a veritable explosion of new kinds of bikes — hybrids, comfort bikes, city bikes, suspension bikes — and new ways to ride them. That's one of the reasons why bicycling is better than ever — and more confusing than ever, too. That's where *Bicycling For Dummies* comes in. The purpose of this book is help you make sense of this still-changing world, to provide no-nonsense explanations of all the genres, sub-genres, and spin-offs, and help you find the bike you want at a price you can afford.

But *Bicycling For Dummies* is more than just a buyer's guide. If you're already perfectly happy with the bike you've got, this book will help you get the most out of it. I'll show you how to ride efficiently and safely, and maybe even get fit while you pedal. And if you don't know an Allen wrench from Allen Ginsberg, this book can teach you how to make simple repairs and adjustments. If you're already a serious rider looking for new challenges, you'll find plenty here for you, too. Whether you're interested in polishing your off-road riding technique, planning a multi-day tour, or even thinking about entering a race, you'll find these pages packed with expert tips and techniques. Something for everyone? This sport — and this book — are nothing if not democratic.

How This Book Is Organized

This isn't *The Bridges of Madison County*. I don't expect you to find a comfy chair and a cup of herbal tea, and read it from cover to cover. *Bicycling For Dummies* is designed as a random access reference. In other words: Go ahead, skip around. To help you out, I give you two tables of contents: a quick overview called "Contents at a Glance" to help steer you to the right section and a more detailed list that shows everything that can be found in this book. Oh, and did I mention the comprehensive index at the back? So start anywhere you want, and don't worry about missing something important along the way. *Bicycling For Dummies* contains extensive cross-references from chapter to chapter, so if there's more information to be found, you'll know where to find it. I do the work so you can save your energy for turning the pedals.

Here's a breakdown of what's covered in each part of the book:

Part I: Buying a Bike: A Consumer's Guide

The section starts with a guided tour of a modern bicycle, giving an overview of the components that all bikes have in common and explaining a little about the theory and practice of how they work. Then comes the meat: A real-world look at each of the new genres of bikes. I explain the features, the tradeoffs, and what kind of riding they're best for. And once you've narrowed down your choices, turn to Chapter 4 for a bike shop survival guide, a practical discussion of the things you need to know before you buy: where to shop, how much to spend, how to take a test ride, and how to get the best deal.

Part II: Techniques and Safety

You've heard the old saying "It's just like riding a bicycle." And it's true, there's a certain part of riding a bicycle that seems almost instinctual. But there's also a world of difference between being able to stay up while you're pedaling and being a real cyclist, the kind of rider who rides safely, efficiently, and, yes, elegantly. These chapters tell you how to get the most out of your bike. I tell you how to handle hills (both on the way up and on the way down); how to negotiate traffic safely; and how to burn the most calories while you're riding.

Part III: The Fix Is In

A bicycle is first and foremost a machine. But unlike most of today's machines, which are crammed with solenoids and microprocessors, a bicycle all but invites you to adjust it, modify it, and even fix it yourself. These chapters are a step-by-step primer — complete with illustrations — to the most common repairs, from simple jobs like changing brake pads to trickier things like maintaining bearings. And even if you're content to leave the greasy things to the mechanic, you'll still want to read Chapter 14, which talks about roadside emergencies. It sure beats walking.

Part IV: Having Fun with Your Bike

The best thing about cycling is that there are so many ways to do it. It's all about your personality. Is your idea of a perfect day taking a five mile ride with your kids? I show you how to plan an intergenerational ride where everyone has fun. Do you want to meet people? Then join a club or a group ride. Do you want to explore? Then take your mountain bike into the woods. I show you how to do it safely and easily. Have the need for speed? Then you might want to try your hand at racing. Want to ride your bicycle 150 mph or jump off a 30 foot cliff? I didn't think so. But it's part of the wide world of cycling, and so I've included a few bike-related things that you might not want to do, but you'd love to hear about anyway.

Part V: The Part of Tens

Everyone loves a list, and that's why this section is so much fun. It covers everything from the ten best bicycle cameos in the movies to the ten best bike Web sites.

Icons Used in This Book

When I want you to pay close attention to a certain blocks of text, I flag them with little pictures called *icons*. Here's what the icons mean:

I use this icon when giving information that will keep you out of harm's way.

Any advice that involves the use of tools or equipment gets flagged with this icon.

When offering a tidbit of information that will make life with your bike fun and easy, I place this icon next to it.

If there's a piece of conceptual information that I want you to, um, remember, then I use this icon.

Part I
Buying a Bike: A Consumer's Guide

The 5th Wave   By Rich Tennant

In this part . . .

I arm you with all the information you need to buy the right bike for you. I cover the different kinds of bikes and help you decide which one best suits your need. I then show you how to measure yourself so that you can choose the right size frame. I provide advice on dealing with bike shops and tell you what to do on your test rides. Finally, I discuss some of the accessories you may need.

Chapter 1

The Anatomy of a Bicycle

In This Chapter

▶ Examining the frame

▶ Looking at materials

▶ Deconstructing the bicycle wheel

▶ Explaining the drivetrain

*W*alking into a bike shop is a little like bellying up to the buffet table at the smorgasbord-to-end-all-smorgasbords. It's a feast for the senses to be sure — you can look at shiny chrome, smell the rubber and, go ahead, spin the wheels. But all that variety can be a little intimidating, too. Big ones, small ones, fat ones, skinny ones, cheap ones, and bikes that cost as much as a good used car. The choices go on and on.

But step back for a second, and it all begins to make a little more sense. For all their obvious differences, all bicycles share most of the same components and operate on the same basic principles. So, I start with a guided tour of a bicycle, explaining how the major components work. Not only do I give you a close up look at one of the engineering marvels of the modern world, I also give you a framework for understanding the differences among bikes, a subject I discuss in more detail in Chapter 2.

The Bones of the Bike: The Frame

The frame is the most important part of any bicycle. It determines the bike's weight, its handling characteristics, and your riding position. Putting great components on a lousy frame is like putting butter cream frosting on cardboard. A little basic knowledge about frames goes a long way toward getting you on the right bike.

Look at it closely and you'll see that a bicycle frame has more triangles than a *Dynasty* rerun. Why, you ask? So that it can make use of a principle called *triangulation*. Sparing you the trigonometry, mechanical engineering, and applied physics, triangulation is the principle that holds that trianglular structures are naturally rigid and quite strong for their weight.

A bike's main triangle consists of three tubes:

✔ The top tube, which runs parallel to the ground

✔ The seat tube holds — you guessed it — the seat, and is roughly perpendicular to the ground

✔ The down tube, which essentially completes the triangle

   (No, I didn't forget about the head tube. I realize that the short tube that joins the fork with the frame actually makes the frame more of a funky trapezoid than a true triangle, but sometimes engineering considerations supercede pure geometry.)

Figure 1-1 shows a bike with the parts of the frame labeled.

The back of the bike has its own triangle, with the seat stays and the chainstays hooking up with the seat tube.

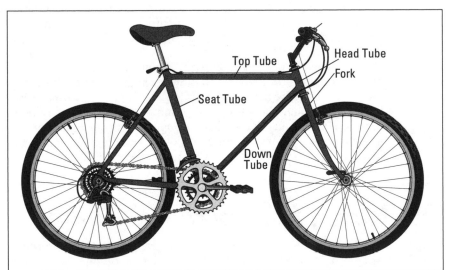

Figure 1-1:
A bike in all
its glory.

The length of these tubes and the angles in these triangles influence how a bicycle rides.

- ✔ Short tubes and tight angles, the kind found on a racing bike, make for a hyperactive machine that handles precisely, turns on a dime, and responds to the rider's input.

- ✔ Shallower angles, like those found on most mountain bikes and hybrids, make the bike stable when you're riding in a straight line, and absorb shock well because longer tubes tend to be more flexible.

Not only important in determining how a bike rides, the frame's geometry determines your riding position: whether you sit upright for comfort, or bent over for aerodynamics, or somewhere in between. The designer's job is to balance the extremes to build a bike that does everything well.

Material Gains: What Bikes Are Made Of

Thirty years ago, this would have been a very short section. Back then all bike frames were made of steel. Some were made carefully of good light-weight steel, some slapped together quickly of cheap heavy steel, but they were all made of steel. If a magnet didn't stick to it, you didn't want to ride it. But while many bicycles are still made of steel, a number of alternative frame materials have elbowed their way into bike shops.

Steel

Steel remains the old standby for a lot of good reasons: It's reasonably inexpensive, easy to work with, moderately light in weight, and quite good at absorbing vibrations. Steel also has a certain feel — a kind of springiness — that a lot of riders love.

Lug story

Lugs are the reinforcing sleeves that strengthen the joints of the finest steel bike frames. While lugs began as functional items, they've gradually become a method of self-expression for the world's most talented frame builders — those rare few who build bikes to order one at a time. These artists hand cut and file lugs with cutouts and curlicues, and braze joints with jeweler-like precision. The result is a bike that's as distinctive as a signature, and too pretty to ride. Well, almost.

The drawbacks are that, while it's plenty strong and light, steel is not quite as strong or light as some of the newer materials.

Steel is the material of choice for el cheapo frames, but it's also used by some of the world's most skilled frame builders to make bikes that are literally works of art.

Aluminum

You may not think that aluminum is inherently strong — consider how little effort it takes to crush a beer can. But the sophisticated aluminum alloys that bicycle frames are made from are much stronger than your average six-pack, and are made stronger still by a heat treatment process. So it's not surprising that aluminum is probably the most popular frame material and gaining popularity every year.

To gain an additional measure of strength, most aluminum bikes use tubes that are slightly larger in diameter than comparable steel tubing, which increases rigidity a lot while increasing weight only a little. Aluminum's drawback is that it's not particularly good at absorbing vibrations, so many aluminum-frame bikes ride a little rough.

Composites

Some of the world's best bicycles are built of space age composites. Employing the same process used to make a tennis racket, materials like carbon fiber, Kevlar, and fiberglass are layered with epoxies in a mold, and then heated. And out pops a fully formed frame. Composite are very lightweight and absorb vibration very well. One of the few drawbacks of carbon-fiber frames is that it must come out of the mold perfectly aligned — you don't get a chance to bend it into precise alignment after assembly the way you can with a steel frame.

What's the downside to buying a bike made of space-age materials? Cost. While prices have come down some in recent years, composite bikes are still quite expensive — composite frames are usually found only in bikes costing $1,000 or more, with some bare frames costing as much as $2,000 without components.

Titanium

Until recently, titanium was generally restricted to aerospace use. But the former Soviet Union is one of the leading suppliers of the space-age metal, and with the Cold War over, a lot of the titanium that would have been used to build MiG fighter jets is now finding its way into bicycles. Talk about a peace dividend.

Titanium combines the light weight of aluminum, the shock absorbing qualities of carbon fiber, the resilient, lively feel of steel, and strength and durability that's unsurpassed. The only drawback is price — even the cheapest titanium frames cost more than $700 without components.

Weld done: How bikes are built

The two basic processes for connecting the tubes in a bike frame are brazing and welding.

Brazing consists of using a torch to heat a brass or silver brazing rod to the melting point, and making the molten metal form a joint between two tubes, or between the tubes and the lug that reinforces the joint. Think of a grilled cheese sandwich with the melted cheese representing the molten brass. Brazing is a good way to build a frame because it only heats the tubes a little, thus preserving their strength.

Welding is more like deep frying. Welding joins two tubes by heating each of them to the melting point. The metal at the tube ends literally melts together. When they cool, they form a joint.

It used to be that only the cheapest bicycles used welded joints, because welding was suitable only for very heavy tubes. But now, a more sophisticated welding process, called TIG welding, in which the welding is done in a bath of inert gas like argon, is used to make high quality frames — especially mountain bike frames — out of steel, aluminum, and titanium.

Buy smart

What do you need to know about frames when you're buying a bike? Basically, you want the best frame you can afford.

Say you're looking at two bikes in the same price range. One bike features some jazzed up components — an upgraded derailleur and a fancy saddle, tricked out bar-ends. The second bike is a little plainer, but it's frame is half a pound lighter, and is built of a better steel alloy. The choice is clear — go with the better frame.

You can upgrade components like handlebars, saddles, brakes, derailleurs, and even wheels as they wear out or as your budget allows, but you're pretty much stuck with the frame you buy. The frame determines the weight of the bike, and that subjective, but very real, yardstick — *feel*.

To determine the quality of a frame, look at the joints. Whether they're lugged or welded, they should be smooth, even and clean. Not sure what that means exactly? Take a peek at a couple of the most expensive bikes in the shop to see what to look for.

The Soul of the Bike: The Wheels

The Temptations had it right: Ain't nothing like the wheel thing, baby. A bike wheel is one of the engineering marvels of the modern world. Ounce for ounce, it's one of the strongest structures ever devised. A wheel weighs less than three pounds, yet withstands untold amounts of abuse, laughing off rocks and potholes and curbs at speeds upwards of 30 miles an hour, and does its job thousands of times, without a squeak of complaint. How does it manage this trick? Through a triumph of teamwork that the Flying Wallendas would envy.

Figure 1-2 shows the components of a bike wheel, all of which are about to be discussed.

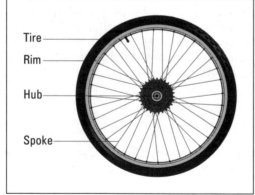

Figure 1-2:
The parts of
a wheel.

Rim shots

Pick up a bicycle rim. The first thing you notice is that it's light — 24 ounces if it's made out of steel, as little as 16 ounces if it's an aluminum alloy.

At first glance a bicycle rim seems pretty strong. But try subjecting it to a very mild torture test: Grab it at either end and try twisting it. Kind of flexible, huh? Then, put it down on the ground, and lean on it gently. It goes a little bit oval before it flexes back. Now find a fat person — John Goodman will do — and have him sit on the rim. Or, you can just take my word for it: Just a couple hundred pounds of force — far less than what a bike encounters on the road — bends a rim. Permanently. But this seemingly flimsy rim, when it's built up into a wheel, can withstand forces more than 100 times greater. Why? Because the rim gets a lot of help from its friends.

Well spoken

The spokes in a bicycle wheel act as a very lightweight and elegant suspension system. The spokes — generally 32 of them — fan out from the *hub* and are tightened so that each spoke pulls equally on the rim. When the rim hits a bump, the impact compresses the spokes at the top and bottom of the wheel a miniscule amount and also stretches the spokes on the sides of the wheel — the equal and opposite reaction that Isaac Newton got so excited about. Those stretched spokes spring back immediately, pulling the compressed spokes back, too, and, so, the wheel stays round.

The key to a strong wheel lies in making sure that the spokes have equal tension. If only one spoke slacks off, or breaks, then all this equal and opposite reaction stuff goes right down the tubes and the result is a dented rim, or in extreme cases what mountain bikers call a *tacoed* wheel. They call it that because a) the wheel is folded like a Mexican specialty b) you have to buy at least one of those specialties for the friend who drives you to the bike shop to buy a new rim.

The spokes cross each other on the way from the hub to the rim. This interlacing, which would make any Shaker proud, gives the rim stability against the forces it encounters when making a turn. Pretty neat, huh?

Tired out

The tire protects the rim, too. The tire provides air suspension for the wheel, and when the wheel hits a bump, the tire shifts an area of high pressure to the point of impact. The first bump causes all the other air molecules to push back, and the end result of all this pushing is that pressure equalizes throughout the tire and prevents the rim from whacking the pavement under most circumstances.

What the bike is used for determines the amount of suspension a tire needs to provide. A mountain bike tire, which has to handle all manner of rocks and ruts, is designed for maximum protection. That's why mountain bike tires are fat — about two and a half inches wide (hence more total air volume) — and carry as little as 40 pounds of pressure. The tire flattens out more on bumps, giving a larger contact area with the trail for more traction.

Rolling, rolling, rolling: A primer on rotating weight

There's a saying in the bicycle biz: An ounce on the wheel is worth three anywhere else on the frame. And it's not only true, it's something to consider when shopping for a bike. Anything that spins on the bike is going to soak up lots of your precious energy if it's unnecessarily heavy. While light pedals and cranks are important, and lighter tires are one of the most cost-effective upgrades you can make to a bike, the place to focus is the rims.

The best rims are made of aluminum alloy, which is much lighter than steel but just as strong. Also take a look at the spokes — stainless steel offers the best balance of weight, strength and resilience. The best spokes are butted — the areas near the hub and the rim which endure the most stress are thicker, while the middle section is thinner to save weight.

The goal of a racing bike tire, on the other hand, is to minimize *rolling resistance* — the friction between the tire and the pavement. So a racing tire is as skinny as Kate Moss — about an inch wide, less than half the width of a mountain bike tire — and is pumped up to a high pressure (as much as 150 pounds per square inch).

You can adjust your own suspension system with one simple tool: a bicycle pump. If your bike feels a little sluggish, pump another 10 pounds of pressure into the tires. If it's bouncing you around on every little divot in the road, try dropping the pressure a little. Likewise, heavier riders need a little more pressure, lighter riders a little less. Needless to say, use a tire pressure gauge when you're doing this, and always stay within the manufacturer's recommended pressure range, which is usually embossed on the tire's sidewall.

The Brains of the Bike: The Drivetrain

Remember when your fifth grade math teacher tried to get you excited about ratios? And you just stuffed your nose back into the latest issue of the Adventures of Nancy and Sluggo and mumbled to yourself "When am I ever going to use this stuff?" The answer that Mrs. Maloney should have come up with: Every time you ride your bike. Ratios make up the brains of your bike's drivetrain.

Have you ever seen a high wheeler? You know, one of those 19th century bikes with a huge front wheel and pedals attached directly to it like a tricycle? Well, if it weren't for ratios, that's what you'd still be riding.

A bike's drivetrain is made up of a few key pieces:

- ✔ **The crankset** is the spidery looking thing that the pedals are attached to.

- ✔ **The chain ring,** aptly named, is the large ring attached to the crankset that the chain rests on.

- ✔ **The freewheel** is the cluster of cogs (also called sprockets) of different sizes attached to the rear hub that the chain goes through. On a one-speed bike, the chain ring is larger than the cog at the back. One turn of the pedals turns the freewheel, and hence the wheel about two and a half times.

Need a picture? See Figure 1-3 for a visual of the crankset, chain ring, and freewheel.

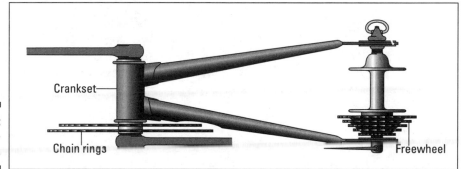

Figure 1-3:
The drive-
train.

Crankset

Chain rings

Freewheel

While that kind of ratio is fine for an average rider on flat terrain, the world, as Columbus proved, is not flat. That's what all that extra drivetrain hardware is for. The derailleurs — the bike's shifting mechanisms — simply move the chain from one chain ring or sprocket to another, altering the ratio up or down.

In the real world, knowing how to use these gear ratios are pretty helpful. After all, the purpose of this knowledge is simply to maximize the perfor-mance of the bicycle's engine; namely, you. When you're feeling strong, or getting a little help from the wind or a hill, increase the ratio by shifting to a larger chain ring or a smaller sprocket. The pedaling gets harder, but your bike covers more ground with each turn of the pedals. And, all things being equal, you go faster.

If, on the other hand, you're approaching a big hill, do the opposite — shift to a smaller chain ring or a larger sprocket. That gives you a lower gear, and a way to inch up the hill. It sure beats walking.

Chapter 2

Just My Type

- -

In This Chapter

▶ Quizzing your way to a perfect match

▶ Understanding a bike's components

▶ Finding your bike type: mountain, road, hybrid, or city

▶ Going non-traditional: tandems, recumbents, BMX bikes

- -

*T*hink about bikes the way you think about dogs. All dogs share a lot of common characteristics: four legs, fur, a cold, wet nose, that sort of thing. At the same time, each breed's a little different. A shar-pei and a golden retriever each has its own charms as well as its own limitations.

Well, the same comparison works with bikes. All bikes have plenty in common — the frame, wheels and basic design I discuss in Chapter 1. But every bike, like every rider, is a little different. Some, like road bikes, are best at speeding down the blacktop, while others — mountain bikes — get their jollies bouncing over boulders. Some are designed for Saturday afternoons on the bike path — hybrids fit that bill — while others — namely city bikes — live for dodging taxi cabs on Monday morning. In this chapter, I discuss the genres and sub-genres within the wide world of bicycles, and, in the process, help you zero in on the set of wheels that's right for you.

Quiz Time: My Bike, Myself

The way to know what kind of bike you must buy, Grasshopper, is to understand first how you will ride it. Yes, there's a Zen-like loop of logic in that bit of advice, but you don't have to shave your head or walk the earth to unravel it. Instead, try a simpler way to get in touch with your inner cyclist: Take this quick quiz.

1. I'm going to ride my bike mostly . . .

    a. On the shoulder of a two lane road.

    b. On a bike path.

    c. On a wooded trail.

    d. Between speeding taxi cabs.

2. My preferred terrain is . . .

    a. Rolling or a little hilly.

    b. Flat as a pancake.

    c. Where mountain goats fear to tread.

    d. Concrete canyons.

3. I like my roller coaster . . .

    a. Big, fast, and wooden.

    b. Near a nice bench that I can watch from.

    c. Upside down, inside out, and standing up.

    d. Who has time for roller coasters?

4. When it comes to bike fashion . . .

    a. I like Lycra.

    b. Sweats work for me.

    c. I go for grunge.

    d. Casual Friday suits me fine.

5. I ride . . .

    a. To rack up more miles than my friends.

    b. For exercise.

    c. For thrills.

    d. Because it's faster than the bus.

6. My favorite riding companions are . . .

    a. Five other fast riders.

    b. My kids.

    c. One close friend who knows when to shut up.

    d. Courteous cabbies.

7. When I'm done riding I want to be . . .

 a. Sweaty.

 b. Half a pound lighter than when I left.

 c. Muddy.

 d. On time.

Now tally up the numbers of As, Bs, Cs, and Ds.

If most of your answers are As, then you like it fast and smooth, Mr. Speed Demon. You're driven, goal-oriented, and a little bit of an endorphin junkie. Try a road bike on for size.

If most of your answers are Bs, you're more interested in fun than thrills. A little bit of exercise, a little bit of fresh air — what could be better? And as for speed, you rush around all week, why get stressed out on the weekends? I see a hybrid in your future.

If most of your answers are Cs, adrenaline's your drug of choice, but you like it in a back-to-nature setting. You're a thrill seeker, but you prefer hairy single-track trails to junk bonds. The mountain biker inside you is waiting to get out.

If most of your answers are Ds, you're a practical person. You need to get somewhere and you figure that a bike is the best way to do it. And if you pass a few gridlocked car-poolers on your way, so much the better. A city bike is the right ride for you.

Components: A Primer

What's a component? Essentially, components are the parts you hang on a frame to make it a complete bike (see Figure 2-1). Here's a guided tour of the components on a bicycle, moving roughly from top to bottom.

- **Saddle:** A fancy name for a bike seat. Most saddles have a plastic base covered with a layer of foam padding and a leather or synthetic cover. Seats vary in shape and padding, but saddle choice is largely a matter of personal preference.

- **Seatpost:** A section of metal tubing that attaches the saddle to the frame. Better seat posts are made of aluminum for light weight and have a clamping system that allows for more precise saddle adjustment. Mountain bikes often have extra long seatposts to allow for a wider variety of seating positions. Some hybrids and city bikes feature suspension seatposts which incorporate a simple spring suspension system designed to take the sting out of small bumps in the road.

✔ **Stem:** A metal fitting that attaches the handlebars to the fork. Better stems are made of aluminum alloy. A few hybrids and lower-end mountain bikes offer suspension stems that pivot when the bike hits a bump. Suspension stems are a compromise at best, adding weight and complexity to the bike while offering only a fraction of the shock absorbing capability of a suspension fork. For more information about stems, see Chapter 3.

✔ **Handlebars:** Handlebars come in three basic configurations. *Flat bars,* found on many mountain bikes and hybrids, are just about as level as the horizon, curving back toward the rider only slightly and upwards not at all. *Riser bars,* found mostly on mountain bikes and some hybrids have an upward sweeping center section — viewed from the front it looks like a flattened U — that allows for a more upright riding position. *Drop bars,* found on road bikes, curve downward — from the side the profile is like a C — which allows for a variety of hand positions and a more aerodynamic posture on the bike. For more information about handlebars, see Chapter 3.

✔ **Brakes:** There are three basic kinds of brakes. *Long arm brakes,* found on most mountain bikes and many hybrids, use two straight brake arms connected by a horizontal cable, and offer great stopping power. *Cantilever brakes,* found on some hybrids and mountain bikes, could almost be called short-arm brakes. They feature two shorter brake arms connected by a triangular cable and offer plenty of stopping power, although not as much as long-arm brakes. *Caliper brakes,* used primarily on road bikes, employ a set of U-shaped overlapping arms that almost encircle the wheel. They're very easy to modulate, but don't offer enough braking power or mud clearance for off-road use. A few high-end mountain bikes use hydraulically actuated disc brakes, similar to the ones on a car. They're phenomenally powerful and equally complex.

✔ **Shifters:** These devices pull a cable attached to your derailleurs, allowing you to change gears. Most mountain bikes, city bikes, and hybrids have shifters that change gears with the push of a button or the twist of a wrist. Which is better? It's largely a matter of personal preference. Most road bikes have brake-mounted shift levers.

✔ **Headset:** This is the set of bearings that attaches your fork to your frame. Headsets come in threaded and threadless varieties. Threadless headsets are lighter and easier to adjust, but the system limits handlebar height adjustment.

✔ **Pedals:** These are the rotating platforms that you turn with your feet to move the bicycle forward. Conventional pedals should have a cage — the part of the pedal that your shoe contacts — that allows for a solid non-slip grip of whatever kind of shoe you wear for riding. Clipless pedals have a mechanism that engages a cleat on the bottom of the shoe.

Components: What's in a name?

It's important to understand that, for the most part, bike companies don't make components, they buy them from third-party suppliers. Which means that Bike A and Bike B made by different companies, are likely to have exactly the same derailleur and brakes which work the same way on each bike.

Shimano, a large Japanese company, owns the lion's share of the component market, especially in mid-priced parts. They make almost every part you can hang on a bike, in more than a dozen different models for virtually every budget and intended use. Bike companies sometimes mix and match components within the Shimano family, picking an upgraded derailleur from one component group, and a set of pedals from a cheaper ensemble.

While no other company offers the sheer number of components that Shimano does, there are other choices. Taiwanese companies like Sun Race make high-quality-for-the-money components found on entry-level bikes. An American company, SRAM, makes the popular Grip Shift twist shifting system, and its derailleurs have become increasingly common on mid-and-high-priced mountain bikes. And Campagnolo, a venerable Italian company, makes beautiful, if expensive, components for road bikes.

- **Cranksets:** The crankset consists of three major assemblies. The *chain rings* have teeth that interlock with the links of the chain, which transfer the motion of the rotating pedals to the chain. The *crank arm* attaches the pedals to the chain rings. And the *bottom bracket* attaches the crank set to the frame, as well as housing the bearings on which the crank rotates. All mountain bikes, most hybrids, and a few road bikes have three chain rings which give you a wider variety of gear ratios. A very small inner chain ring gives you a low gear ratio which allows you to climb hills more easily.

- **Hubs:** Hubs are the devices at the center of the wheel that the axle passes through, allowing the wheel to rotate. Better hubs feature quick release mechanisms, which make it possible to remove your wheels without tools, a real time saver for on-road repairs and putting your bike on a car rack or in a trunk.

- **Freewheel:** This is the set of between five and nine cogs attached to the rear hub, that transfers the motion of the chain into rotation of the wheel. The size of the cogs determines the bike's gear ratios — the larger the largest cog, the lower the low gear, and the easier it'll be to climb steep hills.

- **Chain:** The chain, which transfers your pedaling energy from the chain rings to the freewheel, is a semi-disposable item. Chains occasionally break and definitely wear out in the long run, so you shouldn't be concerned about them at bike buying time.

✔ **Derailleurs:** These are the devices that move the chain from cog to cog. Most bikes have two derailleurs, each operated by its own shifter.

✔ **Rims:** The metal hoops the tires are attached to. Aluminum alloy is lighter and just a strong as steel, as well as offering better braking performance.

✔ **Spokes:** The thin, wire-like devices that attach the hub to the rim. On a well-built wheel, spokes should be tight, and tensioned evenly. You can check this by plucking spokes and listening for a high, even pitch.

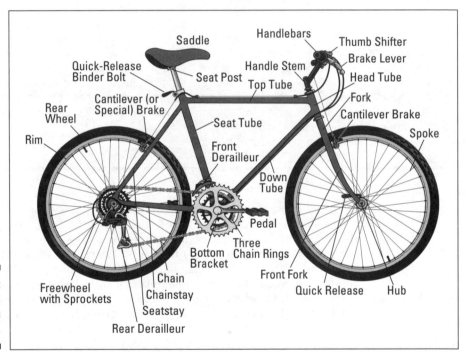

Figure 2-1:
All the
components
of a bike.

The Mountain Bike

The mountain bike is the sport utility vehicle of the bike world — or more accurately, the sport ute is the mountain bike of the auto world. With its ultra-low gear ratios that make hill-climbing a breeze, fat knobby tires, and rugged wheels and frame, a mountain bike is a remarkably versatile vehicle that can take you over terrain that a burro would think twice about. It's rugged and strong. It's nimble and stable. And it's pretty cool looking, too. That's why mountain bikes make up almost 90 percent of the adult bike market. A mountain bike is shown in Figure 2-2.

Figure 2-2:
A mountain
bike.

Photo courtesy of Gary Fisher.

Where it came from

Where did the mountain bike come from? Someone's basement. The mountain bike was born in the mid 1970s when a bunch of riders in Marin County, California took some old balloon-tire, coaster-brake Schwinns and started blasting down hiking trails and fire roads on them. They had so much fun that these pioneers soon began modifying the bikes with parts like caliper brakes with motorcycle levers for effective speed control and wide-range gearing that allowed them to climb as well as they descended. It wasn't long before this type of modification developed into a mini-trend. Some of these same, original mountain-biking guys began building bikes from the ground up, with purpose-built frames and rugged mountain-bike-specific components. The bikes they made were much lighter than their balloon-tired ancestors, but still able to handle off-road abuse. And the rest, as they say, is history.

What it's used for

In theory at least, a mountain bike is most at home blasting down fire roads, picking its way around chicken-head rocks and exposed tree roots, and delivering its rider safely down heart-stopping drop-offs. But, like those folks who buy sport utes to drive to the grocery store, most people who buy mountain bikes stick largely to the street or the bike path. These folks go the rugged route and get mountain bikes because they like the upright riding position, the fat cushy tires, and the bike's looks, and because they like the idea that they *could* enter their bike in the 24 Hours of Canaan race, even if they never plan to do it.

Does this mean that you shouldn't buy a mountain bike if you plan to stick to the pavement? Not at all. First, I hope that you try riding a mountain bike off-road someday. You'll probably love it, and once you're hooked, you won't have to worry about buying another set of wheels. And maybe you really do put your bike through the ringer — Curb? What curb? Or it could be that you think that mountain bikes just look cool. That's reason enough in my book.

If you do buy a mountain bike for on-road use, do it with your eyes open. Be aware of the alternatives — I outline them later in the chapter — that provide most of the advantages of a mountain bike in a more road-friendly package. And be honest with yourself before you head to the bike shop, so that you don't end up paying for expensive features that you never use.

The mountain bike frame

A mountain bike frame is the Rodney Dangerfield of the bike world. It takes plenty of abuse. A number of features help it take anything you can dish out.

- ✔ The tubing is usually large diameter for added durability.
- ✔ The geometry is designed to make the bike stable and absorb shocks over rough surfaces.
- ✔ The frame is built with generous ground clearance — all the better to clear stumps, logs, rocks, and whatever else you find out there.
- ✔ Ample clearance around the chainstays, seatstays, and the front fork help keep the wheels turning and the brakes working no matter how much mud builds up on them.

Another really nice thing is that the frame looks out for you. Notice that the top tube is lower than that of a road bike, and on most models this tube slopes down from the front to the rear. This space between your crotch and the bike is called *standover clearance,* and most mountain bikes are designed to give you more of it. It can be an important safety feature — especially for guys. Those extra few inches are usually enough to render those inevitable falls merely embarrassing instead of injurious.

These days, even mid-priced mountain bikes feature suspension forks to help take the sting out of bumps. A *suspension fork* incorporates some type of shock absorber — usually some combination of springs, polymer bumpers, and air-oil cartridges — that allows it to telescope as much as four inches when it hits a bump. The market is filled with a wide variety of forks, with the most expensive models generally offering higher performance on both large and small bumps in a lighter weight package. The good news about suspension is that it really does smooth out the ride on a rocky trail. The bad news is that a suspension fork adds to the price of a bike ($150 or more) and to the weight (two pounds or more compared to a non-suspension fork). It also adds one more maintenance chore — the forks need to be overhauled periodically if they're ridden in wet, muddy, or dusty conditions (and what other conditions are there on the trail?).

Many high-end mountain bikes — and increasingly, some mid-priced models — feature *rear suspension* as well. This means that the rear wheel pivots or travels to absorb bumps and keep the rear wheel on the ground. To accomplish this takes a lot of engineering know-how, and the result is often a bike that looks more like a suspension bridge — or even Bo Diddley's guitar — than a conventional bike.

Rear suspension has the same pros and cons — weight and price versus comfort — as front-fork suspension, plus one added consideration. Because you're dealing with the rear wheel, the suspension system has the tough job of distinguishing between road shock and the energy from your pedaling. As a result, the first generation of full-suspension bikes bobbed like the S.S. Minnow on a three-hour tour. Today's more sophisticated full-suspension bikes (see Figure 2-3) do a much better job of cushioning the ride without sapping your pedaling energy. But full-suspension models are still expensive and heavier. My advice: Leave this innovation to the serious off-road rider.

Figure 2-3:
A full-suspension bike.

Photo courtesy of Cannondale.

The mountain bike's adrenalized cousins

Take a quick look at a few of the super-specialized bikes in the mountain bike world:

The downhill bike: The idea is pretty simple. Start at the top of a steep, twisty, rock-strewn trail, and ride down it as fast as you can — even if that means doing 60 mph or more. A downhill bike is a pretty specialized animal. It has an ultra-strong frame, long-travel front and rear suspension to soak up big bumps at high speeds, upswept handlebars, disc brakes, and insanely high gearing for pedaling at interstate speeds. In short, it looks as much like a motorcycle as a bicycle. And because it's not designed to go uphill, weight isn't an issue: Most downhill bikes tip the scales at over 30 pounds. Unless your goal is to make it to the X-Games, you ought to pass.

The freeride bike: Picture a downhill bike with a laid-back attitude. A freeride bike is designed for picking off heinously steep descents and catching air off of small cliffs and big rocks. Unlike downhill racers, who shoot for the fastest time and the money that goes with it, a freerider's goal is to be featured in a mountain bike video. Freeride bikes are light enough to be ridden up hills as well as down, so they're somewhat more practical than a downhill bike.

The trials bike: What do you get when you cross a BMX bike on steroids and a pogo stick? A trials bike. These bikes' frames are ultra rigid, the wheels are ultra small, and they often feature a fixed gear that allows pedaling backwards. Trials riders make their way over incredible obstacles — both natural (like logs) and man-made (like picnic tables and even cars). One trials champion even appeared on the Letterman show and casually bounded right up onto Dave's desk.

The single speed mountain bike: Drawing inspiration from the sport's earliest days, a few hardy souls are pitching their derailleurs and riding bikes that sport but a single gear. The light weight makes these bikes ultra responsive on technical terrain, but the lack of gearing for going up hills poses a real challenge for the bike's engine — the rider.

Mountain bike wheels

Mountain bikes sport 26-inch diameter wheels which pay tribute to their balloon-tire roots. The hubs have sealed bearings, which need less frequent maintenance. The rims are rugged to stand up to the abuses that the trail dishes out. And most mountain bikes wear gnarly treaded tires that could put a bulldozer to shame. While I won't deny the appeal of that heavy machinery look, be aware of the tradeoffs in the wheel and rubber game.

If you're riding exclusively on the road, getting the right tires makes your life — or at least your pedaling — easier. Those heavy knobs that sink right into mud or dirt tend to squirm on pavement. And the fat profile that soaks up bumps on the trail, merely slows you down on the road. So if you find that you spend a lot of time on the blacktop, look for a tire that's relatively narrow, and has low-profile knobs, or better yet, grooved tread instead. Some serious riders actually invest in a second set of wheels mounted with high-pressure slick tires for road riding, saving the aggressive rubber for the trail. While this may seem excessive, it's a lot cheaper than buying a second bike.

Remember of course, that tires can be replaced cheaply and easily, and all will wear out eventually, so don't let tires color your bike shopping decision too much.

Mountain bike components

Think of the worst conditions you'd ever ride a bike in. How about up a long, steep, bumpy hill covered in sticky mud the consistency of bread dough? Well that's the kind of day mountain bike manufacturers had in mind when they designed the bike's drivetrain. Mountain bikes have a very small chain ring in the front coupled with a very large cog in the back — which help you inch up even the steepest, sloppiest grade, albeit very, very slowly. Most mountain bikes have between 21 and 27 speeds — three chain rings up front and between seven and nine cogs in back.

You can also do all your shifting without taking your hands off the handlebars; using either a thumb-actuated lever or a twist shifter, which changes gears with a motorcycle-style twist of the wrist.

Mountain bikes also need serious braking power. That's where *long-arm* brakes come in. These brakes are powerful enough to lock up a wheel on virtually any terrain, which can mean the difference between a semi-controlled slide and a messy face-plant.

The Road Bike

If the mountain bike is tapping into the SUV segment of the market, then the road bike is the flashy red sports car of the two-wheeled world. In general, a road bike is built for one thing: speed. If your goal is to cover as many miles a day as quickly as possible, then consider a road bike.

Look at a road bike (one is shown in Figure 2-4) and you can see that everything is focused on maximum efficiency:

- ✔ The downturned handlebars put you in an aerodynamic position.
- ✔ The narrow, high-pressure tires roll very efficiently.
- ✔ The lightweight frame puts you in the most efficient pedaling position possible.

Figure 2-4:
A road bike.

Photo courtesy of Lemond.

Where it came from

The basic road bike design can be traced back to the thoroughbred bikes ridden in the grueling Tour de France as far back as the 1930s. Modern road bikes are remarkably similar to the bikes ridden in that race today. Today's road bike also has a less noble lineage: It's a distant relative of the 10-speed you rode to high school. Those bikes fell from favor for a variety of good reasons: They were heavy, hard to shift, uncomfortable to ride, and the "safety levers" on the brakes (auxiliary levers which often proved unable to actually stop the bike) and stem-mounted shifters were downright unsafe. No wonder the bike boom of the 1970s turned into a bike bust.

What it does

Today's road bikes are a far cry from that old Schwinn Varsity. Even inexpensive road bikes today offer performance comparable to super-expensive custom bikes of two decades ago.

Is a road bike for you? There's really nothing like the feel of you and the bike in perfect harmony, gliding along the asphalt at 20 miles an hour. But getting the most out of a road bike takes a little bit of a commitment on your part. You get the most from a road bike if you wear special cycling shorts and cycling shoes, and even then, there's a period of adjustment as your lower back and your, um, rear, get used to the narrow seat and drop bars.

The road bike's specialized cousins

While a road bike is actually quite versatile, equally capable of entering a race or just rolling around the park, it has some more specialized relatives, suited for higher speeds or longer distances.

Racing bikes: Racing bikes are like a regular road bike, only more so. They're lighter and even more sensitive to rider input, and sometimes their geometry sacrifices rider comfort for efficiency and handling. And of course they're more expensive.

Touring bikes: While many bike tourists have converted to mountain bikes or hybrids, some serious riders still stick to road style touring bikes. Their longer wheelbase and shallower frame angles make them more stable — important for carrying loads — and they feature brazed-on eyelets for fenders and racks. Ultra-low gears make it easier to climb hills.

Track bikes: These are the road bikes for the attention deficit disorder crowd. These ultra light, hyperactive bikes don't have brakes. And the fixed gear doesn't allow the rider to coast. When the wheels turn so do the pedals. While they were originally designed for track racing, where maximum speed is the objective and braking isn't a consideration, track bikes have also caught on with many bike messengers, who like the bike's lightning fast reflexes. And they like the fact that there's no derailleur to get stolen while the bike is parked.

Triathlon bikes: Until recently, drafting — riding behind another rider who breaks the wind for you — was illegal in triathlons, those swimming/cycling/running endurance contests. So a triathlete needed a bike that would give her every edge while riding alone. The result was a genre of ultra aero-bikes, featuring sleek frames, one-piece composite wheels, and handlebars that put the rider in a tight aerodynamic tuck that looked like a praying mantis. The problem is that this narrow position makes steering a dicey proposition. Which is why tri-bikes don't work well in traffic.

But proper bike set up can minimize the discomfort. And when you check your odometer at the end of the day, and realize how many miles you pedaled, you know it was worth it.

The road bike frame

Because the human body is an inefficient engine, a road bike frame often has to serve two masters. On one hand, it has to be rigid enough to transmit energy efficiently from the pedals to the wheels. On the other hand, a frame that's too rigid can buck its rider right off when it hits a bump. The conflict is the same when it comes to the rider's position. A lower, narrower crouch is better for aerodynamics, but if the crouch is too low and compact, the rider can barely pedal, much less see the road. And, while there are a few exceptions — the most exotic racing bikes look like George Jetson should be riding them — the best compromise is the traditional diamond frame with a traditional geometry in steel, aluminum, or if you can afford it, titanium or carbon fiber composite.

Road bike wheels

A road bike's wheels are built for speed. The rims and the tires are narrow — less than an inch wide — to minimize rolling resistance. And the tires are built to withstand more pressure than a bomb squad. Pump them up to 100 pounds per square inch and they'll take it in stride.

The tradeoff of a road bike's easy rolling is a rougher ride. On smooth pavement, that little bit of extra feedback is a wonderful thing — it makes the bike feel alive. But on pavement pocked with potholes, you may wish for the additional shock absorption. You can put a little more plush in your ride just by reducing tire pressure or installing a slightly wider tire.

Road bike components

Remember that *graunnnnnch* every time you tried to shift gears on your old ten-speed? Well, friction shifting, which required you to decide exactly how far to move the lever to execute a shift, is a thing of the past. Index shifting takes all the guesswork out of changing gears — you feel a positive click every time you move the lever — and renders the process completely idiot-proof, even on hills or during hard pedaling.

Today most road bikes have shifters mounted on the brake lever, a system inspired by the bar-mounted setups on all mountain bikes. You push a small lever underneath the brake inward or outward to change gears. Simple. The net result of these innovations makes changing gears so easy that you do it more readily, which means that you're always in the right gear and therefore pedaling with the maximum efficiency. (I talk more about using the right gear in Chapter 7.)

Most road bikes use caliper brakes, which have excellent feel and are very sensitive to small changes in lever pressure, even at high speeds. Unlike mountain bike brakes, these brakes are not designed to lock up a wheel, which, on the road, is just as dangerous for a bike as it is for a car. Think of caliper brakes as ABS brakes for your bike.

Hybrids

The hybrid bike is the intersection where the road bike and mountain bike meet (see Figure 2-5). A hybrid takes a little from column A and a little from column B — both in spirit and in parts — to form a bike that ideally represents the best of those two worlds. Designed primarily for moderate on-road riding, a hybrid features the upright geometry, easy shifting, ultra-low gears for climbing hills, and some of the overall ruggedness of a mountain bike. But taking a cue from road bikes, it's lighter, and it rolls more easily.

How it started

The earliest hybrids popped up in the mid-1980s, not too long after the advent of the mountain bike. And while some of the bikes were pretty good, most were kind of dull, offering a little bit of both road and mountain bikes and not quite enough of either. Only in recent years, as manufacturers have begun to pay more attention to this emerging genre, has the hybrid come into its own. Newer hybrids hit the right mix between comfort, speed, and ruggedness.

What it does

While hybrids can be used for light off-road work, they're really designed for the road or the bike path, which is where most people ride their bikes. They're lighter than a comparable mountain bike — no need to ruggedize them for off-road work — which makes them easier to pedal and even easier to carry up and down stairs. They roll almost as fast as a road bike, but offer a little more comfort because of wider tires. And the riding position meets the Goldilocks standard: it's just right. In short, a good hybrid is a fine choice for the kind of mellow, out-for-a-spin riding that most people do.

The hybrid frame

Hybrid frame features:

- A conventional diamond frame shape
- A low standover height (although not as low as a mountain bike)
- Lightweight steel or aluminum frame
- An upright riding position that balances comfort and pedaling efficiency

The ultimate hybrid

The ultimate hybrid bike is the *cyclocross bike*, which is basically a road bike which features beefed-up brakes, extra mud clearance, and narrow but knobby tires. Originating as off-season training for European road racers, cyclocross is a tiny but growing sub-genre that combines elements of trail running, steeplechase, road bike racing, and mountain bike-like off-roading.

Races are contested over a mile-long course that's partly paved, partly mud-soaked, and which features a number of two-foot high barriers that require riders to dismount and carry their bikes. The races are short, but flat out — a friend who's a cyclocross champion, describes the sport as "an hour of pure puking pain." But trust me, it is fun to watch.

Figure 2-5:
A hybrid.

Photo courtesy of Trek.

What hybrid frames have in common is the way they position you on the bike. A hybrid should fit like a pair of Hush Puppies: You sit comfortably upright, the brakes and the shifters fall right to hand, and your feet just gravitate to the pedals. A well-designed hybrid makes you feel like the bike is conforming to you, and not the other way around.

Hybrid wheels

Most of today's hybrids have 700C wheels, larger than most mountain bikes and the same size as on most road bikes. These are great if you plan to stick solely to the road because they offer low rolling resistance, and if you get more serious about your riding, you can upgrade to a pair of faster, high-pressure road bike tires.

Hybrid components

Most hybrids borrow their components from — you guessed it — road or mountain bikes. Most hybrids have mountain-bike style triple chain rings, but they don't have the ultra-low gears that off-roaders need, which saves weight and makes for better shifting. The brakes are usually long-arm brakes with levers designed for flat bars. The supporting components — the pedals, the hubs, and the headset — are often borrowed from the road bike parts bin, which helps keep the weight of the bike down.

Suspension seat posts offer some cushioning of the ride without the complexity and weight of full suspension bikes. And cushy seats, sneaker-friendly pedals, and comfortable handlebar grips raise the plushness factor.

The City Bike

Why did the bicycle cross the road? To get to the library. Or the grocery store. Or to work. That's the idea behind a city bike: the bicycle as transportation. These bikes are not designed to be ridden for fun or exercise — although you can use them for that — but to get from one place to the other. They incorporate features that make riding in street clothes a pleasure instead of a hassle. Many city bikes have chainguards and fenders to help keep you mud- and grease-free, rubber pedals that grip even leather soled shoes, and can be fitted with racks and baskets so you can carry your books and groceries back home. A recent spinoff from the city bike is the cruiser (shown in Figure 2-6), which retains a city bike's basic simplicity, but has a beefier, retro-newsboy bike look.

How it started

The city bike can trace its roots back to the three-speed English racer of the 1950s. These bikes seemed kind of zippy to Americans accustomed to balloon-tired bombers designed to stand up to the abuse kids can dish out, but in Europe these English racers were the workhorses of the bicycle world. These were the original adult bikes. These were the kind of bikes that people rode to work, to the store, or out to the movies. And while they've lost a little of their luster to fancier 10-speeds and mountain bikes, a lot of those three-speed English racers stayed in circulation, just waiting for the next errand.

A few years ago, manufacturers like Specialized saw the opportunity to revive the city bike for the 1990s, updating the components and adding in a little retro-styling in the way of curved frame tubes, riveted saddles, and backward looking graphics and paint schemes. And while this trend hasn't caught on the way the mountain bike did, you're sure to see more and more city bikes on the bike shop sales floor.

What it does

Designed for on-road use, city bikes are eminently practical, designed to be both efficient and rugged. A good city bike can be ridden every day, no matter what the weather. That's why every real bike buff keeps some kind of city bike in the garage. And cruisers represent a different kind of no-nonsense bike. They sacrifice a little speed in favor of simplicity and ruggedness. That makes them perfectly suited to rolling down the boardwalk or the bike path or just over to Starbucks.

Figure 2-6:
A cruiser
city bike.

Photo courtesy of Raleigh USA.

The city bike frame

A good city bike has an upright geometry — all the better to see and be seen in traffic. The frame, usually made of steel, has to walk the line between being strong and lightweight.

The $20 city bike

If you're not sure you want a city bike, here's the way to find out on the cheap. Check the classifieds or scour a few garage sales and you'll find an old three-speed for less than $50. If you find an old Raleigh Sport, you've got a real classic, but really any brand will do. Give the bike a quick once-over to make sure there are no cracks in the joints and give it a spin down the driveway to make sure that the three-speed hub works — it's pretty indestructible but expensive to replace. Don't worry about rust, chipped paint or general grime; the whole idea is to find a bike that doesn't look like it's worth stealing.

Add a $10 lock to deter ride-away thieves and you've got your own human-powered transportation system. On short trips, your city bike can get you there just as fast as if you were in a car. You won't have to look for a parking space or feed a meter ever again. And talk about multi-tasking. You'll be burning calories, saving money, and helping the environment; all while getting your errands done. Not a bad deal, eh?

A good city bike frame features:

- ✔ Generally curved frame tubes, a change which is really more about show than go

- ✔ An upright geometry, all the better to see and be seen in traffic

- ✔ Reasonably light weight for maneuverability in city traffic (although cruisers are somewhat heavier)

- ✔ Brazed-on eyelets for mounting racks and fenders and chainguards, and even a provision for a kickstand

The wheels

Curbs, potholes, and the like are just a few of the road-borne delights that await a city bike every day. That's why these bikes need rugged wheels (generally 26 inches) and fat but smooth tires that put shock absorption — and rim preservation — above maximum speed. Many riders upgrade their bikes with tubes that feature anti-puncture protection. Cruisers generally have knobby mountain bike tires, which roll slower but look cool.

The bike that shifts itself

While bike drivetrains have improved markedly, making shifting easier, many riders still don't shift, or do so only grudgingly. "Why can't my bike shift itself, like my car?" they wonder. Well at least in a modest way, that dream has become a reality.

Shimano recently introduced a system called Auto-D which allows a bike to shift automatically. The system uses an electronic sensor mounted on the wheel which judges the speed of the bike, and shifts up or down at predetermined points. The system shifts very smoothly, with almost Lexus-like precision. However, at the moment, this system is only available on three and four-speed internal geared bikes, which limits its use to relatively flat terrain.

The Shimano innovation followed the marketing success, if not the engineering success, of another self-shifting bike, the CSA Auto Bike. That bike was the subject of a slick and seductive infomercial which made the bike one of the sales hits of late-night television. However, the bike used a complex mechanical system to achieve the same goals as Shimano's Auto-D, and in practice the bikes were unreliable. As the word spread, the remaining Auto Bikes were remaindered on the Internet at low-but-not-a-bargain prices.

Components

Many city bikes dispense with derailleurs and freewheels in favor of three-or-seven-speed internal hub gearing, which is much easier to maintain, yet more than adequate for most flat riding without a heavy load. The most basic cruiser models are single speed, which is adequate for only the flattest terrain. Riders in hillier locales would do better to choose bikes with derailleurs and wide-range gearing. Old-school city bikes use caliper-style brakes, but some of the new school models use long-arm brakes, which offer better fender clearance.

From the Wide World of Bikes

Some bikes don't fit neatly into the broad categories I use in this chapter, but they help add some welcome diversity to the universe of two-wheeled transportation.

Tandems

You'll look sweet upon the seat of a bicycle built for two. Actually, if Daisy were around today, she'd understand that the tandem is really two beasts. First, there's the kind of clunky tandem that you may find rusting away in the garage at your aunt's summer house, or for rent at some beachfront bike shop. This kind of tandem is clunky, slow, and not much fun once the novelty wears off.

But a serious tandem is a whole other story. Since it doubles the horsepower without doubling the weight or the wind resistance, the result is a machine that eats up the road.

Tandems have benefited greatly from the mountain bike revolution, adopting the rugged components, wider range gearing, the more powerful brakes originally designed for off-road use.

Fatter tires, upright handlebars, and suspension seatposts make the ride more comfortable, especially for the stoker (the back rider), who runs the risk of getting pitched off the seat from bumps she can't see. Many of today's high-quality tandems are actually quite trailworthy, and off-roading a tandem is a small but increasingly popular niche.

A quality tandem is also a great thing for couples — it allows a stronger rider and a weaker rider to stay together, and even have conversations while they're riding. As long as the captain, the front rider, is considerate of the stoker's needs and signals upcoming bumps, turns, and stops, it's actually pretty easy.

On the other hand, using a tandem takes some commitment. The bikes are bigger, harder to transport, and more expensive — good ones start around $1,500.

Recumbent bicycles

What do you get when you cross a bicycle and a Barcalounger? No, it's not a joke. You get a recumbent bike. A recumbent bicycle takes the drivetrain of a conventional bike and rotates it 90 degrees, so that the rider sits up, with the pedals in front, and a pair of handlebars below his or her seat. The long wheelbase makes the recumbent quite stable, and the reclining position is quite efficient, and very aerodynamic. In fact, some of the fastest human-powered vehicles in the world are recumbents fitted with wind-cheating aerodynamic fairings. One drawback: The low profile makes them harder to see in traffic.

Recumbents have a small but growing following, and they're particularly attractive to riders with back or neck injuries that prevent them from riding a conventional bike. A recumbent can also alleviate the ailments caused by too many miles on too narrow seats — guys take note here — and in that way it's bicycling's answer to Viagra.

BMX bikes

Wildly popular among nine-year old boys, these small dirt bikes have become a fashion statement for young adults who like their looks and are willing to put up with the discomfort of pedaling a bike with tiny 20-inch wheels. A cruiser class of 24-inch BMXs make the genre a little more practical for the post-pubescent crowd.

Electric bikes

The good news: You don't have to pedal up hills. A motor powered by a rechargeable battery does the work for you. The bad news: The bikes are heavy — up to 60 pounds — and are only good for about 45 minutes on a charge. Still, these bikes could be an ecological alternative to a car for short trips, and expect the weight to come down and the range to increase as battery technology improves. Think of an electric bike as an environmentally friendly moped.

Chapter 3

Having a Fit

- -

In This Chapter

▶ Measuring your inseam

▶ Finding the right size bike for you

▶ Adjusting the bike for a test ride

▶ Selecting the right bike for your weight

▶ Pedaling, sitting, and other points of contact

- -

*I*n the first couple of chapters, I talk about bikes. Now, I want to talk about you for a minute. Do you have long legs? Short ones? Are your shoulders broad? Are your feet wide? No, I'm not trying to get personal. The answers to these questions determine the single most important part of the bike buying process: finding a bike that fits.

Riding a bike that's the wrong size can cause injuries and accidents, and more to the point, it's not very much fun. In this chapter I show you: how to find the right-sized frame; which handlebars and stem put you in the right position; what type of saddle makes sense for you; and how your weight should influence your bike buying.

Sizing Yourself Up

Sizing yourself up is simple, really: Just measure. Find a wall, a pencil, a tape measure, and a reasonably thick hardcover book: something between *Jonathan Livingston Seagull* and *The Brothers Karamazov* should do very nicely. Here goes:

1. **Stand with your back to the wall wearing the same kind of shoes and shorts you wear when you ride.**

2. **Take the book and put it between your legs as if it were a bicycle saddle, making sure the edge is flush against the wall.**

3. **Reach behind and mark a spot on the wall at the top of the book.**

4. **Measure the distance between the floor and the mark and commit it to memory, or better yet, write it down.**

This is your inseam measurement. You'll be using it often. This inseam is not the same as the one on the tag of your Levi's 501s, but that's why I have you measure.

Getting Framed

The first thing you use your inseam measurement for is to make sure you get the right size frame. Choosing a frame is probably the single most important step in buying a bike, so pay attention.

What do I mean by frame size, anyway? *Frame size* is the measurement along the seat tube from the center of the bottom bracket — the spindle that attaches the crank set to the frame — to the center of the top tube. (A few manufacturers measure their bikes center to top — from the spindle to the top of the frame — these bikes tend to run a little bit smaller, about half an inch, for any given frame size.) Of course the size of the tubes in the rest of the bike also change as the frame size changes. But it's really the relationship between the length of your legs and the "height" of the bike that determines whether a bike fits you or not.

Here's how you choose your frame size:

- ✔ If you're looking for a **road bike,** subtract **10** inches from your inseam measurement.

- ✔ If you're buying a **mountain bike,** which requires more standover clearance, subtract **12** inches from your inseam measurement.

- ✔ For a **hybrid bike,** subtract **11** inches from your inseam.

What this first round of measuring does is put you in the ballpark. The way to see if you've done your paperwork properly is to go to a shop and straddle a bike.

If the bike is the right size, you should have about five inches of clearance for a mountain bike, three inches for a road bike, and four for a hybrid, all while wearing shoes with your feet flat on the floor. Figure 3-1 shows someone checking standover clearance. (This guideline applies to conventional diamond-shaped frames; most unconventional frame shapes give you more clearance, not less.) If you're riding on the top tube, or the top tube's down below your knees, get out the tape and measure again.

Figure 3-1:
Checking
standover
clearance.

Remember that the bike shop is an off-the-rack kind of place. If you have a 32-inch inseam, doing the math puts you on a 20-inch mountain bike. But the bike you're looking at only comes in 19- and 21-inch sizes. So what do you do? Wear elevator cycling shoes?

The old rule suggests buying the smaller of the two sizes. There's some sound logic behind this, as the smaller frame will be lighter and somewhat stiffer, too. But in reality, overall fit is still the most important consideration. If you've got long arms or a torso that's long relative to your legs, you may want to go with the larger of the two frames to give you the extra room for your upper body. On the other hand, if your upper body is proportionately shorter, you'll probably want to go for the smaller frame.

Trying It On

To really see if a bike fits you, you have to make a few adjustments. First, you need to get a ballpark measurement for seat height. (I go into more exact saddle and handlebar adjustments in Chapter 6.)

Loosen the seat binder bolt, which can be found where the seatpost meets the frame, and raise the seat so that the distance from the top of the seat to a pedal in the downstroke position is about a quarter inch longer than your inseam. Remember to retighten the bolt, then check your measurements by getting on the bike. With the pedal on the downstroke and the ball of your foot on the pedal, straighten your leg. You should be able to extend your leg almost completely, without locking your knee.

Next, loosen the bolt on the seatpost that holds the saddle in place. Slide the seatpost forward or back until the nose of the saddle is just about even or slightly behind the center of the bottom bracket. Again, in Chapter 6, I show you how to make this adjustment more accurately once you get the bike home, but for now, eyeballing it works just fine.

To see how the top tube of the frame fits, put your elbow on the tip of the saddle. Your fingertips should just about reach the handlebars. If you're within a couple of inches either way, it's not a big deal. Your dealer can replace the stem with one of a different length to help fine-tune the fit of the bike.

Do you need a girl's bike?

The answer to the question in the headline is yes and no. If you mean the kind of bike that has two parallel down tubes and no top tube, the answer is categorically no. Unless you plan to ride frequently in a skirt, you're better off on a conventional diamond frame. The triangulation principles used in a diamond frame, which I cover in Chapter 1, make a "boy's" style bike frame much stronger than a girl's frame. Not having the benefits of triangulation, "girls'" bikes are especially prone to snap in half right at the bottom bracket. Not fun. Especially if you happen to be riding it at the time.

If you're like most women, you're a little smaller than your male counterparts. And the reality is that most frames are designed to fit an average male. Smaller frames are often just shrunken versions of the mid-size models. They often get the short shrift geometry-wise, with the top tube stretching disproportionately, or a head tube joint that's crowded and messy, with the top tube almost ready to scrunch the downtube.

The advent of the mountain bike, with its smaller 26-inch wheels and reduced standover clearance makes things a little easier for most women. But very small women — under five feet tall — may still need to investigate women-specific bikes. Some designed-for-women bikes, like those by Georgena Terry, feature downsized brake levers and tiny 24-inch wheels. The pricetag, unfortunately, is not tiny, but may well be worth it.

Tailor-made bikes

Just as there are off-the-rack suits and custom-tailored ones, so is it with bikes. If you're willing to come up with the coin — prices start at around $1,500 without components — custom bike builders will build a dream bike that's tailored to you and you alone.

Custom frame making works just like a Saville Row tailor shop. You come in, they take measurements, you fill out a questionnaire, and then go over every small detail. While a few individuals — Shaquille O'Neal comes to mind — simply can't ride an off-the-rack bike, for most of us with relatively average builds, a custom bike is a luxury. But what a luxury.

Once you find a bike that seems to fit, it's time to sit on it. With the salesperson or a friend propping you up, get on the saddle. Put both feet on the pedals and both hands on the handlebars.

Ideally, you're in a good, balanced position and leaning forward slightly with your back anywhere between a 20- and a 60-degree angle to the ground.

About 70 percent of your weight should be on the saddle, with 30 percent on the handlebars This may be a little more weight on the handlebars than you're used to, but if you put too much weight on the saddle, you end up sore. Now look up as if you're trying to read traffic. Are you craning your neck?

Next try pedaling backwards — if you try going forward you'll find yourself zooming across the sales floor. Your pelvis shouldn't rock too much from side to side while you do this. If it does, your saddle is a little too high.

Repeat this process with a couple of different bikes. The key is to listen to your body. One bike is going to fit like your favorite old sweat pants, easing you into a relaxed, neutral riding position. That's the bike you want to take home.

The Great Size Swindle

If you wear a size eight shoe, you don't buy a pair of size nines just because they're a bargain, do you? Don't be tempted to do that with a bike either. If the bike is the wrong size, no matter how cool it looks, or how good a deal it is, don't buy it. More than an inch on either size of your ideal frame size, and the bike won't allow you to achieve a proper riding position, which can lead to injury, and it won't handle properly, which can lead to an accident.

The sizing issue is one way to separate a good dealer from someone merely trying to take your money. Remember that most shops stock a relatively limited array of frame sizes, and the popular sizes often sell out quickly. A responsible salesperson would rather let you walk out of the store to look somewhere else for the bike you want in the size you need than sell you a frame that's the wrong size just because that's what she has in stock. If she keeps saying "It fits," even if your tape measure and your body tell you it doesn't, it's time to walk out.

A Weighty Proposition

How much do you weigh? It's not a rude question. The weight of the rider makes up the lion's share of the bike/rider combination. So naturally it makes sense that the same bike performs very differently whether it has a 100-pound rider on board or a 200-pound rider. If you're at the upper end of the weight scale, look for a more rugged bike with a stiffer frame, beefier wheels, and slightly fatter tires. If you're a lightweight, a stiff bike tends to pitch you around. The better choice is a lighter and more supple frame.

Points of Contact

There are three places and three places only where you touch your bike while you're riding: the handlebars, the saddle, and the pedals — which is why you should pay some special attention to these areas when you're bike shopping.

Handlebars

It's not quite as simple as it was in your youth. Back then, all you needed for your Stingray was handlebars that looked as much like a Harley Davidson as possible. Now there are more options than you can shake a frame pump at.

Most mountain bikes and hybrids come with *flat-bar handlebars,* which are just that. They sweep up or back only a little, and they're stiff which allows for more positive steering. In general, flat bars put you in a good, slightly aggressive riding position. *Bar ends* — they look like little horns bolted onto the ends of the handlebars — are a good idea for any kind of flat bar setup because they offer you a variety of extra hand positions. The stretched-out aerodynamic position on the curved part of the bar end is great for pedaling hard on the flats, while grabbing the straight part of the bar end provides extra leverage for climbing. The next alternative is an *upswept bar* or *cruiser bar,* which gained popularity among downhill riders and is now found on many hybrid and cruiser bikes. An upswept bar offers the same advantages as a flat bar except that your hand position is higher, giving you a slightly more upright riding position.

A few hybrids sport a kind of convoluted bar that starts out like a flat bar, but curves around to the front until it looks a little like the brush catcher on a pickup truck. Whether you like the look is really a matter of personal preference. But these bars don't give you any more useful hand positions than a straight bar with a pair of *bar ends,* and yet they weigh more. Can you say "marketing gimmick?"

Drop handlebars, which curve down and then back, are found on most road bikes. The advantages of drop bars are twofold:

- ✔ The leaned-over position they promote affords far better aerodynamics than a flat bar.
- ✔ Hand positions are plentiful: near the stem, on the brake hoods (the upper middle part of the bar), on the hooks (the lower middle) and on the drops (the very bottom of the bar) — just the ticket for an all-day ride.

Drop bars come in different shapes, and have different amounts of *reach,* the distance forward from the stem, and *drop,* the distance from the top of the bar to its lowest point.

The good thing about handlebars is that they are relatively cheap and easy to replace. So if you feel adventurous, you can try a new pair without taking out a second mortgage.

No matter what kind of handlebars you settle on, it's vital that you get bars that are the right size. The handlebars should be just about the width of your shoulders.

GEAR TALK

Aero bar, anyone?

Some road bikes, mostly those ridden in triathlons, feature handlebars with an elbow rest and a grip that places both hands almost together. These *aero bars* can really increase speed by cutting down on wind drag — American Greg LeMond won the Tour de France because of a fast time trial made possible by his aero bars. But they also make it very difficult to steer the bike and virtually impossible to make an evasive maneuver, which is the reason they're banned in all races except time trials — where only one rider is on the course at a time. Leave this innovation to the really hard core racers.

Even the grips or the handlebar tape makes a big difference in how the bike feels. A set of soft, cushy foam grips smooth out your ride, while firmer rubber grips give you a better feel for the road and make the bike seem more responsive.

Saddles

As the Fonz used to say to Potsie, "Sit on it." Picking the right saddle can make the difference between hours of happy riding, and being miserable on the bike.

The path of least resistance, it would seem, is to go for the widest, cushiest saddle you can find. But it's not that easy. Picking a saddle is a little like buying a mattress; you have to strike a balance between support and comfort. A saddle that's too wide may feel great in the shop, but after an hour of pedaling it may cause chafing, blistering, and all sorts of other dermatological woes that make your life miserable. A seat that's too soft, like some gel models, also absorbs the effort that should be directed into your pedaling. And besides, you'll feel like you're sitting on someone else's butt.

A good place to start is a moderately narrow seat with thick but firm foam padding and a leather cover. It takes a couple of rides to break in the saddle — and you — but making sure the saddle suits you, and vice versa, is the path to long term peace in this quadrant of the bicycle.

Mountain bikers take note: A number of mountain-bike specific saddles are on the market, and whether you buy one or not, you can learn a thing or two by looking at them. These saddles are narrow in the back, all the better for sliding off the back for a steep descent. And the nose is rounded in the front, all the better for applying the kind of body English that some moves require.

Pedals

I'm not being overly dramatic by saying that the pedals are one of the most important, yet frequently overlooked, components on any bike. And because a good pair of pedals can be expensive, bike company product managers sometimes cheap out on them.

Most mid-priced bikes come with what's commonly known as a *rattrap* pedal. It consists of a metal cage — the part your foot rests on — with a few teeth on it for traction, with a couple of garish reflectors to meet safety regulations. And they're really not much good. Rattrap pedals are heavy, clunky, and slippery. All things considered, you're probably better off with a pair of the rubber-treaded pedals that come on kids' bikes and some city bikes.

The cheap way to improve the pedals you've got is with a pair of toe clips, which I recommend for all but the most casual riders. First, *toe clips* improve your pedaling efficiency remarkably by allowing you to pull up as well as push down on the pedals. But toe clips also serve an important safety function; they keep your foot from sliding off the pedal, preventing the sudden and serious kind of fall that happens when your sneaker meets the front wheel's spokes. Yes, there is a learning curve to getting in and out of toe clips, but most riders can master it in an afternoon.

The bigger pedal upgrade is to go to *clipless pedals*. I discuss these in more detail in Chapter 5, but suffice to say that on-road or off, a set of clipless pedals gives you all of the advantages of toe clips and then some, while eliminating their drawbacks. Going clipless is one of the smartest component swaps you can make on your bike.

Chapter 4

Shop Smart:
Buying the Right Bike for You

● ●

In This Chapter

▶ Budgeting for a bike

▶ Choosing between brands

▶ Deciding where and when to buy

▶ Taking a test-ride

● ●

*W*alking into a bike shop can be a pretty scary proposition. You're confronted with dozens of bikes — some are $3,000 racing models, some are pink 16-inch girls bikes with streamers on the handlebars — but they're all yelling the same thing: *Buy me!*

So how do you narrow down your choices and make your decision in the end? You can start by reading this chapter. I show you how to set a budget, how to decide between comparably priced models, how to take a test ride, and how to shop for the best deal. So read on before you ride off. You'll be glad you did.

Bike Budgeting: The Two-Bucks-a-Ride Rule

How much should you spend on your bike? Ultimately, that's really between you and your accountant, but if you want to get the most bang for your bicycle dollar, try the two-bucks-a-ride rule. Got your pencil and paper ready?

1. **Figure out how often you're going to ride the bike.**

   Will you ride about twice a week through the spring, summer, and fall? That rounds out to about 50 times a year. Are you more of a once-a-weeker? Figure on 25 times a year. Will you ride four days a week or maybe a little more? That's about 120 times a year.

Of bikes, budgets, and bang for your buck

The law of diminishing returns — you may remember that concept from college economics. It simply means that the first bit of resources — manpower, money, whatever — that you throw at a problem gets you a lot of results. But after you've thrown a lot of resources at a problem, you reach a point at which you begin to get fewer results per unit resource.

What does this mean to a bike shopper? It means that up to a certain point — say around $600 — spending a little more money gets you a lot more bike. After that point, you end up spending a lot more money to get a little more bike.

At the lower price points, shopping for a bike is a little like being a poor college student going grocery shopping. The budget's tight and every little bit helps — ten bucks gets you Ramen noodles, while thirteen lets you feast on pasta primavera. It's the same way with bikes. A $200 bike may weigh 30 pounds and have steel rims. A $235 bike may weigh 28 pounds and have alloy rims. But apply that same $35 difference to a $2,000 bike, and maybe all it gets you is a trick saddle that's an ounce and a half lighter.

The lesson: Don't be too dogmatic about your budget, especially if you're shopping for an inexpensive bike. Toss a few extra dollars into the transaction, and you're likely to end up with many happy, um, marginal returns.

2. **Multiply your yearly figure by five. (Any quality bike should last you a lot more than five years.)**

3. **Multiply that five-year's-worth of rides figure by two bucks a ride.**

This formula puts a once-a-weeker on a $250 bike. Our twice a weeker on a $500 bike. And our almost-every-day rider will get more than her money's worth out of a $1,000 bike.

Of course, these are far from hard and fast figures. If you've got the money and you want the best of everything, go right ahead and spend more. If you'd have to take a second job to make the payments on the bike the formula recommends, then spend what you can afford. But if you're somewhere between these extremes, this formula should put you in the right ballpark based on how much you'll be riding.

What's in a Name: Brand Shopping for Your Bike

Should you shop by the label when it comes to buying a bike? Well, it depends. The first thing you have to understand is that a manufacturer doesn't really *build* a bike.

Most manufacturers build the frame — or at least design it and have a Taiwanese bike factory build it — and buy off-the-rack components for the wheels and the drivetrain. Every bike maker has access to pretty much the same pool of components, mostly from the Japanese component giant Shimano. And each manufacturer pays just about the same price for these parts. What this means is that there are very few truly lousy bikes out there.

At the same time, a really great bike is more than the sum of its parts. The process of assembling a bike is a little like entering a bake-off: Everyone starts with the same basic ingredients, but the success, or failure, of the recipe depends on the skill involved in combining them. Bike companies have a lot of latitude in designing a frame, and a fair amount in deciding which parts to hang on it.

All product managers face the same hard choices for their low- and mid-priced models: Do I go with an upgraded derailleur for better performance, or buy the fancy saddle that will get the customer's attention on the sales floor? Can I save a few pennies on the components, so that I can afford to use the same frame as the next model up? Do I deliver a bike that's a little more lively and responsive, or one that's very solid and stable?

Every manufacturer — from major companies like Trek, Specialized, Cannondale, GT, and Schwinn to dozens of smaller bike makers — answers these questions a little differently. The result is that some bikes are as conservative as Pat Robertson while others are as flashy as James Brown.

In general, the big companies got to be big companies by making good choices and building bikes that people like to ride. If you want to get past the shopping and on to the riding as quickly as possible, sticking to a major brand is one way to make sure you get a quality ride, even if you end up spending a few dollars more for it. On the other hand, the big guys don't have a monopoly on brains, so you can often find very good values from smaller, lesser known companies, if you're willing to shop around.

The Price/Weight Equation: Less is More, More or Less

How is a bike like a fashion model? Neither one can be too thin. A truly lightweight bike is a wonderful thing; ride one and you feel like *you* lost ten pounds.

Alas, one of the hard and fast rules of the bike world is that the less a bike weighs, the more it costs. Or to look at it another way; more money buys you less bike. Literally. There are good reasons for this:

- Lighter frames are made of thin-walled tubing, which is both more expensive to produce and requires more time and skill to braze or weld.

- Lighter components are made of expensive aluminum alloys, instead of steel, and are built to closer tolerances.

- Lighter wheels must be built and trued with special care or they fold like an origami convention the first time they hit a bump.

For most riders the best way to gain the benefits of a light bike is to focus on the pounds, not the ounces. Get a bike with a good light frame and light wheels and you're ahead of the game. Once you reach about 23 pounds for a road bike and about 27 pounds for a mountain bike, you come to that ol' point of diminishing returns I talk about earlier in this chapter. After you reach that point, you can spend hundreds, even thousands of dollars and save only ounces, not pounds. Truly gossamer bikes use space-age materials like titanium and carbon fiber that were originally developed for use in fighter jets. Leave that stuff to the Pentagon. It can lighten your wallet a lot faster than you can lighten your bike.

This, That, or the Other: How to Compare Bikes

Now that you have a pretty good idea what kind of bike you should buy and about how much you should spend on it, it's time to target your search a little. You can do this a couple of ways.

The first way is to do some homework. Check out the buyer's guide issues of some of the cycling magazines. Look at some bike manufacturers' Web sites. Pick up some of the manufacturers' literature.

And, after you finish looking at the pretty pictures and reading the flowery descriptions, flip to the specifications page.

- Find out about the frame: What's it made of? What's the frame geometry (remember that shallower angles and longer tubes generally mean a more relaxed ride)? (Check out Chapter 1 for a discussion of frame geometry.) And look at the next model up or down the line. Does it sound like the same frame? If it does, it probably is. In this situation, you want to stick with the lowest priced bike with the highest end frame.

✔ Move on to the components: What kind of brakes, derailleurs and hubs does the bike have?

✔ Skip to the bottom line. How much does it weigh? Don't just take the catalog's word for it — listed weights are notoriously optimistic. Instead, use a test from a magazine, or better still, put the bike right on the shop's scales and make sure you're dealing with bikes of the same size or you're comparing apples to oranges. The lighter the bike, the faster and easier the ride.

Write all this stuff down, and go to the next manufacturer's propaganda and do the same thing. Soon, you have a chart that gives you a pretty good rundown of your options. Remember to take it along to your next stop, the bike shop.

Where to Buy Your Bike

Once upon a time, you had two choices for where to buy a bike: the corner mom-and-pop bike shop, or the sporting goods section of a big department store. Now, it's not quite as simple. Small chains of bike shops around major cities have most of the buying power of big department stores. Large sporting goods stores are becoming more specialized, often creating a store within a store completely dedicated to bicycling. And those small independent dealers are enticing you with a combination of friendly service and competitive prices. What's a consumer to do?

This is a good time for a little networking. Ask your friends and neighbors where they bought their bikes. And, of course, ask them if they are happy with the way they were treated, and happy with the bike they took home. The next stop is the Yellow Pages. It can tell you which shops carry the brands you're interested in.

Keep in mind that you need both a quality shop and a smart salesperson. A quality shop carries a good selection of brands, has well-established guarantee and return policies, and a fully-equipped repair shop to handle any adjustments or repairs that you may need down the line.

But it's the salesperson's brain you pick when you shop. A good salesperson knows all the bikes in the shop, and takes the time to help you focus your needs. She won't push you into spending more money than you need to, because having a happy customer is more important than making a quick sale.

While a good salesperson should ask you a lot of questions, don't be afraid to fire a few right back. The following questions can give you some insight into your salesperson's experience, prejudices, and motivation.

    ✔ Where do you usually ride?

    ✔ How long have you been working here?

    ✔ What kind of bike do you own?

    ✔ Do you work on commission?

No, this isn't a job interview, but if you don't like the answers you get, remember that it's a free country. Spend your money somewhere else.

When to Buy Your Bike

The way to get the best price on a bike is to think like a bike dealer. In April, riding is on everyone's mind and plenty of people come into the shop. Bikes are priced on this basis: "Well, if this guy doesn't buy it, the next guy will." But in late summer or early fall the dealer may ask herself, "Do I really want to look at this bike until next spring?", as she fills out a price tag.

Buy during the off season

The time between September and early November is one prime buying season. The next begins in mid-January until about mid-March, when you can buy last year's models just as the new models are arriving. (Often the only differences from season to season are paint colors or decal schemes.)

The key to taking advantage of this counter-seasonal strategy is being flexible and doing your homework. If you've got your heart set on owning this year's hottest model in a common size, you're going to have to buy early in the season, and pay what the market will bear — usually close to list price. But if you're willing to wait and play the field a little, you can often save some money or convince the salesperson to throw in a small accessory or a free lifetime maintenance package — something many quality shops offer. Still, it may take a little effort on your part to track down a shop with the model and size you want at a price you're willing to pay.

While it's important to be flexible about brands and models, don't ever buy a bike that's the wrong size, no matter how cheap it is. You'll regret it until the day you sell it.

Don't buy on weekends

Whatever time of the year you shop, do it any day but Saturday. On weekends, bike shops are so crowded that it's hard to even get a salesperson's attention. Walk in on a Tuesday afternoon, and not only can you take your time, you're often waited on by the owner or the manager. You'll get the personal attention that will help ensure that you roll home on the right bike.

The Test Ride: The 15-Minute Moment of Truth

Once you narrow your choices down to a couple of bikes, give the finalists the Goldilocks test, in the form of a test ride. You want to find the bike that's "just right." The definition of "just right" is different for every rider. A bike that feels responsive to one rider feels twitchy and unstable to another. A bike that's sturdy and rigid to a heavier rider feels like a bucking bronco to someone who weighs 50 pounds less. And a bike that just doesn't fit your body — it's got a long top tube and you've got a short torso — is like wearing someone else's shoes.

Your test ride should include as many riding conditions as possible. Take the bike up a hill and back down. Try it on some rough patches as well as smooth pavement. Turn a few corners. Come to a full stop.

Try to concentrate on the overall feel of the bike, rather than on troubleshooting. A noisy derailleur or overly grabby brakes can usually be solved with a couple of turns of the screwdriver once you get back to the shop.

Finally, ask yourself the ultimate question: Is this the bike I want to be riding week in and week out for the next five or ten years? If the answer is an unqualified yes, you've got yourself a ride.

Add-ons: Why your accessory shopping should wait

It's a very emotional moment when you fork over your plastic for a new bike — a time of joy, a time of relief, a time of anticipation. And every salesperson this side of Willie Loman knows that it's that's a great time to add on some accessory sales while you're excited about the bike. Resist the temptation for these very good reasons:

✔ First, if you're working on a tight budget, you should spend as much money on the bike itself as you can. You can always save up for accessories.

✔ Secondly, after riding the bike for a while you'll have a better idea of what you really need and what will be just so much extra baggage.

✔ And third, you get to spread the fun of buying new toys out over weeks or, even months.

Of course there are exceptions to every rule, and this rule is no exception. (Follow that?) Anyway, buy a bicycle helmet if you don't already have one. And getting a tire pump and a spare tube is a pretty good idea, too, because, after all, riding beats walking. For more information on accessories, see Chapter 5.

Chapter 5

Gearing Up: The Right Accessories for Your Bike

In This Chapter

▶ Your helmet: The crucial accessory

▶ Lights, bells, and other cool items

▶ Clothes that make the biker

Remember your first bike? No sooner were you done thanking Mom and Dad than you started thinking about how to make it really your own. As soon as you got your allowance, it was off to the bike shop where you debated over the best way to customize your bike: A headlight or a speedometer? A basket or a bell? A raccoon tail or handlebar streamers?

The more things change, the more . . . well, you know the rest. Every bike shop is filled with accessories designed to make your biking life easier and safer and to make your bike feel more like your own.

But if you buy everything that looks like it might be useful, your bike soon looks like a prop from *Back to the Future III*.

So how do you decide which accessories you can't ride without and which ones are simply destined to clutter up your basement? Read on.

A Helmet: The Accessory You Can't Live Without

I have only one rule about cycling. I never ride without a helmet. Not in the park on a sunny summer Sunday. Not to the corner to buy a newspaper. Not even down my driveway.

I look at it this way. My skull may be hard, but the ground is harder.

What happens when a skull hits pavement? It's not pretty. Picture your brain as a molded gelatin dessert — your brain is actually about that size and consistency. Your skull is the Tupperware bowl it sits in. Now, if that bowl accelerates and then stops suddenly — say you drop it onto your kitchen floor — the gelatin sloshes hard back and forth against the inside of the bowl. That's what happens to your brain in what ER docs call a closed head trauma and sportscasters call a concussion. All that sloshing destroys brain cells and blood vessels, which causes the brain to swell. The result, if untreated, is permanent brain damage or, yes, even death.

It isn't a pretty picture. Unfortunately, it doesn't take a collision with a Mack truck to start this chain of events. Serious injury can occur even in a very low-speed impact — like when you fall and hit your head on the pavement after swerving to avoid a squirrel.

The good news? A helmet can prevent most serious head injuries. The open-cell foam in a helmet — a material not unlike the Styrofoam in a coffee cup — compresses on impact, dissipating the energy from the fall, literally sacrificing itself to save your head. Pretty nice of it, eh?

Sure, there are plenty of lame excuses for not wearing a helmet: "They look silly." (A skull fracture looks sillier.) "Helmets don't help in all kind of accidents." (But they help in a lot of them.) "I'm always careful when I ride." (But sometimes the people you share the road with aren't.)

This sermon concludes with this one lesson: Go out and buy a helmet. And wear it every single time you ride. It may save your life.

Buying the Right Brain Bucket

How do you make sure that you get the right helmet? Well, your helmet doesn't have to be expensive — quality helmets start at around $30, and these mid-priced models are fine for most riders. High-end helmets weigh slightly less, and offer more sophisticated ventilation systems, cooler graphics, and add-ons like sweat bands. Nice, but definitely optional.

From a safety point of view, most bicycle helmets are pretty much equal. Virtually all helmets sold in the United States are certified by ANSI and/or the Snell Memorial Foundation, two testing organizations that put helmets through a battery of torture tests before lending their approval. But remember that hockey or equestrian helmets aren't designed for bicycle use. In case you're not sure what a bike helmet looks like, one is shown in Figure 5-1.

Figure 5-1:
A bike
helmet.

But even the best helmet won't work if it doesn't stay on your head. So make sure you get the right fit. A helmet should fit snugly without squeezing your noggin. The Styrofoam shell itself — as opposed to the pads inside it — should conform as closely as possible to the shape of your head.

Not only do helmets come in different sizes, different manufacturers have slightly different ideas as to what shape constitutes an average head. So try on different models from a few different companies before plunking down your plastic.

And don't forget to secure the straps when you're trying a helmet on. Most straps have a wide adjustment range, but a buckle that pinches your ear can really put a crimp in your riding.

If you're planning to ride off road at all, consider a model designed specifically for mountain biking. These helmets feature a strap system designed to keep the helmet on your head even over rocky terrain.

No matter what type of helmet you decide on, take the shake test. With the straps secured and the front of the helmet sitting on your forehead, not your hairline, shake your head from side to side, from front to back; every which way. (No, people won't think you're weird — at least the salespeople won't; as for other customers, or passers-by, I make no promises.) If the helmet doesn't slide around on your head, you've got a winner.

Let There Be Lights

There are two kinds of lights: lights that help you see, and lights that help you be seen.

Lights that help you be seen

If your goal is to let cars know that you're there, what you need is a small, simple, foolproof light that gets a lot of attention. Manufacturers like Specialized, Vista, and others make a variety of LED-based lights that screw onto a reflector mount or clip onto your clothing and flash like the Vegas strip on a Saturday night. They're light, inexpensive, uncomplicated (one switch and a battery), and they do a great job of telling drivers that you're there. One is shown in Figure 5-2. A good supplement to one of these basic lights is a reflective vest or helmet ring which can be seen from as much as 1,000 yards away when the light from a car's headlamp hits it.

Figure 5-2:
This lightweight LED light attaches to a reflector mount.

Photo courtesy of Trek.

Lights that help you see

Seeing-in-the-dark lights have improved a lot in recent years with the advent of nocturnal mountain biking and 24-hour mountain bike races, which has been a blessing for commuters and other folks who need or want to ride at night. The handlebar- or helmet-mounted systems from companies like

Nightsun feature high-power halogen light, usually with both high and low beams, and heavy-duty rechargeable batteries that mount in a water bottle carrier or a pack that straps to your frame.

This kind of serious lighting technology doesn't come cheap ($150 or more), but if the alternative is running into a tree — or getting your wheel caught in a sewer grate on a poorly lit road while you're commuting home in December — it's not a bad way to spend your money.

Rack 'Em Up: Making Your Bike a Beast of Burden

Sure a rack on your bike says "Hey, look at me, I'm a history professor." But if you plan to use your bike for errands, a rack is one of the handiest accessories you can buy.

A good rack with a spring clip can hold a newspaper, a tennis racket, and a small pizza. Get a couple of bungee cords and you can carry a small bag of groceries or even a briefcase. For this kind of moderate, everyday use, a simple aluminum rack like the Swiss-made Pletscher does fine. If you're using your bike for errands, you might want to consider adding a handlebar mounted wire basket for extra carrying capacity.

If you do any kind of touring, even extended day trips, rack-mounted bags called *panniers* put the weight low and close to the rear wheel where it affects handling the least. For this kind of heavy duty use look for a welded steel rack — front or rear — like the ones made by Blackburn and Bruce Gordon.

I'm Coming: Horns, Bells, and Other Warning Devices

There's no reason to think that French philosopher René Descartes ever rode a bicycle in traffic, but if he had he may well have said "I beep, therefore I am." There's a lot to be said for letting people, especially people behind the wheel of a motor vehicle, know that you exist. And you can choose from a variety of ways to do this:

✔ The **bell** is the "excuse me" of the bike world. It's not wimpy; it's simply polite. A little ding tells that in-line skater and that stroller-pushing dad that you're coming, without giving them a heart attack. Bells are especially useful off-road, where tensions between hikers, bikers, and equestrians using the same trail are high enough without honking or yelling. (And if you think that a frightened in-line skater is scary, you've obviously never seen a freaked out horse.)

✔ A **horn** is a more demonstrative way to announce your presence. No, we're not talking about the ah-ooh-gahh trumpet horn that you had on the Raleigh Chopper banana bike you had as a kid. Today's bike horn is powered by compressed air (it's actually a downsized version of a boat fog horn) and it lets anything short of an 18-wheeler know to get out of your way. If you ride a lot in heavy traffic, it's worth a shot, but use it to avoid collisions, not to vent your frustrations.

✔ A variation on the living loud theme, usually reserved for bike messengers jamming in heavy city traffic, is the **police whistle**. It's small and it's attention-getting, but if you really feel the need to use one, maybe you'd better cut down on the caffeine instead.

The Lock Mess

My father used to quote an old saying: Locks are made for honest people. He meant that most locks are designed to deter casual thieves and provide just enough deterrence that your normal, average citizen won't succumb to the temptation of an easy score. But if a real, professional thief wants to steal something, he'll find a way to do it.

It's a good thought to bear in mind when you think about bike security. The only foolproof way to keep your bike from getting stolen is to not let it out of your sight, and in certain big cities, even that's no guarantee. If you leave your bike alone for any length of time, and a professional thief takes a fancy to it, she'll be able to get through any lock you can buy in a matter of seconds.

But to deter less serious thieves, you can choose between two basic varieties of locks:

✔ **A cable or chain with a shackle lock that you loop around the frame, through your wheels, and around a stationary object.** These do a good job of deterring ride-away thieves, but a determined crook can bypass them in short order with a hacksaw or a bolt cutter.

✔ **A U-lock like the ones made by Kryptonite.** Very strong for their weight, these locks resist bolt cutters and hacksaws very well, but — and there's always a but — they shatter if they're super-cooled with a can of Freon and smashed with a hammer.

TIP

Anti-theft camouflage

What's the cheapest way to protect your bike from getting stolen? Dirt. Next time you're in a big city, look carefully at a bike messenger's bike. It'll be filthy and the frame may even be covered with electrical tape, stickers and who knows what else. But strip off that grime, and you're likely to find a De Rosa track bike or a Fat Chance mountain bike worth thousands of dollars.

Let their looks be a lesson. If you plan to leave your bike parked for any length of time, you may want to dress it down a little. Or at least not wash it too often.

The best defense? Don't let that bike out of your sight. But if that doesn't work, try a combination strategy. A thief who sees a bike that's secured with both a cable and a U-lock is likely to be unprepared to get through both locks quickly and easily. And even if he is, he's likely to move on to an easier target. (For more information on where to lock your bike, see Chapter 20.)

Keeping Tabs: The Cycle Computer Story

How fast am I going? How far have I gone? How long have I been riding? Those are pretty basic riding questions. A *cycle computer* tells you all that and more. Want to know your cadence (the number of pedal strokes per minute)? Your average speed? Your mileage for the year — or since the last time you replaced the battery? With a cycle computer the answers are just the push of a button away. The miracle of microprocessors make today's electronic cyclometers cheap, reliable, and almost too smart.

Even today's cheapest models are very accurate and easy to install. You mount a rotating sensor on your wheel, which sends information to a stationary receiver that clips to your fork and is attached by wire to a handlebar-mounted display unit. More expensive models, naturally, have lots of extra trick features ranging from a heart rate monitor to an altimeter that keeps track of your climbing. Some even feature wireless operation, eliminating the wire that runs from the receiver to the display.

REMEMBER

Just be careful about becoming a slave to your odometer. I know riders who actually refuse to ride when their cyclometer is broken because they won't "get credit" for the ride.

Fender Bending

Getting wet is no fun. So if you live and ride in one of those places where it rains a lot, think about getting a set of fenders. They keep the road spray off you, which is especially nice if you're wearing a suit while riding to work.

And while the fenders on your old three-speed were kind of heavy and they rattled, today you can buy cool plastic fenders that clip on when you need them and pop off when you don't.

Mirror, Mirror On . . .

With all due respect to baseball great Satchel Paige, I suggest that you *should* look behind you because something might be gaining on you — like a big truck or a student driver. The best way to find out what's gaining on you is with a small helmet- or eyeglass-mounted rearview mirror. You get a lot of peripheral vision for not very much added weight. Large handlebar mounted mirrors are bulky, heavy, and can even be dangerous in a fall.

Water, Water Everywhere

Once upon a time hydration was called drinking, and a water bottle and a fountain were all you needed to stave off thirst while you rode.

Now, increasingly, riders fuel up with energy drinks, and carry those drinks in backpack hydration systems. Say what? Made by Camelbak and several other companies, these hydration systems consist of a nylon pack containing a large bladder attached to a tube with a bite valve on the end. The bottom line is that you suck. Literally.

The advantage is that you can carry a lot more liquid — about 40 ounces compared to 12 ounces for a water bottle — and you can drink without using your hands.

While no-hands drinking is a legitimate advance for serious mountain bikers and roadies, most casual riders are better off with a water bottle and cage. Most bikes have brazed-on fittings for at least two bottle cages, and they can be installed in five minutes with one hex wrench. And water bottles are easier to clean, too. Can't ride and drink at the same time? Then stop, sit under a tree, and take a swig.

Four accessories you probably don't need

✔ **Gel saddle pad:** Your own butt is amply padded.

✔ **A tool kit:** Yes, you need tools. But the ones that come prepackaged in most tool kits are junk, which you discover the first time you try to use one. See Chapter 11 to find out how to assemble a really good set of tools *à la carte*.

✔ **A CO2 tire inflator:** It's certainly trickier than a plain old frame pump. But it's hard to inflate a tire *just a little* with one, a necessity for repairing a flat. And a little clumsiness in loading the cartridge could leave you with the most frustrating scenario of all: a fully-patched tire and nothing to pump it up with.

✔ **A kickstand:** You can lean your bike against a tree.

Cool Threads

I always say that it's not a sport if you can't dress for it. But until recently, cyclists had to take that to extremes. Serious cycling wear — skin tight Lycra shorts and even tighter jerseys advertising a Belgian bank or French dairy products — made you look like a refugee from the Tour de France. But thanks in part to mountain bikers who would — and did — prefer to wear bowling shirts instead of roadie clothes, today's cycling clothes are a little more fashion forward.

Figure 5-3 shows many of the the items discussed in the following sections.

Jerseys

Cycling jerseys have one big thing going for them — pockets in the back. Put something in a front pocket and it sags while you ride. In the back, it's just along for the ride, and still easily accessible if you reach around. The synthetic fabrics found in most of today's jerseys are much more comfortable than cotton. They wick away sweat, which keeps you feeling drier. Wool does the same thing, and has some retro-chic appeal as well. And while a jersey doesn't have to have that painted on look that European riders favor, you don't want it too loose or it flaps around in the breeze. A front zip that extends all the way to the navel is a great ventilation option — at least for the guys.

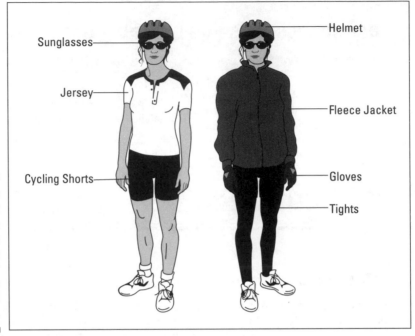

Figure 5-3:
A couple of cyclists dressed to the nines: one for warm weather and one for cold.

Sunglasses

Jersey

Cycling Shorts

Helmet

Fleece Jacket

Gloves

Tights

Shorts

Looking inside of a pair of cycling shorts goes a long way toward explaining how bike racers can ride all day on those hard, narrow saddles. Riders carry their padding *with them* in the form of a *chamois,* a padded patch of soft leather or synthetic material for that tender area where the bicycle and you interface.

This padding is a good thing — it allows you to determine the amount and kind of padding you need, and lets you wash it frequently. (Don't laugh. Eddy Merckx, considered the greatest road racer of all time, once had to drop out of the Tour de France with an infected saddle boil.)

As for shorts, the basic black styling is more practical than it looks: It doesn't look dirty, it doesn't chafe, and figure-wise, it's the next best thing to control top panty hose. Mountain bike shorts are more stylin', and just as functional. They feature the baggy cut and soft feel of your favorite laying-about shorts, and add a padded chamois and technical fabrics for on-the-bike performance.

Gloves

Every serious rider wears gloves, and you should too. Cycling gloves have a padded leather palm and a Lycra, mesh, or terrycloth back, and only half fingers. The padding does a great job of insulating your hands from road shock whenever you ride, and when — I mean if — you fall, they protect your palms from road rash. At about $25, they're a lot cheaper than stitches.

Foul weather gear

Remember one thing: When you're pedaling a bicycle, you're encountering a breeze of 10, 15, or even 20 miles an hour or more all the time. So it's not surprising that you often need a little extra warmth. A long-sleeved jersey is generally a good investment, as are biking tights.

For truly cold weather, you can choose winter gloves, Gore-Tex helmet covers, neoprene shoe covers, and fleece balaclavas to keep your neck from getting frostbitten, but wearing all this is reserved for days when most of us are resigned to heading for the gym.

And finally, a rain shell is an important addition to any cycling wardrobe. It should be long enough to cover your butt while you're on the bike, and tight enough that it doesn't flap around too much. A hood is strictly optional — most restrict you peripheral vision too much. If you opt for a water-proof, breathable nylon shell, it can serve as a windproof outer layer on dry days.

Cycling shoes

For casual riding, tennis shoes are perfectly fine. But if you get a little more serious about the sport, cycling shoes are a smart investment. They help you literally ride longer and faster without any additional effort.

A cycling shoe has a very stiff sole, all the better to transmit the power from your legs to your pedals. Most cycling shoes allow you to secure your shoes to the special clipless pedals with cleats that bolt onto the sole. The system works much like a ski binding — the shoe clicks in when you step on the pedal, and you twist your foot out slightly to release it. Clipless pedals allow you to pull up on the pedals as well as push down. The result is a far more efficient pedal stroke. As you may have guessed, road and mountain bike shoes, while they share these stiff soles and cleats, are otherwise quite different.

Road shoes are made of thin leather and have a super stiff, slippery sole that resembles nothing so much as a pair of pumps with the heel broken off. Needless to say, they're not all that easy to walk in, as I found out the time that I put my elbow through a window when I slipped while carrying my bike out of the house.

Mountain bikers, however, often have to dismount to push or even carry their bikes around or over obstacles. So while they're not exactly Air Jordans, mountain bike shoes are much better suited to walking than road bike shoes. Most models have a knobby tread and a rugged upper that makes them look like a trail-running shoe or a lightweight hiking shoe.

However, if you're not willing to make the commitment to clipless pedals and dedicated cycling shoes right now, there's an intermediate solution. First, find a pair of hiking or running shoes that have relatively stiff soles. Then mount toe clips and straps to your current pedals. This combination will make for more efficient pedaling, without pushing your shoe closet into Imelda Marcos territory.

Part II
Techniques and Safety

The 5th Wave   By Rich Tennant

"I don't know if the deluxe helmet is safer or not. It keeps tipping him over."

In this part . . .

*J*ust in case you don't already know, I tell you how to ride a bike. After showing you how to set up your bike, I discuss riding in traffic, biking for fitness, and even doing a little training.

Chapter 6

Getting Ready to Ride

. . . .

In This Chapter

▶ Fine-tuning the fit of your bike

▶ Dressing properly

▶ Gathering the stuff you need

. . . .

*O*kay, you've got a bike. You're ready to put on your best sunglasses, leave a note for your significant other, and hit the road, right? Not quite yet. Not if you want to escape the fate of a lot of riders who get back from that first ride pretty bummed out — tired, sore, and disappointed — and end up turning on *Wheel of Fortune* and putting the bike back down in the basement to rust. The reason? Their bikes didn't fit right. But you can be happy on your bike from day one — this chapter shows you how.

As it comes from the bike shop, your bike is like a pair of off-the-rack dress pants; You may think the fit is all right, but with only a few minor alterations, you can look like you stepped right off the runway.

It's the same with your bike. In less than an hour — two reruns of *Green Acres* — you can fine-tune the fit of your bike using the same principles developed by scientists, and tested by top riders in every discipline. And when you're done, your bike will fit so well that even though you may not want to spend eight hours a day in the saddle, it's nice to know you could.

And speaking of things sartorial, I'm also taking this opportunity to talk about cycling clothing. You'll find out what to wear when, and how to adapt your existing wardrobe to the semi-specialized demands of riding.

Going In for a Fitting

The first thing you need is a bike that's the right size. (Refer to Chapter 3 for a discussion about size.) Trying to personalize a frame that doesn't fit is like — warning, clothing analogy alert — taking a pair of jeans with a 36-inch waist to your tailor and asking her to make them fit your 31-inch waist (or vice versa). It can be done — at least up to a point — but it's a whole lot easier to start with the right size in the first place.

This final fitting of the bike is something you can do at home, or you can have a bike shop do it. Some shops will charge for the service — the same way clothing stores charge for alterations — while others will do it free, especially at the time of purchase.

 Before you start your final fitting, gather a few simple tools: a pencil, a tape measure, a plumb bob (a string with a small weight attached to it), a book (besides this one), a calculator, and tools to loosen your seat, seatpost, and handlebars (usually a 5- or 6-millimeter Allen [hex] wrench will do).

Setting the seat height

Seat height is critical to the way your bike fits and feels. Follow these simple steps to perfect seat height.

1. **Determine your inseam measurement.**

   (If you did this in Chapter 3, and wrote it down — you did write it down, didn't you? — you can skip to the next step.) Stand facing a wall, with your riding shoes and a pair of shorts on, and put a book that's not this one between your legs as if it were a bicycle saddle. Making sure the book is flush with the wall, put a mark on the wall where the top of the book is. Measure the distance from the mark to the floor to get your inseam measurement. Write it down, somewhere you can find it. There'll be a quiz later.

2. **Get out your calculator and multiply your inseam measurement by 1.09.**

   Why? Because I said so, that's why. Actually this formula is the result of some very serious biomechanical research, in which top-flight exercise physiologists put world-class cyclists on stationary bikes and tinkered with their saddle positions until they determined the exact formula to achieve the optimum saddle height for efficient and injury-free riding. Satisfied?

3. **Adjust your saddle to that height.**

Loosen the Allen bolt that holds the seat tight — it's just below where the seatpost meets the seat tube. Then, with the crankarm parallel to the seat tube (which should put the lowest pedal in about the seven o'clock position), move the saddle up or down until the measurement from the top of the lowest pedal to the top of the saddle is exactly the same as the results of your calculations in Step 2. The key word in the last sentence is *exactly*.

This measurement shouldn't be accurate to within an inch, or half an inch, it should be accurate to within a sixteenth of an inch. A discrepancy of as little as a quarter of an inch can, and does, cause knee and back injuries to racers.

Your seat may seem a little high initially, but give it a chance. A seat that's too low is an invitation to knee problems. Some mountain bikers riding on technical terrain with obstacles and steep drop-offs lower their saddle height just a bit to facilitate getting on and off the saddle as they surmount obstacles, but they spend most of their time riding above the saddle anyway.

Your seatpost should have a maximum height mark, showing how much seatpost must remain in the seat tube for safe operation. Be sure not to exceed this height or the seat post could break and cause a serious fall.

4. **When you're sure this measurement is right, retighten the seatpost.**

Make sure the seat is really tight — there's no bigger drag on a ride than a seatpost that slowly sinks to the south. A seat post that sinks quickly can be a real safety hazard.

To check your work, get on the bike, and have someone hold it upright by straddling the front wheel and holding the handlebars by the stem. Now pedal backwards, with the ball of your foot on the axle of the pedal. If your leg is almost, but not quite, fully extended on the downstroke, and your hips don't rock back and forth, congratulations, you nailed it! If not, go back, check your measurements, and readjust the saddle height until you can pass this test, too.

Saddling up

Now you can move on to the position of the saddle itself. The goal of this adjustment is to fine-tune the position of your knee over the pedal, which helps you to pedal efficiently and avoid injury.

You can adjust the seat fore and aft as well as its tilt. Follow these steps:

1. **Loosen the bolt that holds the saddle in place.**

   You can find it either on the side or the top of the seatpost.

2. **Hold the string of your plumb bob on the nose of the saddle.**

   Note where the string crosses the bottom bracket.

3. **Slide the saddle forward or back until the plumb bob string is between one and two inches behind the bottom bracket.**

   You're in business!

4. **Now, set the tilt of the saddle.**

   The saddle should be parallel with the ground. While you can eyeball this adjustment with the help of a yardstick placed on top of the saddle, for a truly accurate adjustment you should use a carpenter's level. If the saddle tilts downward, you'll slide off. If it's tilted up too much, well that can be pretty uncomfortable.

5. **Finally, tighten up the seatpost bolt, again making sure that it's _really_ tight. If it's not, you could fall when it slips.**

To check your work, get on the bike, move the pedals to the three o'clock and nine o'clock positions. Now hold the string from the plumb bob on the front of your three-o'clock kneecap. The line should bisect the pedal axle. If it doesn't, adjust the saddle forward or backward accordingly. Figure 6-1 shows how things should line up.

Passing the bars

Now you're ready to move on to the adjustments for your upper body, the handlebars and stem. The stem is the basic means for adjusting handlebar position. It has two basic parts — the *quill*, which sticks vertically into the steerer tube of the forks and determines the height of the handlebars, and the *extension*, which extends forward, usually at an angle, to attach the quill to the handlebars, and determines how far the handlebars are from the saddle. Unlike seatposts, stems generally come in a fixed length, but you can adjust your setup by getting a new stem, which come in a wide variety of extension lengths and angles.

The two basic kinds of stem setups are as follows:

  ✔ **A conventional stem** fits inside the head tube of the fork in much the same way that the seatpost fits into the seat tube, and is secured with an internal wedge inside the quill that expands when you tighten the bolt. These stems offer a wide range of height adjustments by moving the quill up and down inside the steerer tube.

Figure 6-1:
A line from
your knee
should
bisect the
pedal axle.

✔ **A threadless stem/headset combination** is a feature of many newer
bikes. In this system the extension fits around the outside of the steerer
tube of the fork and is secured by an external bolt. As you may have figured out, this system essentially eliminates the quill of the stem. The
good news is that the system is simple and lightweight and makes
adjustment of the headset bearings easier. The bad news is that handlebar height is basically constrained by the height of the steerer tube. If
you need to go up more than that, you have to consider switching to a
stem with more *rise,* the upward angle of the stem from the steerer tube
to the handlebars. Another alternative is to change to riser handlebars,
which sweep upward, allowing for a higher hand position.

When you're adjusting the height of a conventional stem, be sure to leave
enough of the quill inside the steerer tube. There should be a maximum height
mark on the stem, and don't exceed it. If you don't insert the stem far enough,
it can break, causing a serious fall. And don't try to adjust the height of a
threadless-style stem. Any attempt to do so could compromise the strength of
the stem and/or steerer tube and may cause a failure and serious fall.

Obviously if you just bought your bike and you can't adjust the handlebar
position to where you want it — it's too high or too low, too far or too
close — you go back to the shop and trade for a new stem. The proper reach
of a stem (how far away the bars are) is largely a matter of personal preference. You don't want to feel you're all scrunched up or too stretched out. But

there is one trick for determining stem length. Look down at your front wheel while you're riding. If the handlebars just obscure your view of the front hub, the stem is the right length. If the hub is well in front of the bars, the stem is too short; if it is well behind, it's too long.

Some newer bikes with threadless headsets feature adjustable stems with a pivot that allows you to adjust both bar height and *reach* — the distance from the saddle to the bars — at the same time. The drawback of this system is its added weight and complexity, and since handlebar height is a one-time adjustment, a fixed stem that's just the right size is really a better alternative.

Stem height

To adjust the stem height on a conventional stem, first mark the current height with a piece of tape against the top of the headset. Then loosen the hex nut in the top of the stem. Straddle the front wheel and pull the bars straight up. There's no need to pull the bars all the way out.

Threadless stem systems also have a hex nut in the same place, but it adjusts headset preload, not stem adjustment. Unless you're a skilled mechanic, leave this adjustment alone.

Handlebar height is more subjective than saddle height; it's primarily a comfort issue. For recreational riders, a good starting place is to set the bars at about the same height as the saddle. For improved aerodynamics, racers set their handlebars from two to as much as five inches below the saddle. But you shouldn't sacrifice comfort for efficiency at this point, and you can always lower the bars a little later. When you're happy with the height, make sure that the stem extension is perfectly parallel with the front wheel and then retighten the stem securely before pedaling away.

Handlebar tilt

The final adjustment you make to the handlebars is to their tilt. To adjust this, loosen the bolt at the front of the stem near the bars. If you have drop bars, the bottom of your handlebars should be parallel to the ground. With flat or riser bars, tilt the bars slightly until you have a hand position you're happy with. Then retighten the bolt securely.

If you have *bar ends* — small extenders that attach to the end of your handlebars — adjust them separately with a bolt on the bar end itself. A reasonable starting point is between 15 and 25 degrees of upward tilt, making sure, of course, that each bar end is tilted the same amount. When you're holding on to your bar ends, you should be stretched out and leaning forward, not sitting straight up. If you feel the need to tilt your bar ends until they're almost vertical, then your handlebars are too low. And besides, they're there to help you steer your bike, not to make your bike look like a steer. Moo.

Guess what? You're almost done. The only thing left to do is go back and make sure that each of the bolts you loosened is completely retightened. Check? Now you're prepared for optimal pedaling. While the position may seem a little strange at first, give it a chance. Within a few rides, your bike should feel as comfortable as your favorite pair of jeans. If you're still uncomfortable, experiment with your position, but do it conservatively. Move your saddle in one direction at a time — up or down, forward or back — no more than a quarter inch at a time. This way if you make it worse it's easier to get back to this home position.

Dressing for Success

The one inalienable rule of cycling: Get dressed first. Unlike say, volleyball, cycling is one sport that's unquestionably best done clothed. But seriously folks, wearing the right clothes can make the difference between a great ride and a cold, wet, messy one.

I discuss shopping for cycling clothes in Chapter 5, but now it's time to walk over to your dresser (or that pile of clothes next to the hamper) and answer that eternal question: What to wear?

It's cool to dress warmly

The first basic question is how warmly to dress. And the answer, of course, is: Warm enough, but not too warm. First, remember that even on a calm day you pedal into a self-generated 10- to 20-mile-an-hour wind. Those air molecules may not be moving, but you are. Because of this human-powered wind-chill factor, even on temperate spring days you want to dress a little warmer than if you were going running. One of the best ways to do this is with a lightweight but breathable shell that keeps the wind off your skin, but still allows sweat to evaporate.

On the other hand, this isn't a walk in the woods. You burn 500 calories an hour or more while biking, so after you warm up, you sweat plenty. Which is why you shouldn't overdress. My personal rule is that if I go out for a ride in the spring, or early in the morning, and I'm a little chilly, but not downright cold after the first mile or so, then I'm dressed appropriately. If you plan to stop along the way, or expect the temperature to drop during the course of the ride, an extra layer is prudent.

The key to successful dressing is layering. Layering is a time-honored cycling tradition, as racers add or peel off layers — shells, jerseys, and yes, even tights, while riding at 25 miles an hour. Needless to say, I suggest stationary stripping for most recreational riders. An ideal ensemble for an early spring or late fall ride may be a wicking synthetic long underwear shirt, a cycling jersey over that, and a light shell to top it all off. And even for a ride in warm weather, it's not a bad idea to pack that shell anyway — stuff it in a pocket or bag.

Shorts or tights? That's a debate that's been raging in cycling longer than Coke or Pepsi. But it's not totally a matter of personal preference. The synovial fluid that lubricates your knee gets thicker when it gets cold, and like the oil in your car, doesn't work as effectively. A good general rule is that if the temperature is below 68, go for the tights. The great compromise — and a lifesaver when you expect the temperature to change — is wearing shorts with leg warmers, which are essentially the lower two thirds of a pair of tights. Leg warmers allow you to adapt to changing temperature, and, just as importantly to strip in public without embarrassment.

See and be seen

Good cycling clothing does more than make a fashion statement — it makes an epistemological statement as well: "Yo, guy in the Taurus, I exist."

While basic black may work fine for a first date or a job interview, on the road it simply makes you invisible. So when you're choosing your riding attire, channel the colors of traffic signs — bright reds, oranges, and yellows. Drivers are attuned to paying attention to those colors, and you can tap into that subliminal programming.

And even if you're riding off-road, ditching the earth tones isn't a bad idea. Remember that Bambi shares the same woods with you, and where there's deer, there are deer hunters. Wearing a bright color is one of the best ways to make sure you don't accidentally get plugged by some Elmer Fudd wannabe during hunting season.

Other Important Things You Shouldn't Forget

You're dressed; your bike is up to snuff; you're ready to ride . . . almost. You need just a few more things.

Sunglasses

You remember what your mother always said: It's only funny until someone loses an eye. Your mom was right: You should always wear sunglasses with impact-resistant lenses or some other eye protection when you're riding. It's rare, but cars, trucks, and even other riders occasionally kick up pieces of gravel and other small debris. So, if you just happen to be in the wrong place at the wrong time, you can find yourself in the market for an eye patch. Unless of course you take this advice, in which case you're in the market for a new pair of sunglasses. Or you can wear shades just because they look cool.

If you're a mountain biker, consider a pair of clear or amber glasses. On the trail, you've got to contend with the additional problem of low-hanging branches and the like, and clear or lightly tinted glasses keep you out of the poke-in-the-eye-with-a-sharp-stick scenario while allowing you to see clearly in the lovely, deep darkness of the woods.

Sunscreen

Can you say *mel-a-noma?* I knew you could.

Money for a cab

You never know when you're going to need to take a cab ride home. Or stop for a double latte.

Change for a phone call

To call that cab. Or just to let your significant other know you're taking the long way home.

An ATM or credit card

In this increasingly cash-free society, it's always good to have a way to cover unexpected expenses: a big repair at a bike shop, an impromptu dinner, or a longer cab ride home.

Your phone number

Even if you leave your wallet at home as many of us do, remember to bring a paper with your name, address, and phone number on it. It should also have your health insurance number, and the name of the hospital where you'd like to be taken in an emergency. If you're in an accident and you can't speak for yourself, that piece of paper can save your life.

Zen and the art of pedaling

Oh, there is one more thing you need before you're ready to ride your bike: a reason. If you're having trouble answering that eternal question — why am I riding my bike? — this classic bike shop/philosophy department joke ought to help:

A Zen teacher saw five of his students returning from the market on their bicycles. When they arrived at the monastery, the teacher asked the students, "Why are you riding your bicycles?"

The first student replied, "The bicycle is carrying the sack of potatoes. I'm glad that I do not have to carry them on my back." The teacher praised the first student, "You are a smart boy. When you grow old, you will not walk hunched over like I do."

The second student replied, "I love to watch the trees and fields pass by as I roll down the path." The teacher commended the second student, "Your eyes are open, and you see the world."

The third student replied, "When I ride my bicycle, I am content to chant 'nam myoho renge kyo.'" The teacher smiled at the third student and said, "Your mind will roll with the ease of a newly trued wheel."

The fourth student replied, "Riding my bicycle, I live in harmony with all sentient beings." The teacher was pleased, and said to the fourth student, "You are riding on the golden path of eternal peace."

The fifth student replied, "I ride my bicycle to ride my bicycle." The teacher sat at the feet of the fifth student and said, "I am your student."

Chapter 7

Riding Right: The Fine Art of Turning the Pedals

In This Chapter

▶ Starting elegantly

▶ Pedaling properly

▶ Turning with ease

▶ Braking safely

▶ Riding with no hands

▶ Climbing and descending hills

"*I*t's as easy as riding a bike." Hey, not so fast. While riding a bike isn't as complex as, say, playing Beethoven's Moonlight Sonata or hitting a split-finger fastball, as with all things in life, there's a right way to do it and a wrong way.

That's what this chapter's about: The right way. The right way is about gliding effortlessly along the pavement, coaxing the maximum amount of speed out of every turn of the pedals. It's about being as comfortable in the saddle as you are in your favorite chair. And it's about handling whatever the next mile throws at you — hills, turns, sudden stops — and doing it with an almost Zen-like ease.

In these pages, I discuss how to pedal comfortably, efficiently, and safely in three easy lessons. You find out how and when to shift. You discover how to take hills in stride, both up and down. You find out how to turn, turn, turn. And you can even find out how to ride no hands. Look, ma!

I assume you're already past the training wheels part, so my focus is on giving you tips on how to ride better.

Because most of these tips and techniques are situational, I'm not going to tell you, as much as *show* you (or at least as well as I can in the pages of a book). You and I are setting off on an imaginary ride, and I'll highlight those little secrets that separate real riders from mere pedal pushers. So get out your riding clothes, and get ready to tag along.

(I also assume that you're already dressed appropriately — see Chapter 6 if you're not — and that you completed a quick pre-ride safety inspection of your bike as outlined in Chapter 8.)

Getting Underway

A former editor at Marvel Comics once told me that the reason comics capture people's imagination in a way that TV and movies don't is that you never see superheroes in transitional moments. For example, you don't catch Superman in that awkward half-squat between sitting and standing. The lesson I've taken from that observation is that the key to being graceful is finessing life's transitions: If I don't look like the Green Lantern, at least I don't look like a total geek. (I hope.)

Cycling's biggest transition is pretty obvious — the one between standing still and getting moving. The key to getting in motion gracefully is proper preparation.

1. **Before you even start, make sure that your bike is in a suitable gear — something low enough so that you can spin the cranks easily, but not so low that you end up going nowhere fast.**

2. **Then, standing to the right of the bike, take hold of the handlebars and lean the bike toward you a little.**

3. **Swing your left leg over the top tube and find the pedal with your foot.**

4. **Spin the cranks backward so that the left pedal is at the 2 o'clock position, ready for the power part of the pedal stroke.**

   Figure 7-1 shows you what I mean when I refer to a clock position.

This pedal rotation is the key move. Put the pedal in a position so that you can get going easily and perhaps even gracefully. If you start with the pedal at the 5 o'clock position, you'll probably lose momentum and have to scooter with your other foot to get going.

In case you haven't figured it out yet, it takes a lot more balance to ride a bicycle slowly than it does to ride one fast. So, the secret to a clean getaway is gaining momentum quickly. And that comes by picking the right gear and getting a solid first turn of the cranks.

Once you're in motion, find the right pedal with your right foot. If you're using toe clips or clipless pedals, don't worry about them quite yet — wait until the second or third pedal stroke to clip in.

Figure 7-1:
No problem
finding the
2 o'clock
position
now.

The Three Secrets of Proper Pedaling

Pedaling is actually a pretty basic skill — just look at a 3 year-old on a Big Wheel. But pedaling properly? Well, that's an art. Because a proper pedal stroke — unlike a grown-up version of Big Wheel pedal mashing — asks your feet to perform a complex, counterintuitive task, and do it precisely, thousands of times in an hour of riding, all while your conscious brain is occupied with small matters like avoiding that double-parked Toyota.

As with most complex skills, pedaling can be broken down into simple steps. Here, then, are the three secrets of pedaling properly.

Position your foot

How about some introductions. Mr. (or Ms.) Foot meet Mr. Pedal. Mr. Pedal, meet Mr. Foot. Now that we have that out of the way, I can get to the serious business of pedaling. The first thing you've got to get straight is your relationship with Mr. Pedal. Every pedal has an axle that attaches it to the crank arm. Your mission, and, no, you can't choose not to accept it, is to put the ball of your foot on that axle, and keep it there while you're pedaling. And I mean the ball of your foot, not your arch, not the front of your heel. It's possible to pedal a bike while using the pedal as an arch support, but not very well, and definitely not without looking like a geek. Serious riders who use cycling shoes and toe clips or clipless pedals (which are not a bad idea for even casual riders, as I explain later in this chapter) spend hours trying to get this ball-over-the-axle position exactly right, because they know that efficient and injury-free cycling begins with a good foot position.

Getting the ball of your foot over the axle is more than half of the battle, but there are a few finer points. It's also important to keep your foot relatively straight while you're pedaling — not pigeon toed or duck footed. How can you tell if your foot's properly aligned? If you look down and see that your thigh is roughly parallel to the top tube of the bike, your foot position is probably pretty good.

As for the vertical relationship between your foot and the pedal, just go with the flow. If you just pedal naturally, at the top of the pedal stroke (12 o'clock) your toes are about even with your heel, while at the bottom of the stroke (6 o'clock) you're likely be on your "tiptoes" a little, with your heel above your toes (refer to Figure 7-1). Keeping a loose ankle joint to allow for this subtle movement makes for a smoother pedal stroke, but the active "ankling" motion that some cycling books advocate is really overkill and will likely leave you with nothing more than sore ankles.

Choose the right gear

The second step to righteous pedaling is choosing the right gear. Most beginning cyclists tend to choose too high a gear, figuring they'll go faster or get a better workout that way. Nope, it doesn't work that way, any more than you can win a toll booth drag race by starting your Chevette off in fourth gear. The problem with pushing a higher gear is that you also pedal slower. If your pedaling feels like you've been doing squats for an hour, then you're riding in too high a gear. Pedaling in too high a gear is also one of the quickest ways to sore knees.

Souplesse

One of the wonderful things about bicycling is its rich multi-lingual vocabulary. *Souplesse*, a French word without a strict English equivalent, is the ability to turn the pedals in a natural, supple, effortless way. When applied to your pedaling style, it's high praise indeed. Think of it as pedaling a bike the way a bird flaps its wings. Sound like fun? It is. And if you follow the simple tips outlined in this chapter, you'll be well on your way.

The key to riding efficiently is to keep your pedal cadence high — scientific studies suggest that humans pedal most efficiently at between 80 and 100 revolutions per minute.

How do you know how fast you're pedaling? Well, you could just get your watch and count. But that's kind of a drag. You could buy a cycle computer with a cadence function. Not a bad idea if you want one anyway. But you can get the same information for free at your health club. Most stationary exercise bikes have a cadence (or rpm) readout. Pay attention to it the next time you're there. If you're trudging away at 70 rpm, then lower the resistance until you get to that magic 90 rpm mark. Try to stay in that range during your next few workouts — it'll soon become second nature.

Now, take that lesson on the road. On a flat stretch of road, tap into your muscle memory to get to that magic 90 rpm mark. If you err, err on the side of pedaling too fast.

- ✔ If you find it too hard to pedal, then shift to a smaller gear — go to a larger cog on your freewheel.

- ✔ If you feel like a mouse in a Habitrail, scurrying furiously but getting nowhere fast, then shift to a higher gear/smaller cog.

The idea is to find a gear that lets you feel some resistance, but not too much.

Get that feeling of pedaling loose and easy into your muscles. The whole purpose behind those 24 gears is to allow you to pedal that way on any terrain and under any conditions. The following tips should help:

- ✔ Riding into a headwind? Shift down.

- ✔ Got a tail wind at your back? Shift up.

- ✔ Feeling frisky at the beginning of the ride? Shift up.

- ✔ Feeling tired at the end of the ride? Shift back down.

- ✔ Hills? I talk about them in the "To Hill and Back" section, a little later in this chapter.

Pedal in circles

Take a close look at the chain ring on your bicycle. What is it shaped like? A banana cream pie? A smiley face? A PJ Harvey CD? No, this isn't a Rorschach test. Whatever you think it looks like, it's round.

And doesn't it follow, therefore, that your pedal stroke should be round, too? That's easier said than done. For the moment, think about your chain ring as a clock face. Most people pedal a bike a little like they walk — push down with one foot, then push down with the other. In short, they do almost all of their pedaling between 2 o'clock and 4 o'clock. Now you can move the bike like this, but there is a better way.

The key is to use more of the clock. When your foot crosses the 12 o'clock point, consciously think about pushing forward. The downstroke between two and four o'clock more or less takes care of itself.

When your foot reaches four o'clock, shift your focus and think about pulling back.

One of the best places to improve your pedal stroke is at the gym. A studio cycling class, which features bikes with a fixed-gear flywheel system, forces you to pedal in circles — the pedals virtually pull your legs around. A conventional stationary bike is also a fine place to start. Without having to worry about little things like balance and traffic and whether that's your neighbor driving that new BMW, you can concentrate on one thing: turning the pedals.

All studio cycling bikes and most stationary bikes have some kind of toe clips, so you can get a first-hand (or should I say first-foot?) feel for how clips can help your pedaling. They can also help you realize that getting in and out isn't as much of a hassle as you thought.

Making contact

The hardware side to a strong pedal stroke is good, solid contact between your shoes and the pedal. You don't have to be a physicist to understand why it's hard to push forward or pull back if your foot is slipping off the pedal. The first solution is to make sure you're wearing the right shoes — something with grippy soles. Penny loafers and anything else with leather soles can be downright unsafe.

A better solution is clipless pedals or toe clips (see Chapter 5 for more details). Most riders are pretty concerned about getting into — and especially out of — their toe clips or cleated shoes. "What if I get up to a stoplight and my foot's stuck in the pedal?" you ask. "Won't I just topple over like a turtle?" Well, I'd be lying to you if I said that this never, ever happens to anyone. But it's actually pretty rare, and that kind of slow-motion fall is generally more bruising to the ego than to the body.

Contrast this with the flying-foot fall, in which your unsecured foot slips off the pedal, goes flying into your spokes, and the bike flips you like an also-ran at the Calgary Stampede. This is not a good way to fall. This is why toe clips or clipless pedals are a good idea.

There you have it. If you want to pedal like a pro, just remember these three "S"s:

- Set your feet.
- Shift to the right gear.
- Spin the pedals.

Your Turn

While it should be obvious by the lack of six-way power seats and cruise control (not to mention the monthly payment), your bicycle is not a car. So don't try to steer it like one. This may be news to you, but you don't make a bicycle go where you want by simply turning the handlebars. In fact, if you turn the handlebars too hard, you'll likely end up on the ground.

Good turning technique requires more than a little body English. You want to lean your body to the inside of the turn while turning the handlebars only gently (see Figure 7-2). Centrifugal force takes care of a lot of this for you — you're probably leaning the bike a little without even realizing it.

Figure 7-2:
Leaning into
a turn.

But truly effective cornering entails giving Mr. Newton's forces a hand. The first thing you have to do is stop pedaling and move your inside pedal to the 12 o'clock position and the outside pedal to 6 o'clock so you don't scrape your pedal on the ground. Some coaches also suggest pointing your inside knee toward the ground — but you have to realize that the important thing is not the knee move so much as the adjustment you have to make at your hips to make it happen. Ideally, you want to lean into the turn with your hips while keeping your shoulders relatively level. If you're doing this right, it should almost feel like you're doing a side stretch, with the "long" side on the inside of the turn. Another tip is to consciously push down on the handlebar on the inside of your turn. This helps shift your weight to the inside of the turn and keeps the wheels tracking as if you were on rails.

The other part of the turn business is tactical. The first thing you need to remember is to control your speed before you start the turn. Hitting the brakes in the middle of a turn can make the rear wheel slide out, taking you with it.

Your goal, when traffic and other obstacles allow, is to take the shortest, straightest line through a turn. The bike — take my word for it — tends to go in a straight line. So you want to find the line that lets the bike do what comes naturally. Start at the far end of a turn, go straight across the apex — the inside point of the turn — and end up on the far side of the corner, the way a race driver might.

Them's the Brakes

One thing you have to say about a car — you don't have to think about the brakes very much. Not so with a bicycle. Treat them with skill and respect, and they'll be your friends. If you don't though . . . well. Good braking is largely a matter of subtlety.

The tricky thing — and the cool thing — about a bike is that you control the front and back brakes independently. Used wisely, this feature gives you great power — braking-wise at least.

Let me clue you in to a couple of laws of nature: First, understand this: Your front brake is by far the more powerful of the two. Stop the front wheel, and the back is sure to follow. That's the law. But the corollary to that law is that if you stop the front too suddenly, the back continues to move — remember inertia, that "Bodies in motion tend to stay in motion" stuff? So if you use the front brakes to stop too quickly, the bike — and you — end up doing a somersault. Not fun.

So here are some simple rules for effective braking.

Always use both brakes

A decent application of the rear brake virtually guarantees that the vaulting-over-the-handlebars scenario remains nothing more than an interesting exercise in theoretical physics.

Use the front brake more

It's easy to get freaked out by the possibility of doing a Mary Lou Retton on your bike and then overcompensate by trying to stop by just wailing on the rear brake only. Don't. It's the front brake that's really going to stop you when you need it, and in an extreme situation using the front brake can mean the difference between a close call and getting up close and personal with the rear bumper of a minivan. So squeeze that front brake hard — on level pavement, a 60-40 split between the front and rear brakes is about right. On hills, favor the rear brake a little more. Using the rear brake too much or too early can make the back wheel skid. Not cool.

Leave 'em unlocked

The key is to brake as hard as you need to, but not too hard. Maximum braking power happens just before your brakes lock up. But the bad news is that as bad as it is locking up your brakes on a car, it's an even bigger problem on your bike. If you lock up your brakes while traveling with any speed, you'll probably fall. (Yes, mountain bikers occasionally deliberately lock up a rear, or even both wheels, but only under very specialized circumstances like a steep descent on a loose surface, in which the ground surface is actually moving even though the wheels don't. But on pavement, locking your wheel is a bad idea.)

You've got to be the ABS brain of this brake system. The first thing to do is find out just how much pressure it takes to make your brakes lock up. So you've got to do a controlled experiment. Riding very slowly on a smooth, level, lightly trafficked road, apply your brakes firmly. Then start rolling again, and make another stop, this time applying the brakes a little more firmly. Keep doing this until you feel your wheels start to skid just a little. That's your lockup point. The idea is to brake as hard as you can without locking your wheels up.

"Look Ma, No Hands"

Riding with no hands — it's a rite of passage for youngsters everywhere, fitting solidly in the space between first steps and first dates. But, wait, you say you missed out on that course of your cultural education?

Why ride no hands? So that you can . . .

- Stretch your back
- Drink while you're riding without dribbling on your bike
- Eat a banana or a PowerBar
- Read a map
- Wipe your sunglasses
- Put on a rain jacket or take one off
- Show the world that you can ride no hands

In short, so that you can make the most of your opposable thumbs while your legs are getting you where you want to go. Obviously, some of these are more advanced moves, and you don't want to be riding hands free in heavy traffic, on a bumpy road, or a narrow shoulder.

Don't worry. It's so easy an adult can do it. The first order of business is finding an appropriate stretch of road — someplace flat, wide, smooth, and free of traffic. Riding no hands is largely an act of faith. Assuming that your bike is in reasonably good *alignment* (one wheel is right behind the other) and the wheels are more or less *true* (are round and don't wobble side-to-side), in the absence of any steering input from you, your bike tends to go in a straight line.

Nice theory, but you're not going to risk a case of road rash on it, are you? To find out for yourself, start out gradually. Ride in a straight line, pedaling smoothly, and slowly lighten your grip on the handlebars. Bike's still going straight, right? Now try letting go, gently raising your hands just an inch or two from the grips. Still going straight?

Actually, balancing is easier if you sit all the way up, a position that puts your shoulders right over your hips, and relax your arms. But what about those little steering corrections that keep your bike going in the right direction?

It's body English time. As the bike moves slightly in one direction, shift your weight ever so slightly — that's far enough — in the opposite direction. You're probably doing this anyway almost without realizing it, so don't exaggerate the move; it should be all but imperceptible. The skinny: You almost feel like you're steering the bike with your butt.

Wrist Management

Let's talk about your wrists. This is not a subject that comes up much in cycling circles: Lots of talk about quads; lots of talk about backs. Not a lot of talk about wrists.

You don't hear a lot about upper-body position in cycling — until someone gets injured.

That's what happened to me the first year I started to pile up significant mileage on my bike — back before I had my learner's permit. I read lots and thought lots about my cadence and my gear selection. I gave no thought whatsoever to my upper body until one day my right wrist started hurting a little. And a little more. And a lot more. And within a few hundred miles I could barely open a door. And worse, I could barely grip the handlebars.

I sought the counsel of some older riders, who immediately figured it out. I was riding with my elbows locked, which transmitted all the road shock to my wrists. I didn't realize it at the time, but I was in the early stages of what occupational therapists call repetitive stress injury — the kind of overuse syndrome that turns classical pianists into conductors. It was a one-way ticket to Tendonitis City.

The solution? A couple days of rest, an icepack, a pair of padded cycling gloves. And most importantly, a new position on the bike. From then on I've made sure I ride with my elbows bent so they can act like shock absorbers. I also loosened my grip on the bars to give my wrists and fingers a break, and learned to change hand positions pretty frequently. (That's why road bars are shaped like they are, and you can get the same benefit with flat bars by using auxiliary bar ends.) The end of the story? My wrist stopped hurting. I kept on riding. I eventually got my learner's permit. I still kept riding.

To Hill and Back

Okay, you're pretty cool riding on the flats. But uh-oh, here comes a big hill. Do you:

    a. Shift to a lower gear.

    b. Shift to a higher gear.

    c. Get off and start walking.

    d. Abandon hope.

Actually, while hills can be pretty intimidating, they don't have to be that difficult. Follow these simple rules and you can be a virtual mountain goat.

Shift

That's why your bike has all those gears, to make this hill climbing stuff easier, if not actually easy. The good thing is that, unlike Saabs, hills don't sneak up on you. They pretty much stay where they are, so when you see one ahead, you have plenty of time to prepare.

The first thing you need to do is assess the hill. How long is it? How steep is it? Is the pitch pretty consistent or does it vary a lot? Say you encounter something that's more of a molehill than an actual mountain. If you're riding in a middle-of-the-road gear (on the middle chain ring and one of the middle cogs) make a moderate downshift with your rear derailleur — move to the next biggest cog on your freewheel — before you get to the hill.

A more formidable obstacle — a long hill, or a shorter one that's very steep — requires a little advance planning: Use your front derailleur to shift to your smallest chain ring, while staying on one of the middle cogs on your freewheel.

The key is to make your shift — or at least your first shift — before you get to the hill. Your eyes should tell you that a hill is coming. If you wait for your legs — grunt, gasp — to tell you that you're there, you've lost the battle.

Shifting early gives you the chance to maintain an optimum cadence. It allows you to adjust your gear choice. And derailleurs do their best shifting when they're not under too much pressure. When you're straining, you're drive-train is too.

Figure 7-3 shows some shifting points for a sample hill.

Figure 7-3:
The right
places
to shift on
this hill.

Upshift on a hill? No, that's not the cycling equivalent of jumbo shrimp. Most hills don't have a consistent slope, and many start out steep, flatten out for a while, and then get steeper near the peak. So be prepared for that flat middle section, and if you're feeling up to it, upshift a gear.

Spin

On moderate hills, your goal should be to pedal the same way you do on the flats. The spin-in-circles style of pedaling works great on hills too. Stay in the saddle, keep your cadence high, downshift if you're getting bogged down, and you're at the top before you know it.

Stand

If you're addressing a long hill, or a very short, steep one, standing is a great change-up strategy. No, not literally standing — I mean pedaling out of the saddle. Just getting your butt off the saddle allows you to change positions and allows you to pedal in slightly higher gear. So at the point where you're ready to downshift, try pedaling out of the saddle for a few strokes, and allow the bike to move naturally from side to side beneath you. Some racers rock the bike very aggressively as they stomp the pedals, but that's more for show than go.

Psyche yourself up

Hills are psychological, as well as physical, obstacles. There comes a time during every hard climb when hitchhiking seems like a very attractive option. The key is to harness your inner doubts, to send your inner critic off to play with your inner child. After all, you need to *see* yourself at the top of the hill before you can *be* at the top of the hill. Enough of the self-help book claptrap. Here's some real world advice.

Set intermediate goals

When you're at that point where you're really hurting, you need a distraction. Count pedal strokes. Pick a landmark. Hum the theme song to *Gilligan's Island*. Anything that breaks up a big, formidable task into manageable segments can help you reach the top.

Don't fall on the fallback

Unless you're crossing the Continental Divide (and especially if you are), don't immediately shift into your absolute lowest gear. If you do that right away, and the hill gets unexpectedly steeper, or you tire more quickly than you thought, well, you're walkin'. Consider that lowest, bailout gear as if it's your nest egg: Don't go there unless you really need to. When the going gets tough, it's a big psychological boost to know that you have a fallback position. And when you get to the top without having used it, you feel like you've accomplished something.

Pat yourself on the back

Not literally. But climbing a hill is an accomplishment. So when you get to the top, reward yourself, even if it's only with a swig of water or a bite of banana.

The Down Side: A Few Words about Descending

Okay, you made it to the top, and now you've got gravity on your side. Excellent. Your role has changed pretty dramatically — you can stop being the engine and start being the pilot. On steep hills, you can pretty much forget about pedaling. Put your hands in an optimal steering position — on the grips or the brake hoods — where you can reach the brakes easily. Move the cranks to the 3 o'clock/9 o'clock position and move your butt back on the saddle a little for extra stability.

Then watch where you're going. Since you can easily end up going twice as fast on a long downhill as you do on the flats, you need to anticipate obstacles — sewer grates, uneven pavement, cars, pedestrians, and anything else you can think of. If you have to steer around an obstacle, do it gently. Jerk the handlebars around and you'll probably fall. Same with the brakes. Apply them oh-so-gingerly, favoring the rear brake slightly. Especially on a long hill, you don't want to "ride" the brakes. Apply them gently and then release them — the friction of a long downhill run has been known to literally melt brake pads. But mostly, enjoy the ride. This is your reward for making it to the top of the hill.

Chapter 8

You're Saaaafe: Dealing with Road Hazards

. . . .

In This Chapter

▶ Inspecting your bike

▶ Riding in traffic

▶ Dealing with dogs

▶ Riding on bike paths

. . . .

*B*icycling isn't bowling. It's not one of those activities that draws you in, serves you a beer, and lets you escape from the world. It's a game that gets you out in the world in all its 3-D glory. The good part, of course, is that every ride is different, its own little adventure. The bad part is that the world can be an unpredictable place, and occasionally forces — like bumpy roads, inattentive drivers, overeager watch dogs, and yes, even other riders — conspire to make your adventure, well, a little too adventurous. In short, once you leave your home, you've got more to worry about than whether the lanes were waxed last night.

That's what this chapter is about: dealing with those on-road surprises and riding safely in an at-times unsafe world. In this chapter, I lay out cycling's fundamental rules of the road: How to anticipate road hazards. How to ride safely and confidently in traffic. How to make sure that dog stays man's best friend. Which non-moving obstacles can be just as dangerous as the most reckless driver and how to avoid them. And a lot more.

In truth, this is the most important chapter in the book. Buy the wrong bike or pedal in the wrong gear, and those mistakes can be rectified. But if you miscalculate your relationship with a 2,000 pound chunk of metal, the implications can be far more serious. The ultimate goal of every ride, after all, is to get back home safely. All the better to ride another day.

A Pre-Ride Checklist

Safety begins at home. I know this for a fact. Let me explain. Once upon a time, I was ready to put my $2,500 custom-built racing bike into my girlfriend's $400 car — a 13-year-old BMW named Billy — to go for a ride. As I turned the bike upside down to remove the front wheel, what I saw scared me more than a Wes Craven movie: There was a crack halfway around the back side of the right fork blade. At the moment I didn't know whether I should be miserable about a big, expensive problem with my beloved bike or relieved that I found it this way instead of by ending up on the ground at 25 miles an hour after my fork collapsed on the third bump I hit. In the intervening years I've gained a new respect for how difficult it is to repair the human body, and I've come to consider this one of the happier moments of my life. And ever since, I've made it my business to go through this five-step, 60-second safety tour of my bike every time I roll it out.

Wheelie important

The first thing to do is to check that your front wheel is really, truly and completely attached to your bike. Check that the axle is securely held by the *dropouts* — the u-shaped slots on the end of the fork — and that the bolts or quick-release mechanism are holding tight. If you're not sure how the axle's supposed to fit, or how the quick release is supposed to work, turn to Chapter 14 and/or ask someone at your local bike shop. It's that important. Then, while you're at it, check the rear wheel. It's not as crucial, but if it slips, it could still result in a fall.

Give it a brake

Try both brakes. They should feel firm when you squeeze the levers and snap back positively when you release them. Some brakes have a quick-release mechanism that opens the caliper wide to make it easier to remove the wheel. Make sure that this in the closed position. For mountain/hybrid brakes, make sure the transverse cable is seated correctly on both sides of the brake arm and/or the cable hanger. Then spin each wheel quickly and make sure that the brake pads rub against the rim only when the brakes are on and don't rub against the tires.

Pressure situation

Now, check your tires. If you've got a gauge, use it, but if you don't, just push a thumb into the sidewall of your tire. It should feel firm, but not quite rock hard. Tires tend to lose air even while the bike's just sitting down in the basement, and underinflated tires are much more prone to flats. If you haven't ridden your bike for a while, check to make sure that the tire itself isn't cracked or split. (For more information on tire pressure, see Chapter 13.)

Bar associations

Look at your handlebars and make sure that they're perfectly perpendicular to your front wheel. Lean on the handlebars a little to make sure that the *binder bolts* — the bolt that attaches the bars to the stem, and the bolt that attaches the stem to the fork — are both tight. And don't forget to listen — a cracked handlebar will often creak before it breaks.

The frame thing

Yes, frame failure is very rare thing, but if you've been in an accident, or if your mountain bike gets off-road use/abuse, check for it anyway. Simply look at the main joints of the frame and make sure that there aren't any gaps that weren't there before. Then check the dropouts and the *fork crown,* the joint at the top of the fork near the brakes. Suspension forks on mountain bikes are especially vulnerable to impact damage in a crash, so give them special attention. Rust is also a big danger sign. Of course, if you see anything that looks at all suspicious, don't chance it. Take the bike right to a bike shop to have it evaluated by a competent mechanic.

Cars Are Cars

Repeat after me: Cars are evil. They are the enemy. It's them or us.

No, not really. Most drivers are actually pretty attentive and courteous. That's how you are when you're behind the wheel, right? The problem is that most motorists are not really attuned to sharing the road with bicyclists. Some get kind of freaked out, figuring that anyone on a bike has the attention span of an eight-year-old and is about to swerve right in front of them. So they honk the horn, slow down to nine miles an hour and pass you with an eight-foot berth, while holding up everyone behind them. Others concede your right to the road grudgingly. They'll zoom by right on the edge of the shoulder, their door handles passing within inches of your handlebars.

But, in truth, most drivers are too busy making cell phone calls, changing the radio station or spilling hot coffee on themselves to notice that you even exist. Most of the time this is fine, but occasionally, your invisibility works against you. Like when a driver wants to make a right hand turn, and you happen to be crossing the intersection.

Here are four basic rules for happy coexistence with your four-wheeled friends.

Be decisive

The biggest key to safe riding is to send clear signals to those around you. Act like you know just where you're heading and how to get there. (If you don't know where you're going, how can you expect that guy in the Explorer to figure it out?) Ride in a straight line. Keep a consistent pace. Signal your turns (covered later in this chapter). If you get involved in a "You first . . . No, *you* first" situation with a driver, be the one to take initiative. Give an appropriate hand signal and either proceed quickly or yield decisively.

Be alert

Save the spacing out for the stationary bike. You need to scan the road even more conscientiously than when you're behind the wheel of a motorized vehicle. Watch for cars in front of you and beside you, and listen for cars as they approach (and when applicable take a peek over your shoulder or into your rear view mirror). And don't forget to look at the road in front of you for glass or road debris — especially prevalent on the shoulder where you'll be riding.

Be prepared

Sometimes, despite your best efforts to be proactive, something happens that takes you by surprise; a car turning in front of you, a dog chasing you, a car door flung open in your face. So try to think through some of these scenarios in advance. While your first instinct may be to grab for your brakes, remember that it's usually easier and faster to steer around an obstacle than to try to stop on the proverbial dime. But don't swerve too far to the left — you could move right in front of a passing car.

Be a vehicle

This is the golden rule of riding in traffic. In fact, most states and municipalities don't make distinctions between bicycles and motor vehicles in their traffic codes. Every now and then this results in a humorous news item about a guy who gets arrested for DWI while riding his bike. But this legal distinction (or lack thereof) has much more profound implications. On the one hand, you have a right to a place on the road. Just because your top speed is 25 miles an hour doesn't mean you're a second-class citizen.

But with that right comes responsibilities. Don't assume that you get special favors because you've got two wheels instead of four. Follow all traffic laws, even when it's not convenient. Specifically, I mean don't run red lights or stop signs. You shouldn't feel any sillier sitting at a traffic light at a quiet intersection than if you were in the same situation behind the wheel. If you want respect, you've gotta earn it.

Traffic School

How much do you really know about riding on the road? Get out your number two pencil. Fill out the boxes completely. No looking at your neighbor's paper. You've got 10 minutes, starting now. Good luck.

1. **On a city street, you should ride . . .**

    a. Against the flow of traffic

    b. With the flow of traffic

    c. With no regard to the flow of traffic

    d. As fast as possible

2. **You're riding on a two-lane road and the shoulder abruptly ends. You should ride . . .**

    a. On the sidewalk

    b. As far to the right as possible

    c. Right on the yellow line between the two lanes

    d. To a payphone to call your Senator (You pay taxes, don't you!?)

3. **When you come to a red light at an intersection, you should . . .**

    a. Stop

    b. Get off your bike and walk across

    c. Slow down, and then proceed before the light turns green

    d. Turn around and go back home

4. **Before you make a left turn, you should give the driver behind you . . .**

    a. The right of way

    b. A hand signal

    c. A long look in your mirror at his license plate

    d. The finger

5. If you're involved in an accident with a car, you should . . .

    a. Call your lawyer

    b. Call the police

    c. Call an ambulance

    d. All of the above

Answers:

1. B. While runners are taught to head into traffic, bicycles are vehicles and must follow the flow of traffic at all times. And besides, isn't it better to go with the flow?

2. B. If there is a shoulder, you should ride on it. If there isn't, ride as far to the right as you can to give drivers as much room as possible to pass you on the left. Calling your senator isn't a bad idea, but wait until you get home.

3. A. No, this isn't a trick question. The same applies to stop signs.

4. B. Inform your fellow road users of your intention with a left turn signal — an outstretched left hand.

5. D. Well, not necessarily in that order. Obviously the ambulance (if necessary) comes first. Then the police to file an accident report. (You have the same obligations as if you were driving a car.) And while juries have been historically unsympathetic to claims made by bicyclists, you owe it not only to yourself but to your fellow cyclists to get whatever compensation you can if you were injured through the negligence of a motorist.

The route of the problem

Want to avoid most of the hassles of riding in traffic? I'll let you in on one of the best kept secrets in cycling: Choose your route carefully. An ideal route has the following things:

- A reasonable speed limit — 35 miles an hour or less.
- Little or no traffic.
- A wide, clean shoulder.
- Few, if any, major intersections.
- A distance long enough (or short enough) to fit into your schedule. And if it's scenic, so much the better.

So how do you find this kind of ideal route? You scout. Ask other riders. Ask at your friendly neighborhood bike shop. And be on the lookout when you're driving. Obviously, you'll have to stray from your regular route — if you're happy to take those roads on a car, then they're probably too fast for low-stress bicycling. Instead, search out those side streets and back roads that are too pokey for four-wheeled transit. Chances are that most other drivers feel the same, and you and your bike can have those roads more or less to yourself.

Your turn signals

You probably learned the bike hand signals when you were in a kid. In case you forgot, check 'em out in Figure 8-1. Then use them.

Left Turn   Stop   Right Turn

Figure 8-1:
How to
signal your
movements
on the road.

The lefty

The left-hand turn is kind of the post-graduate move of riding in traffic. Doing a good one takes a fair amount of advance planning, because you have to be aware of traffic in two different directions. First, take a peek behind you to judge the traffic, not only the presence of cars, but their speed as well. If the coast is clear, scan ahead and look at the coming traffic in the opposite lane, and then for traffic on the street you're turning onto.

Here comes the tricky part: You need to coordinate all that information. First you have to merge from the shoulder into the flow of traffic — remember to signal first — and then move quickly toward the center line to get ready for the turn. Make sure that the coast is still clear in the opposite direction on your destination street. The key to a good turn is to slow down if you need to, but avoid stopping if at all possible. If you have to come to a full stop, you're essentially a pedestrian, because a standing start on a bike isn't much faster than walking.

Figure 8-2 depicts a good left turn.

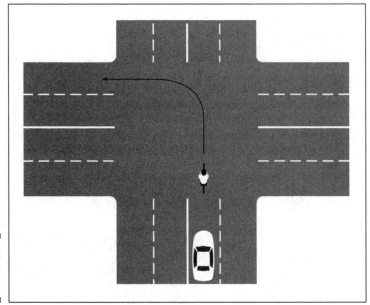

Figure 8-2:
Making a
left turn.

The case for common courtesy

Okay, I admit it. I've given the finger to my share of drivers who cut me off, passed too close, or otherwise endangered my life while I was riding my bicycle. I've shouted a few things I wouldn't say in front of my two-year-old son, too. No, I'm not advocating this strategy, except under extreme duress and only when the car is well out of swerving range.

On the other hand, I also go out of my way to acknowledge courteous driving. If, surprise of surprises, some one yields to me, I smile. I wave. I even yell "Thank you" to let them know that their small act of civility didn't go unnoticed.

And when I'm at a stop light, I check behind me to see if a car is waiting to make a right. If so, I pull my bike to the left to make way for the car's right turn on red. It doesn't cost anything, and it keeps traffic moving.

In part, I consider these small actions positive reinforcement, a way to turn the minivan into a Skinner Box. Drivers who are rewarded for their courtesy are more likely to repeat it. And in the bigger picture, it's public relations. By showing drivers that cyclists can be civil, courteous, and even downright friendly, I hope to engender some good feelings that'll encourage them to smile at a cyclist somewhere down the line — or maybe even go for a ride themselves.

But I also recognize that this door swings both ways. So for this reason, I'm not above giving a lecture to a cyclist — especially a young cyclist — who I see violating traffic rules or riding in an unsafe manner. For better or worse, all of us on two wheels get painted with the same broad brush, so let's make sure it's sable and watercolors, not tar and feathers.

The hidden dangers of stationary cars

Approach a parked, but occupied, car the way you'd approach a sleeping grizzly bear — very carefully. Cars, you see, have doors. And while most drivers peek over their shoulders or check their mirrors before pulling out, they almost never do that before opening the door. If you happen to be five feet behind the car, moving at 15 miles an hour, when this happens, the results can be disastrous. If you hit the door, it's bad news (see Figure 8-3). I've heard of bike/door collisions in which the force of the impact was so great that it actually folded the door back against the fender. Likewise, in trying to avoid the opening door, you can end up instinctively swerving to your left, and out into the flow of traffic. Again, bad news.

Figure 8-3: A disaster about to occur.

In general, give parked cars at least a couple of feet of clearance, enough to avoid getting doored. If you're on a really tight street, you have to focus almost as much attention on the parked cars as the moving ones. If a car's got a head in it, check the brake lights. If they're on and they go off, it's likely that the door's ready to open. Which means that you should prepare for evasive action. Be especially careful around taxi cabs — they're prone to making sudden stops, and passengers rarely think twice before opening the door.

A few words about trucks

If cars are like the rhinos of the road-going world, then trucks and buses are the elephants. They're so big and lumbering that they can cause problems without even meaning to. Their height and length make it difficult for drivers to see small cars, much less a bicycle. (As the bumper sticker says, if you can't see a truck driver's mirrors, then she can't see you. And if you can see her mirrors, she probably can't see you anyway.)

So the best strategy is avoidance. Give a passing truck as wide a berth as possible, especially near intersections where a wide right turn is a definite possibility. And remember, buses make frequent stops, so view every bus stop as an occasion to reach for the brakes. Or better still, get to know bus routes and stops so you can stay out of their way altogether.

Slippery when wet

In case you hadn't figured it out by now, the road system in most of North America was not designed with bicycles in mind. And the logical extension of this is that plenty of things that cars take in their stride can send a bicyclist tumbling to the ground. Here are a few of those dangerous obstacles and how to handle them.

Wet and slick pavement

In the first few minutes of a rainstorm, riding on asphalt can be like riding on a skating rink with no Zamboni in sight. Especially if it's been a while since the last rain, the water brings the small amounts of oil on the road to the surface and the result is a microscopic re-creation of the Exxon Valdez scenario.

Ride gingerly, avoiding excess body movements. Leave extra space for stopping — caliper brakes can become all but useless in a heavy rain. Be especially cautious while cornering — slow down before the turn, take a conservative line, and don't lean the bike over too much in the turn.

Potholes

Let's put it this way. If a monster pothole can collapse the suspension of a Buick, what chance do you think your front wheel has?

The strategy: Avoid big potholes at all costs, and if you can't see the bottom because of a puddle of water, assume it's deeper than it looks. Small potholes or other kinds of broken pavement can be dealt with by basic rough road technique: Stop pedaling, pull your pedals parallel to the road, lift your butt off the saddle, and let the bike bounce around beneath you, with your bent elbows and knees absorbing the shock.

Sewer grates

The granddaddy of all road hazards. Some sewer grates run parallel to the direction of the road and have slots wide enough to swallow a bicycle tire (see Figure 8-4). If this happens, you'll come to an unbelievably abrupt stop and get pitched over onto your head. Not a pleasant prospect. The strategy: Look for grates and steer around them.

Train tracks

Mass transit is a good thing. But train tracks and their associated crossings sometimes have little gaps that can catch a bike tire. And at worst, they can be bumpy enough to toss you down if you're not expecting them.

The strategy: First slow down. Then assume the bumpmeister stance you use for potholes. And to avoid those gaps, cross the tracks as perpendicularly as possible so that your wheel is never perfectly parallel to a gap. Be especially careful around wet tracks, which are as slippery as the proverbial eel. And needless to say, always obey grade crossing signals. You can't *possibly* be in that much of a hurry.

Figure 8-4:
Doh!

Metal grates and plates

Bridges are often covered with metal gratings and big expansion joints. By the same token, when a road is under repair, the road crews often lay big metal plates to temporarily cover their mess. Both situations have much in common. Metal grates and coverings can be a) very slick b) bumpy enough to taco a wheel c) and have gaps that can swallow a wheel just like a sewer grate. The strategy: It's combination tactic time. Slow down and approach with extreme caution. Avoid any unnecessary movement by riding in a straight line and not applying sudden pressure to the pedals or brakes. Ride with special delicacy when the grates are wet. On bumpy sections, use the techniques I describe in the preceding "Potholes" section. And then thank heaven for asphalt.

No Dogs Eating Bicycles

Back in my college days in Chicago's South Side, I subsisted on chicken from Harold's Chicken Shack — $3.18 for a half a chicken and fries, 425 grams of fat, no extra charge. Harold's was a no-frills kind of place — the cashier stood behind bulletproof glass, and one of the few accoutrements in the waiting area was a sign that read: No Dogs Eating Bicycles. While he undoubtedly omitted the commas inadvertently, Harold also hit on a fundamental truism about cycling. Dogs and bikes don't mix.

When I'm on foot, I love dogs as much as Betty White does. When I'm riding, I'd really rather have them be occupied with a rawhide bone than my rear derailleur. Or my left calf.

Don't blame it on Rover. It's just human, um, canine nature. Dogs are very territorial, and when you're pedaling in front of their house, you represent a threat to their pack. Plus, like their hunter ancestors, they like to chase things, and on your bike you make for much more sporting quarry than the neighbor's cat. These are the reasons dogs chase cars. But while even a Geo has enough horsepower to outrun a frisky Lab, any reasonably athletic dog can catch you and probably knock you off your bike.

Here's how you and Fido can co-exist peacefully.

Watch for dogs

Keep your eyes open. Assume that every front yard has a German shepherd who's under-exercised and over-stimulated. Eventually, you'll be right.

See Spot run

If Fido does set out after you, you're faced with a variation on that classic fight or flight dilemma. All things considered, you're better off riding away, *if,* and this is a big if, you're sure you can outrun your four-legged foe. If you're a reasonably fit rider, and it's a small dog, this isn't a bad gamble. However if the dog does catch you, he's likely to try to herd you like a sheep, and that may mean darting in front of you — a situation which could result in painful interaction for both you and Fido. So, if it's a big dog, or your sprinting skills aren't up to par, consider Plan B below.

See Dick walk

The most foolproof way of defusing the situation is simply to get off your bike and walk slowly away. This can help Fido realize that you're just a human being in funny pants and he'll lose interest. But just in case, keep the bike as a barrier between you and the dog. Talk to the dog, in either a gentle "Nice doggie" tone, or a more commanding "No! Stop this . . . now, Rover" groove. Whichever you choose, it's true that dogs can tell if you're afraid, so do your best to keep your cool.

On very rare occasions, a dog will continue menacing you, even after you've dismounted. Some riders carry a can of aerosol pepper spray for just such occasions, but a squirt from a water bottle can distract the dog almost as well. If the dog appears ready to pounce, use the bike as a shield, and call for help. "Fire!" works well in these situations.

And one more thing. If you encounter the same dog day after day on your regular route, be proactive. After all, it's not really the dog's fault. So call the owners, and suggest politely that they may want to keep the dog tied up or fenced in. Explain your encounters with the dog, bearing in mind that referring to the dog as Cujo probably won't help the situation. Focus not on yourself, but on the welfare of the dog. If these encounters continue, the canine in question is likely to bite someone or get hit by a car. Or even a bicycle.

The Path to Enlightenment

Ah, the bike path. Your sanctuary. Your oasis. Your Xanadu (minus Olivia Newton-John). With no cars to worry about, you can either zone out or hammer at full speed, right? And you believe in the Easter Bunny, too, I'll bet. Look around. The path is crowded with in-line skaters, Dads pushing jogging strollers, power-walking senior citizens, toddlers chasing squirrels, and other riders who aren't paying attention. If it's nirvana, it's more like the Kurt Cobain kind.

But there is one big difference between the road and the bike path. In this figurative food chain, you're on the top. You're the biggest, fastest, and arguably least maneuverable path-user. Which is why you've got to pay attention not only to yourself but to everyone around you, too.

Who to watch out for

Here's a list of the hazards you're likely to encounter on a friendly, neighborhood bike path:

Runners

Good news: They tend to keep a pretty predictable pace. And they look so miserable that it makes you feel lucky to be riding a bike.

Bad news: They're so into their endorphin high or that Gloria Estefan tape, that they're pretty much oblivious to anything outside their little circle of stride.

Skaters

Good news: They move fast, and a lot of them at least wear helmets.

Bad news: A lot of skaters are in over their heads and seem especially close to disaster on hills.

Pedestrians

Good news: They move slowly. (No easy-target jokes, okay?)

Bad news: They have absolute right of way, and they tend to abuse it.

Kids

Good news: They're cute and cuddly.

Bad news: They're creatures of the moment, and if the biggest fun of the moment consists of dashing across the path to chase a squirrel, that's exactly what they'll do, regardless of whether you're bearing down on them at 15 miles an hour or not.

Animals

Good news: I'm not only talking about dogs here. I'm talking about that squirrel, the preoccupied pigeon, and a stray ferret. Most semi-wild animals do have enough good sense to move out of your way.

Bad news: If you've ever taken even a casual interest in the road kill smorgasbord that lines our roads and highways, you'll recognize that this is hardly a hard-and-fast rule.

Bike path survival strategies

So what do you do to stay safe when you have all manner of humans and animals sharing the bike path with you? Follow these simple rules:

Yield

Exercise your imagination for a moment. Assume, if you will, that every tree has a yield sign on it. Assume that at any moment someone is going to do something wholly unpredictable. Now you're in the proper mindset.

Signal

When you're coming up behind slower traffic, simply say politely, "On your left" if you plan to pass on the left. But be prepared for the possibility that the people you want to pass a) didn't hear you or b) misunderstood what you said and are going to veer to the left, right in front of you.

Slow down

Just because you're the fastest thing on the path doesn't mean you have to be really *fast*. The best ally in dealing with the unexpected is a moderate speed. When you're on a packed part of the path, just slow down.

Hit the road

Sometimes you should just take the path of least resistance. And if the path is super-crowded, maybe you should be riding on the road. At least cars are predictable (usually).

Chapter 9

Fitness: The Final Frontier

• •

In This Chapter

▶ How cycling stacks up to other exercises

▶ What, when, and how to eat

▶ Why water is important

▶ How to prevent and treat injuries

• •

*I*t's not like when you were a kid. Back then, the only questions were "Is it fun?" and "Will Mom get mad if she catches me?" Now, when you're working up a sweat, a few other questions come to mind: How many calories am I burning? What are the cardiovascular benefits? Will I get injured? And you thought adulthood would be all credit cards and R-rated movies.

Well, the great thing about cycling is that it not only satisfies your inner child, it will also do good things for your outer grown up. Bicycling, as they say in those late-night infomercials, is a great form of aerobic exercise. It's low impact, it can be done at a wide variety of intensities, and, unlike most of those machines you can buy for five easy monthly payments of $99.99, it's fun, so you're likely to keep on doing it.

For the skeptical among you, I'll get down to the numbers and discuss just how cycling will make you more fit and, yes, help you melt away those unwanted pounds and inches. Then I'll get to the nuts and bolts. I discuss how a proper diet will make you a better and happier rider, and I even talk about the most important nutrient there is. (*Hint:* It's free.) I'll share the good news about cycling injuries — or lack thereof — and how to prevent and treat those that do crop up. I discuss staying healthy through stretching, massage, and proper warm-up. And as if that wasn't enough, I even talk about how cycling affects your sex life.

Bicycling: The Perfect Exercise?

Is riding a bike good exercise? The answer to that is definitely yes. Is it the best exercise there is? Rational people have certainly made that argument. Is cycling better than running? Well, it gives you the same kind of aerobic workout and burns calories just as efficiently as running, but you don't run nearly the same risk of developing the chronic injury that can put you on the sidelines. Swimming? It's fine, and it's low impact, but you need a pool. And if you stay in too long, you come out looking like a prune. Cross-country skiing? Wonderfully aerobic, but hardly a year-round sport, unless you live in the Yukon. And most other activities simply don't compare when it comes to giving you a workout. Activities on the low end of the scale — golf, bowling, watching TV, even aerobics — just aren't vigorous enough. And high-output activities like full-court basketball, boxing, and jumping rope are so intense that most weekend warriors can't keep them up for an hour, much less two.

What does cycling have going for it? As you can see in Table 9-1, cycling burns calories as efficiently as any other sport. You can go out for a 20-minute spin or ride your bike hour after hour at a steady aerobic pace, while you watch the scenery go by. You can easily increase the intensity of your cycling workout — and the number of calories you burn — by boosting your speed without worrying about subjecting your joints to increased pounding. Perfect? I'll leave that to the philosophers to decide. All things considered, as good as any other exercise? If you don't believe me, take a look at the table.

Table 9-1	Calorie Burning and Common Exercises	
Activity	*130 Pound Woman*	*170 Pound Man*
Cycling 12-14 mph	499 calories/hr	653 calories/hr
Cycling 14-16 mph	624	816
Cycling 16-19 mph	749	979
Running 12 min mile	499	653
Running 10 min mile	624	816
Running 8 min mile	780	1,020
Walking 15 min mile	281	367
Swimming, crawl	686	898
Swimming, backstroke	499	653
Cross-country skiing	593	775
Basketball	499	653

Activity	130 Pound Woman	170 Pound Man
Boxing	562	734
Jumping rope	624	816
Tennis	437	571
In-line skating	437	571
Low impact aerobics	343	449
Raking the lawn	250	326
Golf, using a cart	218	286
Bowling	187	245
Watching TV	47	61
Sleeping	39	51

Weight watch: Ride on, slim down

Do you want to lose weight? Then you can start having a shake for breakfast, a shake for lunch, and a sensible dinner. Or, if you ride at a moderate pace for an hour three times a week, and don't change your diet, you'll burn enough calories to lose about half a pound per week. (For you show-me-the-math types, you need to burn about 3,500 calories to lose a pound.) Sound good?

The myth of fat burning

If you read diet books or ads for exercise equipment, you hear a lot of talk about how aerobic exercise burns fat. And yes, it's true, when you're doing low-intensity exercise, your body uses fat directly as a fuel. But what this doesn't take into account is the fact that while higher intensity exercise doesn't burn fat directly, it contributes to a daily calorie deficit, which allows you to burn fat when you're not exercising. The bottom line is that for weight purposes, a calorie is a calorie. Think of it like a checking account: If you deposit more than you spend, your balance will increase. If you spend more than you take in, your balance will go down. It doesn't much matter whether you deposit $100 bills or rolls of pennies and nickels. And it doesn't matter much whether you withdraw the money from an ATM or write a check. It's the same with food and exercise.

If you ride a lot — whether it's fast or slow — and eat less, you'll lose weight. It's as simple as that.

And that doesn't even take into account the collateral benefits of exercise. Cycling raises your resting metabolism for a few hours after your ride so that you actually burn a few extra calories while you're sitting in front of the television or the computer screen. Exercise also increases your lean muscle mass, which again boosts your resting metabolism. And, best of all, it beats having to wait all day for that sensible dinner.

The best medicine

What if I told you about a medicine that can reduce your risk of heart disease, stroke, many kinds of cancer, diabetes, osteoporosis, and even the common cold? What if I told you it was inexpensive, there were no adverse side effects, and it was a lot more fun than eating broccoli? You'd get right in line, wouldn't you? Well, there is such a medicine, and it's called *exercise*. Even a moderate exercise regimen — 20 minutes of aerobic activity three times a week — has been proven in study after study to help in the prevention of any number of diseases. Now if we could just get your HMO to buy you a bike.

My Food, My Self

You know the old saying, "You are what you eat." So do you really want to be a Big Mac, a large order of fries, and a chocolate shake riding up that next big hill? When you're on your bike, food isn't food, it's fuel. Which is why you need to think before you chew.

Before the ride

This is a balancing act. You need to eat enough to give you sufficient energy for the ride, but not so much that you end up slowing yourself down. In practical terms, it's not so much a matter of limiting *how much* you eat, but *what* you eat. As you found out after you left the all-you-can-eat buffet at Enchilada World, some foods are more easily digested than others. Generally, this means focusing on carbohydrates and keeping fats to a minimum. If you're riding in the morning, cereal or yogurt is a better bet than a triple cheese omelet with a side of sausage. (I found this one out the hard way on a particularly strenuous ride following a particularly indulgent brunch.) For lunch, it means bypassing the bacon double cheeseburger with a crème brulée chaser and going for the grilled chicken salad with the dressing on the side.

Why are foods that are okay when you're chilling out such a no-no when you're exercising? Chalk it up to evolution. Back in the days when your ancestors were being chased by sabretooth tigers, they needed all the help they could get. So your body developed a response to this fight-or-flight situation. When you're running away from a wooly mammoth — or just pedaling up a big hill — your body funnels most of its resources to your muscles, postponing non-essential functions, like digestion. So eating easily digestible foods allows you to keep your muscles well fueled and keeps your stomach from rebelling. In short, you could say that it's about staying on the right side of the line between eating and being eaten.

During the ride

Should you eat when you ride? Probably. If you're just going out for a half-hour spin, you can wait until you get home. But if you're going to ride for an hour or more, you should plan for some on-the-go refueling, and do it sooner rather than later.

No, I don't mean you should stop at the drive-through window. A couple of bites of an energy bar or a little bit of fruit is enough. And keep in mind, I'm defining eating in the broadest possible way; that is, taking in calories. And if you chug some fruit juice or a sports drink, as far as your body's concerned, that's eating.

What should you eat? Well, it should be neat so that you don't get crumbs all over your jersey. And from a nutritional standpoint, it should be mostly carbohydrates, with a little bit of fat to mellow out the blood sugar spike that can come from too big a hit of sugar. There is a multi-million dollar industry trying to get you to choose energy bars and energy gels for your in-ride nutritional needs. They're generally easy to eat, and nutritionally, they've done most of the thinking for you. If you like the way they taste and they make you feel more like a triathlete, go right ahead. But they're not magic. You probably have some perfectly good energy foods in your cupboard. Take a look at Table 9-2.

Table 9-2	Good Cycling Food			
Food	*Calories*	*Carbohydrates*	*Fat*	*Protein*
4 fig bars	200	46 g	0 g	2 g
3 Rice Krispie treats	225	45 g	4.5g	1.5 g
1 Milky Way Lite bar	170	34 g	5 g	1 g
1 PowerBar	225	42 g	2.5 g	10 g
2 bananas	220	58 g	0 g	2 g

The bonk

Are you one of those people who hates to stop at a gas station? You'll run your car until it's almost at E, right at E and even a little bit below E. Did you ever push it too far? Well, when your body runs out of fuel, it's called *the bonk*. While all endurance athletes can experience the bonk, cyclists are particularly susceptible. Unlike, say, running, it's easy to push yourself so hard on the bike that you literally can't stand up, but you can manage to turn the pedals, just barely. The symptoms are sudden, extreme weakness, often accompanied by lightheadedness, nausea, and/or severe hunger. In short, it's not fun. Fortunately, the prevention is simple. Eat before you ride. Eat small amounts frequently while you're riding. And don't wait until you feel hungry. By then, it's probably too late. A linguistic note: In French, the bonk is called *la fringale*, a word so euphonic that a fine French restaurant in San Francisco adopted it as its name. Funny how the French can make something so unpleasant sound romantic.

As you can see, there's not all that much difference between performance food and what your mother would dismiss as junk food. All have a good amount of carbohydrates and an acceptably low level of fat, and they can be eaten easily while you're riding. And if you stop to eat, your choices widen even further. Pretzels, low-fat muffins, and just about any kind of fruit, from orange to kiwi, will help keep your energy up and the bonk (see "The bonk" sidebar) at bay.

After the ride

Here's the time for refueling. Eat some carbohydrates within a half hour of getting home. It'll speed your recovery from a long ride. Later, focus on a well-balanced diet with an eye toward your long-term energy needs. It's a good time to fuel up with protein — something lean like a chicken breast, a pork tenderloin, or a piece of fish. Some veggies add fiber and all sorts of nutrients to the mix. And round out the meal with a small side of complex carbohydrates — a baked potato, a portion of pasta, or even just some bread. As for the fats, just keep it in perspective. In moderation, fats are a necessary part of a balanced diet. While an occasional pat of butter or sprinkle of grated cheese won't hurt you, you should pass on the ribeye steak.

The Hydration Quotient

Do you ever get home from a ride, and before you step into the shower, you step on the scale? "Three pounds lighter than this morning," you congratulate yourself. While it's certainly gratifying to watch those numbers go down, the reality is that you're probably a little less fat and a whole lot dehydrated.

There are a lot of reasons why water is the most important nutrient there is. All cellular activity takes place in a water bath, and your body tends to conserve that water at all costs. Water — in the form of sweat — helps your body regulate its core temperature, and if you don't replenish your body's supply, it's like running your car with the radiator only half full. When you mix dehydration with exertion, the result can be heat exhaustion and, even rarely, heat stroke.

Drinking on the road is almost a Zen thing. You need to drink before you're thirsty. If you wait until you're thirsty, you're already dehydrated, and you're fighting a losing battle. Fortunately, bikes have water bottles, and they're not just there for decoration. Just plan to take a drink every 15 minutes — more often if it's really hot — and you'll be fine.

Post-ride, it's still important to continue rehydrating yourself. However, the key is doing it right. Your body's prime function is to keep your electrolytes balanced, and when you sweat, you not only lose water, you also lose electrolyes. If you fill up with plain water while your electrolytes are down, your body will sacrifice its hydration needs in order to keep its electrolyte balance from being further distorted. The bottom line: You'll just urinate away almost all the water you took in. That's the idea behind energy drinks, which replace electrolyte stores while replenishing your fluid. Or you can use your diet to replenish your electrolyte stores. Eat a banana to replace your potassium. Have a few pretzels to replace the sodium. And most of all, be grateful when you put back two-and-a-half pounds of that three pounds you lost.

The Big Hurt: Injuries and Their Prevention

Next time you walk past your bike, give it a pat on the saddle. Why? Because more than your skis or your running shoes or just about any other piece of sporting goods that you own, your bike is kind to your body. That's why racers in the Tour de France can ride more than 100 miles day after day for three weeks straight, while a marathon runner has to chill out for a couple of months after running a two-hour and ten-minute race. The act of turning the pedals is so inherently efficient that, done correctly, it doesn't place undue stress on any part of the body. But that's not to say that injuries can't occur.

There are basically two kinds of injuries: *overuse* injuries and *acute* injuries. An overuse injury happens when you're doing basically the right thing but doing too much of it. An acute injury is much less subtle. One minute you're fine; the next you're yelling because of a pulled muscle or a sprained joint. Most acute injuries in cycling occur as the result of a fall.

Proper warm-up

Most recreational runners won't run down to the corner without doing 15 minutes of stretching, for fear that they're going to end up — ker snap! — like the guest of honor in a wishbone pull. But most bicyclists head right out their door and start pedaling without a second thought. After a little warm-up of spinning in a low gear, Steve Johnson, director of development for USA Cycling, suggests using the enforced waiting period of a stoplight to do a little stretching. To stretch your quadriceps, just stand on one foot and pull your foot up to your butt, and hold it there for 20 seconds. You can stretch your hamstrings by stepping off the bike, putting one leg on the top tube, and bending forward at the hips. And of course when you get home, do a full program of lower-body stretches, covering your quads, your hamstrings, and your calves.

Quadricep Stretch   Hamstring Stretch

Overuse injuries

Remember this old joke:

Doctor: "Does it hurt when you do that?

Patient: "Yes."

Doctor: "Then don't do that."

Well, there's more than a grain of truth to this. If you suffered an acute injury — a sprained ankle while carrying your bike on the trail or a pulled muscle — just get it better and be more careful the next time.

However, if you're hurting from an overuse injury, you've got a problem. Because if you keep "doing that," it'll just come back. Which means that you have to do more than just treat the injury, you have to address its root causes.

In general, overuse injuries tend to sneak up on you. You're a little sore one day, a little better the next, a little more sore the day after that. And then one day you wake up and you can't walk down the stairs. As I said earlier in this chapter, cycling is pretty kind to your body, so while overuse injuries aren't unheard of, they're not nearly so common as in, say, running, and most are preventable with proper technique and bike setup. What follows are some common complaints and some suggested remedies.

My knee hurts

Will it get better on its own? No. The bad news: The knee is the most vulnerable joint in the body, and even on a bike it can take a beating. The good news: Unlike in most other sports, most cycling-related knee injuries on the bike are preventable and are related to bike setup or riding style. If you experience general diffuse pain behind the kneecap — known in the trade as *patellar/femoral* pain — treat the symptoms and then run down this checklist of potential causes:

The technique solution: Ride in a lower gear. Riding in too high a gear is like doing deep knee bends for an hour. No matter how fit you are, it's going to hurt your knees. Try counting your cadence, and find a gear that allows you to keep it comfortably over 90 rpm. A pre- and post-ride stretching program can prevent or alleviate some knee problems.

The gear solutions:

- ✔ **Raise your saddle.** A saddle that's too low is one of the prime causes of knee pain among less experienced cyclists. A saddle that's too high often results in pain in the back of the knee. To set your saddle height precisely, see Chapter 6.

- ✔ **Align your feet on the pedals.** Improper alignment of your foot on the pedal is another key culprit of knee injuries. Without even realizing it, you probably walk a little duck-footed (quack-quack) or pigeon-toed (coo-coo). So when you're pedaling, it's important to allow your natural gait to be reflected in the position of your feet on the pedals. Alignment is especially important if you're using toe clips or shoes with clipless pedals. Try adjusting the cleats on your shoes — or have a bike shop do it — to help achieve a comfortable position. If your knee pain continues, ask your doctor about *orthotics,* specially molded insoles designed to place your foot in a neutral position.

> ✔ **Move your saddle forward.** While it's not as big a culprit as saddle height, the fore-aft position of your saddle can have an effect on your knees. First, do the basic setup that's covered in Chapter 6. If your saddle's not where it should be, then fix it. If it falls within the acceptable range, you might try nudging your saddle forward just a little — a quarter-inch at a time.

My neck hurts

Will it get better on its own? Maybe. If your position is fundamentally sound, the additional strength and flexibility that comes from riding could resolve this problem.

The technique solution: Try straightening your back, which should naturally raise your head and put your neck in a more relaxed position.

The gear solution: Try raising your handlebars or possibly shortening your stem, which will put you in a more upright position.

My wrist hurts

Will it get better on its own? No. In fact it's likely to get worse and can develop into a very serious case of tendonitis.

The technique solution: Try flexing your arms more so that shock is absorbed by your elbows instead of transmitted to your wrists.

The gear solution: Shorten your stem to shift some of your weight to your butt. Try cycling gloves with more padding.

My butt hurts

Will it get better on its own? Yes. Almost every rider experiences some pain after getting back on the bike after a long layoff. After a few rides, the tissues around your sit bones "toughen up" and you can ride pain free. (However, if you've been riding regularly and you start experiencing intense saddle pain, you could be developing saddle boils, an extremely painful, and potentially serious infection of these tissues. If you suspect this problem, consult your doctor.)

The technique solution: Try bending more at the hips to shift more of the weight to your handlebars.

The gear solution: Lower your handlebars and/or lengthen your stem to support more of your weight with your hands. Try a pair of padded cycling shorts or a new saddle.

A warm knee is a happy knee

Admit it. You like showing off your legs. Most cyclists do. And while it does good things for your ego, it may not be doing good things for your joints.

Your knee, you see, is lubricated by something called synovial fluid. "If the knee joint gets cold, it makes the synovial fluid thicker," Steve Johnson, Director of Development for USA Cycling, explains. "Normally, it's the consistency of warm honey. When it gets cold out it's like cold honey, and it doesn't work so well." How cold is cold? Well, most European coaches make their riders wear tights or leg warmers anytime the temperature drops below 70°F.

If you've got chronic knee problems, you might just want to do the same.

Acute injuries

Most acute injuries in cycling occur as the result of crashes, whether on the road or on the trail. The bones and joints of the upper body — most notably the collarbone — are especially vulnerable. If you're experiencing severe pain, numbness, or restricted movement in a joint after a fall, see your doctor immediately to rule out a broken bone or a serious dislocation of the joint.

For less serious injuries — mild sprains or bruises — follow the RICE regimen outlined later in this chapter.

One of the most common acute injuries is road rash. Unfortunately, the name is a lot funnier than the malady. Road rash is the result of soft skin scraping against hard, abrasive asphalt, essentially a jumbo version of the kind of skinned knee you used to encounter when you were a kid.

The key to treating road rash is making sure it's clean. In order to prevent infection, you need to remove all the foreign material from the open wounds. If the risk of infection doesn't spur you to action, understand that those little bits dirt or pavement will become a permanent tattoo if you leave them under the skin. Here's what to do:

1. **Clean the area with plenty of water and an antibacterial soap, scrubbing with a washcloth or even a brush (ouch) if necessary.**

2. **Cut away any loose skin.**

3. **Apply some antibiotic ointment and cover the wound with mesh gauze and a non-stick bandage.**

4. **Change the dressings twice a day, and keep applying ointment to keep the wound moist, which will keep the scabs from cracking.**

   The new skin that forms is very delicate, and applying a moisturizing lotion until it's completely healed will prevent or minimize scarring.

"If you ride a lot, sooner or later you're going to fall." That's the hard truth according to Steve Johnson, director of development for USA Cycling. That's why he suggests taking some preemptive action against your next case of road rash. The next time you go to your doctor, have him or her write a prescription for xylocaine ointment. If you happen to crash, apply it to an open wound, wait a few minutes for it to get numb, and then you can scrub with the kind of impunity that you need to clean out a wound thoroughly.

Treating injuries

The basic treatment for most joint and muscle injuries is pretty similar, regardless of the cause. The standard RICE regimen is the place to start:

- ✔ **R** is for rest. That means stay off it, although some recent research suggest that gentle, range-of-motion exercise can speed healing.

- ✔ **I** is for ice. As soon as possible, put an ice pack on the affected area to keep down swelling and inflammation during the first 48 hours after the injury.

- ✔ **C** is for compression. This means wrapping the joint to keep down the swelling. In the short run, it means not taking off a shoe or a glove or a pair of tights until you can get home to ice it.

- ✔ **E** is for elevation. That means raising the affected body part to keep the swelling down.

Cycling and Impotence

Is riding a bike better than sex? Do we really have to make that hard choice? Bike-induced impotence in men has been an, um, sensitive topic in the cycling world lately.

The physiology is relatively simple. The arteries and nerves that supply blood and sensation to the male genitals can be found in the *perineum,* which is inconveniently located between your sit bones. And where your body contacts the saddle. Some urologists have suggested that prolonged pressure on these areas can damage these nerves and blood vessels, causing temporary or even permanent impotence. Traumatic injuries, such as falling onto the top tube in a crash, can also damage these delicate structures.

Got your attention? However, doctors also point out that cycling can help prevent arteriosclerosis, diabetes, high blood pressure, and heart disease, which have also been implicated as causes of impotence. In light of that, moderation and monitoring seems to be a reasonable course of action. Also consider these tips:

- **Check your riding position:** Make sure your saddle is adjusted properly, not only for height (a saddle that's too high puts additional pressure on the perineum) but for tilt (keep your saddle level or slightly nose down).

- **Avoid aero bars:** Triathlon-style bars tend to encourage sitting on the nose of the saddle which can exacerbate this problem, so you should avoid using them for long periods of time.

- **Consider a new saddle:** Seat manufacturers have gotten on this bandwagon in a hurry, introducing new models with cutaways and pads which are designed to minimize pressure in this sensitive area. (Be warned, though, that some gel saddle pads and other seemingly cushy alternatives may actually increase the pressure in this area.)

- **Relieve the pressure:** Get off the bike every hour or so, and pedal out of the saddle for, say, 30 seconds, every 10 minutes. And on rough pavement or trail, ride out of the saddle.

- **Try a recumbent:** The seated position of a recumbent all but eliminates the risk of damage to the perineal area.

- **Watch for symptoms:** If you notice any kind of transient numbness in your genital area, change your riding position or get off the bike. If you suffer a groin injury while riding or experience persistent numbness or any kind of erectile dysfunction, then stop riding and go see a doctor immediately.

There's the rub: The benefits of massage

Even if you've never thought about being a professional bike racer, there are at least a few minutes each day you probably envy them. Because as soon as a rider crosses the finish line, the next stop is the massage table. Most cycling teams employ at least one and often several full-time masseurs. Massage is one of the most effective ways of ridding your muscles of lactic acid — the stuff that makes you hurt all over after a long day in the saddle. And while hiring your own massage therapist may be a little excessive, you can prevent some soreness by trying a little do-it-yourself rubdown. With your legs elevated, simply knead the big muscles in your legs to break up the tension, and then rub along the length of the muscle to help flush out the lactic acid.

Chapter 10

Getting Serious: The Easy Way to Train

In This Chapter

▶ Measuring your fitness

▶ Developing endurance, power, and speed

▶ Trying the three kinds of training rides

▶ Devising a workout plan

▶ Exercising in the off season

Ride lots.
— Eddy Merckx

*I*t happens gradually, almost imperceptibly. You wake up one morning and you discover that bicycling is no longer a pastime, it's a hobby. Well, maybe not a hobby, more like an obsession. No, not an obsession exactly. More like a compulsion. Yeah, that's it. Or an addiction. Well, no, not quite.

As hobbies, obsessions, and compulsions go, cycling is a pretty good one. It's healthy, it's cheap, and it's fun. But when you start getting serious about cycling, it changes the way you look at the sport. You want to ride more often, ride more miles, ride faster, ride more challenging terrain. Riding becomes not so much a means to an end — one part of your total fitness program — but an end in itself. It's no longer enough to ride to get fitter. You want to get fitter to ride better.

This is a chapter about (shhh) *training*. Now don't get freaked out by the T-word. The reality is that your actual riding won't be much different than what you're doing now. It's merely a matter of setting some goals, focusing your riding, and keeping track of your progress. Yes, it's true that most of these techniques are based on training programs used by racers. After all, who's more concerned about improving their performance? But you certainly don't have to be a racer to use them. Whether you want to finish a century ride, shave 10 minutes off your personal best commuting record, or enter a road race or a mountain bike race, the same basics apply. It's really about squeezing the maximum fitness benefit out of the minimum amount of time. Sounds a lot better than using the T-word, right?

And the best part is the progress you'll see. You'll be fitter, faster, and stronger — able to climb steep hills in a single bound. And if, after a month or two, you can suddenly fit into a pair of jeans that you thought were two sizes too small, so much the better.

In this chapter, I introduce the three major components of fitness and how you can improve them. I talk about how you can chart your fitness quickly and easily. I explain why sometimes the best training is taking a day off. And best of all, I show you shortcuts for supercharging your riding, both on and off the bike.

The Fitness Yardstick

The great thing about fitness is that it's quantifiable. Practice your new arrangement of "Billy, Don't Be a Hero" on the Steinway for a month, and you have to depend on the kindness of your friends to tell you how much better you've gotten. When it comes to riding your bike, you can just look down at your wrist or your handlebars and see a number that proves beyond a shadow of a doubt how much stronger, faster, and fitter you are than you were 30 days ago. Trust me, it's a great feeling.

That's why every good fitness program needs good measuring tools. The three essentials are a cyclometer, a heart rate monitor, and a training diary. They form what a consultant might call a synergy. The cyclometer tells you how far you rode; the heart rate monitor tells you how hard you worked; and the training diary lets you keep track of your progress. And all three together motivate you to get out, identify your strengths and weaknesses, and help you get the most out of your riding time.

While keeping track of distance is pretty basic, heart rate monitoring is something that only elite athletes did until recently. At its most fundamental level, your heart rate is really the measuring stick of your cardiovascular fitness. If your speed goes up while your heart rate stays the same, then, congratulations, you're fitter. But even more importantly, your heart rate is the most reliable indicator of how your body is producing energy — more on that later — which gives you the opportunity to target your training that much more accurately.

And though you can take your pulse by just putting a finger on an artery on your wrist or on you neck, while you're exercising it's more convenient, not to mention safer, to keep your hands on the handlebars and just peek at your heart rate monitor.

"But," you say, "I'm not a racer." All the more reason why you need a heart rate monitor. Racers actually have sort of a built-in heart rate monitor, a sixth sense about how hard they're working, developed over years of training. They mostly use their mechanical heart rate monitors to confirm what their bodies are already telling them.

Ironically, the riders who can benefit most from a heart rate monitor are the least likely to own one. Less experienced cyclists are more likely to judge their workout by speed than real workload, so they're likely to overdo it when they're faced with some rolling hills and loaf a little when they're riding with a tailwind.

Do you fall into that camp? Try this test: During your next ride, guess your heart rate just before you stop for a traffic light. Then take your pulse while you're waiting for the green. If you're not consistently within five beats, you definitely need a heart rate monitor.

A buyer's guide to training aids

A cyclometer's job is to provide you with an accurate tally of your daily mileage. And virtually any model on the market, once it's properly calibrated, can provide that. All the other functions — speed, average speed, and cadence — can be good motivators, not to mention that they can alleviate the boredom of waiting for 15.1 miles to flip over to 15.2, but they're not essential.

A heart rate monitor should have a readout that's big enough to read while riding, and a handlebar mount is nice, although you can make one of your own by wrapping a piece of PVC pipe insulation around the bars and securing it with — you guessed it — duct tape. The monitor's buttons should be big enough that you can manipulate them while you're on the road. The elastic chest strap, which actually takes the reading, should be comfortable both while you're standing and while you're riding. One very useful function, which does raise the price some, is the capability to set a target heart rate range with an audible alarm that beeps when you're above or below it. As for the more sophisticated programming options — anything from a post-workout readout of average heart rate to a full record of the workout that can be downloaded to your computer — let your love of gadgetry, or lack thereof, be your guide.

Your training diary can be as simple or elaborate as you like. You can buy a printed training log at a bookstore or just use a yellow legal pad. If it makes you happy, you can write it on your bedroom wall, the way William Faulkner outlined *Intruder in the Dust.* At the minimum, you should record how far you rode and whether you did an endurance workout, a speed workout, or a power workout. On the numbers side, you might also add your average speed, your morning resting heart rate, and your heart rate while you were out on the bike. On a subjective level, you might record the weather, how you felt when you got up, what you wore, and, how you felt before, during, and after the ride. When you achieve a goal, big or small, write that down, too. For that matter, you can write down the funniest bumper sticker you saw that day, or the fact that you saw the first piping plover of the season. Whatever floats your boat, so to speak.

Having trouble getting a reading from your heart rate monitor early in your workout? Try licking the sensor. Most rely on the conductivity of your sweat to work properly, and saliva is the best substitute.

Maxing Out

One bit of information that you need before you start on a training program is your maximum heart rate (MHR). Throughout the rest of this chapter, different training intensities are expressed as a percentage of maximum heart rate. Here's the simplest way to determine your MHR:

- Women, subtract your age from 226. (A 33-year-old female ends up with a maximum heart rate of 193.)
- Men, subtract your age from 220. (A 33-year-old male calculates a maximum heart rate of 187.)

While this number should give you a reasonable ballpark figure, it doesn't take into account such factors as heredity and your fitness level.

The other way of determining your maximum heart rate is by pushing yourself until you get there. The safest and most accurate way to do this is with a treadmill stress test administered by your doctor. And of course, before embarking on any exercise program, you should consult your doctor.

The Building Blocks of Better Riding

So what's the difference between training and just plain riding? Well, on a training ride you build at least one of three things: endurance, power, or speed.

These are the building blocks of all fitness — whether it's on a bike, a basketball court, or the skating rink. Every sport more strenuous than chess calls upon these three basic qualities in various proportions. And what makes cycling such a great challenge is that it requires a balance of all three. But before I talk about how to build our fitness, I need to define the terms.

Endurance

Endurance is a pretty straightforward concept. It's the ability to ride a little further today than you did yesterday. Sure, some part of endurance is mental — this is how people can swim the English Channel or ride a bike across the United States in less than nine days. But it's also a physical attribute, the ability of your muscles and your connective tissues to keep turning the pedals strongly and consistently throughout a long ride. And when you have the urge to turn an hour-long ride into a two-hour ride, it's nice if your body doesn't protest.

Power

It's easy to get power confused with speed, so think of it this way: Speed is a Porsche, and power is a tractor-trailer. While speed is all about high rpms, power is about working under a load. Power comes into play when you're climbing a steep hill, pushing a big gear on the flats, riding a bike that's loaded down with camping gear, or riding into a headwind for an hour.

Speed

Speed, as I'm defining it, isn't about how fast your bike goes, but how fast you turn the pedals. (Although the two are generally related, you can turn a big gear at a slow cadence and still go quite fast.) The ability to pedal fast can be very useful when you're being chased by a dog or you want to move quickly through a potentially dicey situation — around a double-parked car for example. Speed is especially important when riding in the city because the ability to keep up with the flow of traffic gives you an added margin of safety.

The Three Kinds of Rides

Okay, so you understand what your goals are. Now how do you increase your abilities? Any balanced training program should incorporate three different kinds of workouts, each one addressing each of these three cornerstones.

Long, steady distance

To improve your endurance, you're going to do LSD — long, steady distance, that is. LSD rides seem easy, and in a way, that's the problem. When you're riding relatively slowly, you feel like you should be doing more, and so you push yourself beyond the point at which you're getting maximum training benefit. Discipline yourself to stay away from big hills and stay out of your big chain ring. During an LSD workout, pedal in a low gear at a cadence between 90 and 100 rpm.

The myth of medium hard

What's the most common training mistake among cyclists? Going at one speed.

"Most people ride their long rides way too hard," (which limits the opportunities to build endurance and recover), says Steve Johnson, director of development for USA Cycling, "and their hard workouts are way too easy" (which limits the power and speed they can build). The end result is that every workout is done at a pace Johnson calls "medium hard." That's why he suggests working with a heart rate monitor, and if possible, enlisting the help of a coach.

By building endurance, LSD rides provide a base for your training schedule. They train your body to use fat as a fuel, which is the most efficient way to power your muscles for long-distance workouts. They also allow your body to recover from the stresses that your power- and speed-building workouts place on your body.

Heart rate

Shoot for between 50 and 70 percent of your maximum heart rate on LSD rides. While it may be difficult — you feel like you're riding sooooo slowly — it's important to keep your heart rate down. As soon as your heart rate exceeds 70 percent of your maximum, even for a minute or two, your body begins to abandon its fat burning regimen and recruit other "fast" energy sources. And even brief anaerobic efforts sabotage your recovery plans.

Typical workout

Ninety minutes of riding in a low gear on level terrain at a constant heart rate of 50 to 70 percent of your maximum heart rate.

Power intervals

A power interval is simply an extended effort at a higher resistance. The goal is to build strength. You can increase the resistance of your workout in any number of ways. Hills, of course, provide great power workouts. The same goes for a strong headwind. Or you can create your own resistance by pedaling in a higher gear. And remember that while you should find it harder to turn the pedals, you're not doing leg presses here. If you can't keep up a cadence of at least 80 rpm, then shift to a lower gear.

In search of absolute power

Psst. Wanna get stronger without turning a pedal? Then head to the gym. A good balanced program of weight lifting can increase your strength, help prevent injury, and even help you look better in a bathing suit. "You want to do a basic whole-body workout," explains Steve Johnson, development director for USA Cycling. This training can take the form of a machine-to-machine circuit or a series of light free-weight exercises. If you've never lifted weights before, ask a trainer at your gym or club to show you proper form and help you design a workout plan. The key, according to Johnson, is stick-to-it-iveness. It'll take about 12 to 16 weeks, working out two to three times a week, to really build your strength. As a cyclist, your goal isn't to get pumped up Schwarzenegger-style. Adding too much upper-body muscle can actually slow you down by adding a little power for a lot of weight and reducing your flexibilty.

Heart rate

You want to be near your aerobic threshold — just below the point at which you start consuming oxygen faster than your lungs can replenish it. That's at about 80 to 85 percent of your maximum heart rate, but you can tell you've reached that point when you feel like you're working a lot harder — and your heart rate continues to climb — but you're not really going much faster. That's the beginning of your anaerobic zone, where your body is pumping out lactic acid. Back off a little and you're at your aerobic threshold. Over time, power training helps move your anaerobic threshold higher, enabling you to ride faster with less effort.

Typical workout

Try a 20-minute LSD warmup, a series of three 7-minute power intervals with 5 minutes of LSD-pace recovery in between, followed by a 10-minute cool-down.

Speed intervals

To get fast, you need to do sprint intervals. The idea is to pedal as fast as you can for a short time — between 10 and 20 seconds. Then catch your breath and do it all over again. Though you'll need to upshift a cog or two from your LSD gears, the goal is really high rpms — a cadence of 110 to 120 — at a medium resistance.

Failing to succeed

How hard should you be pushing yourself during a sprint? Harder. No, harder than that. No, even harder. According to Steve Johnson, director of development of USA Cycling, intervals should be done until "failure." What does that mean exactly? It means that on your last set, you simply can't quite turn the pedals fast enough. On a micro level, you have tried and you have failed. And on a macro level, you have most definitely succeeded.

In every muscle, there are fast-twitch and slow-twitch fibers. While an individual's proportion of fast-twitch to slow-twitch fibers is largely determined by genetics (Olympic sprinters got there by choosing their parents well), you can increase your percentage of fast-twitch fibers somewhat by speed training.

Speed training also helps smooth out your pedal stroke.

Heart rate

Your heart rate should go completely into the anaerobic zone, the place where your body pulls out all its energy trump cards. This corresponds to a reading of between 85 and 100 percent of your maximum heart rate.

Typical workout

Do a 20-minute LSD warmup, followed by six 200-yard all-out sprints with a minute of LSD-pace recovery between each effort, followed by a 10-minute cool-down.

Building a Workout Plan

In order to maintain a consistent workout regimen, you need to get out your calendar. What follows is a 12-week training program, divided into three phases, guaranteed to get you in top shape in as little time as possible.

Phase 1 of the program focuses on building an endurance base. You start out riding three days a week, all LSD rides. By the end of the program, you're riding four days a week and doing some power workouts.

Phase 2 of the program focuses on maintaining your endurance while building your power (Pow). You start out with one power workout a week and increase it to two, while introducing some speed work by the end of phase two.

Phase 3 of the program focuses on maintaining your power and endurance, while adding some speed work (Spd).

Workout Plan: Phase 1, Weeks 1 – 4

Sun	*M*	*T*	*W*	*Th*	*Fr*	*Sat*
45min LSD	rest	rest	30min LSD	rest	rest	20min LSD
60m in LSD	rest	rest	30min LSD	rest	rest	25min LSD
60min LSD	rest	20min LSD	rest	30min LSD	rest	30min LSD
75min LSD	rest	30min Pow	rest	30min LSD	rest	30min LSD

Workout Plan: Phase 2, Weeks 5 – 8

Sun	*M*	*T*	*W*	*Th*	*Fr*	*Sat*
75min LSD	rest	30min Pow	rest	40min LSD	rest	30min Pow
90min LSD	rest	40min Pow	rest	40min LSD	rest	30min Pow
100min LSD	rest	40min Pow	rest	40min LSD	rest	30min Pow
100min LSD	rest	30min Spd	rest	50min LSD	rest	30min Pow

Workout Plan: Phase 3, Weeks 9 – 12

Sun	*M*	*T*	*W*	*Th*	*Fr*	*Sat*
30min Pow	rest	30min Spd	rest	40min LSD	rest	110min LSD
40min Pow	rest	30min Spd	rest	40min LSD	rest	110min LSD
40min Pow	rest	40min Spd	rest	50min LSD	rest	110min LSD
50min Pow	rest	40min Spd	rest	50min LSD	rest	110min LSD

Workout Plan: Maintenance

Sun	*M*	*T*	*W*	*Th*	*Fr*	*Sat*
90min LSD	rest	40min Spd	rest	50min LSD	rest	40min Pow

No, the program isn't carved in stone, and you can feel free to adapt this training plan to your schedule and your level of fitness. However, note that there are some overriding principles in any good training program:

- ✔ Alternate your power and speed workouts with LSD days or rest days to allow for recovery.

- ✔ Make your longer LSD rides on a Saturday or a Sunday, to give yourself more flexibility in scheduling them.

- ✔ Increase your time on the bike gradually from week to week by no more than 25 percent a week during the endurance phase, and no more than 15 percent a week during the power and speed phases.

What do you do when you reach week 12? Try the maintenance week schedule for a few weeks, which replaces one of the speed workouts with an LSD ride.

Charting your progress

How will you know that you're getting fitter? The best way is on a stationary bike or trainer. Set the time and see how far you can go, or set the distance and see how quickly you can complete it. If you'd rather ride outside, correlate your heart rate and the speed on your cyclometer on one of your LSD rides. On consecutive weeks, ride the same loop, preferably something in a park or an open road where you won't be interrupted by stop lights, at the same maximum heart rate. If you complete the loop faster, you're fitter. On a less scientific basis, you can simply check your cyclometer and your heart rate monitor at the same time. If you're riding faster at the same heart rate, or your heart rate is slower at the same speed, then you've made a fitness breakthrough, and feel free to write it in your training log — right next to the gold star.

In recovery

Here's the news you've been waiting for. If you want to get fitter, it's just as important to rest well as it is to ride hard. Elite athletes know this. Racers in the Tour de France literally don't do anything except eat, sleep, and pedal their bikes. They get daily massages. They request rooms on the ground floor so they don't have to walk up an extra flight of stairs. They'd probably request sedan chairs if they thought they could get away with it. They understand that while they're resting, their bodies are recovering from the day's exertion. "Recovery is just as important as the workout," says Steve Johnson director of development for USA Cycling. "The purpose of the workout is to stress the body and let it repair itself. The benefit of the workout only happens after you've recovered."

Because you're not riding 150 miles a day, you don't have to be quite so inactive. But you should plan to take a couple of days off during the week and restrict yourself to "active rest." Get out from behind the desk (or off the couch) for a little while and help your body help itself. Do some gentle stretching. Take a walk. Go out and shoot a few baskets. Mow the lawn. Do something that gets you moving without really breaking a sweat. This keeps your muscles from getting stiff and helps get the blood circulating to the connective tissue in your hips, your knees, and your ankles. But as long as you take it easy, your body can divert its energy reserves into helping repair the damage that yesterday's intervals inflicted, and build stronger muscles in the process.

Overtraining

There is such a thing as too much of a good thing. If you don't believe me, go ask the third runner-up in a hot-dog eating contest. The same goes for fitness. There's a fine line between building up and tearing down, and it's easy to veer onto the wrong side of it. How do you know if you're training too hard? Listen to your body. Do you feel chronically tired? As if you're constantly on the verge of getting sick? Are you having trouble sleeping? Or having trouble getting out of bed?

These admittedly vague maladies can all be symptoms of overtraining, especially if you've increased your mileage or intensity in the past week or two. The most objective way to monitor your training is to check your resting heart rate before you get out of bed in the morning. If your program's working, your resting heart rate should stay basically the same or even gradually drift slightly downward as your fitness increases. If you see your heart rate increasing, it's a sure sign that your body's under stress.

Fortunately, unlike the common cold, there's a cure for overtraining. Just simply take a day or two off, and when you go back to training, take it a little easier until your first-thing-in-the-morning heart rate settles back down.

The Off Season

So what do you do when winter sets in? If you live in, say, Arizona, you put on a jacket and keep right on riding. But for riders in the rest of the United States, the months between November and March offer both a challenge and an opportunity. While you can just bundle up and keep riding, it's often beneficial to use the change of seasons as a way to change your workout schedule. You might try cyclocross, a cold-weather hybrid of road biking, mountain biking, and trail running. Or you can try cross-country skiing, or join a basketball league. Anything that keeps you active, while giving you a break from your daily riding routine, will help you pick up right where you left off in the spring.

The other alternative is bringing your riding indoors. Here's a quick buyer's guide to the machines that make it happen.

A stationary bike

What it is: Basically, it's two-thirds of a bike.

The pros: It's relatively inexpensive, it's quiet enough that you can watch TV or crank your favorite Modern Lovers CD, and most don't take up much space. And some even have trick readouts that'll let you race a virtual Tour de France on your computer.

The cons: If you're looking to log some serious miles, be aware that it's hard, if not impossible, to duplicate your regular riding position on a stationary bike. The saddles are fat and often don't adjust in small increments; the bars tend to be narrow and high; and the pedals probably don't let you wear your cycling shoes.

The skinny: A perfect way to burn a few calories while watching *Wheel of Fortune.* "I'd like to buy a vowel, Pat!"

A training stand

What it is: A small stand that mounts on your rear wheel and holds it off the ground. When you turn the pedals, your rear wheel turns a small roller attached to a small fan or a magnetic resistance unit.

The pros: The biggest benefit is that you get to use your own bike, so the saddle and the handlebars and the pedals are set up just the way you need them. When it's not mounted to your bike, the stand is actually pretty small — it should stash under your bed — and it's relatively inexpensive.

The cons: Stand trainers tend to be noisier than a stationary bike — especially if you're using a mountain bike with knobby tires or any kind of bike with a wheel that's slightly out of round. When it's set up, it takes more space in your living room. And — no, this is not a joke — your bike can rust or corrode from the sweat you drip on it, at least if you're not vigilant in wiping it up afterwards.

The skinny: Be it ever so noisy, there's no place like bike.

Rollers

What it is: Picture a little treadmill for your bike (see Figure 10-1). Your rear wheel turns one of two rollers in the back, one of which is attached to a single roller in the front by a rubber belt. When you pedal, the rear wheel spins those rear rollers, and the front roller spins your front wheel, and voilà, you're riding.

The pros: Because there's nothing holding you up, besides centrifugal force, it's the best way to improve your bike handling. For the same reason, it also forces you to smooth out your pedal stroke. And there's a certain feeling of accomplishment in just staying upright.

The cons: Since the rollers are only about two feet wide, it's possible — some might say inevitable — that you'll ride off the side. This means that you can't simply zone out. And unless your rollers have a resistance device, you

Figure 10-1:
Rollers.

also have to pedal pretty fast to stay up on them, making rollers better for high-intensity workouts than for long aerobic slogs. And unlike a stationary bike or a stand, you can fall, which is why beginning roller riders should start in a doorway.

The skinny: A workout meets a party trick. Impress your friends — by staying up. Assuming, of course, that you *can* stay up.

A studio cycling bike

What it is: It looks like a stationary bike on steroids, but with one big difference. The cranks are directly attached to a large flywheel by one gear, which means that you can't coast.

The pros: Studio cycling bikes have a lot of the advantages of a stationary bike, plus a few of their own. They generally have good saddles, bars, and pedals, and the ability to dial in your setup as accurately as on your own bike. The flywheel literally pulls your feet through the whole pedal stroke, much like a track bike. This teaches you to pedal more powerfully and efficiently. The best part of having a studio cycling bike at home is that you get all these cool advantages without the neo-aerobics class atmosphere of most studio cycling classes.

The cons: This kind of bike demands your full attention. If your foot flies off the pedals, you can get seriously hurt. That's why health clubs only let you use them during a class. They're also more expensive than most stationary bikes.

The skinny: It's like being a bike messenger in the comfort of your own home.

Part III
The Fix Is In

The 5th Wave · By Rich Tennant

"Listen, thanks. I'll return them as soon as I *get* the wheels fixed."

In this part . . .

I cover many of the ways that you can adjust and repair your bike. After presenting the tools you need, I walk you through some of the repairs you can make to your drivetrain, tires, wheels, and brakes. Then I cover some emergency fixes you may have to make while on the road.

Chapter 11

The Tools of the Trade

● ●

In This Chapter

▶ The basic tools you need

▶ Tools to take on the road

▶ A note about cables

▶ Some tool rules

● ●

> *Fix a man's bike and he'll ride for a day.*
> *Teach a man to fix his bike and he'll ride forever.*
> — Anonymous

The bicycle is a marvel of engineering, and not simply because it can support a rider many times its weight and carry her twice as fast as her feet alone can manage. The real wonder of a bicycle is its fundamental simplicity. How simple is simple? So simple that you — yes, you — can fix it.

Think about that. Hundreds of machines populate your daily life — VCRs, food processors, electric pencil sharpeners — and when any of them go on the fritz, you make sure they're plugged in and then head to the repair center or, more likely, out to Circuit City to just buy a new one.

That's what I do . . . except when it comes to my bike. My bike has no microprocessors, no circuit boards, no little decals that say *No user-serviceable parts inside.* With most of its components sitting out there in plain sight, a bike all but invites you to tinker, to adjust, to repair.

But I'm not saying that *simple* means *completely self-evident.* I'll never forget a phone call I got from my brother-in-law. He's a professional mechanic, in the best sense of the word. He can turn a few odd pieces of wood into a cabinet or drop a transmission in his sleep. He can also answer hundreds upon hundreds of my stupid questions when our dishwasher's broken or the lawn mover won't start.

But when he was assembling a bike for my niece, it was role reversal time.

"Allen, the gears aren't shifting right," he told me.

When I went over, I took one look at the back of the bike and diagnosed the problem. The rear derailleur was upside down. Within ten minutes, my niece had a slick-shifting little ten-speed. And I proved that I wasn't a complete and total klutz.

So maybe you won't get a sense of validation from fixing your bike. But you will get a bike that runs like a Swiss watch. And you'll have the sense of security that comes from knowing that if something goes wrong while you're on the road, you won't be walking home. And, last but not least, if you pay attention to this chapter and chapters to come, your derailleur won't be upside down.

The Basic Tool Chest

The first thing you need to work on your bike is:

    a. A good set of tools

    b. An uninterrupted block of time

    c. A cold beer

    d. The phone number of a good bike shop

    e. All of the above

And the answer is . . . d?

You're right . . . and you advance to our grand challenge round, where the questions get harder and the prizes get bigger!

Seriously, having a set of high-quality tools doesn't make you a good mechanic, but trying to work with a lousy set can turn anybody into Dork Mechanic. You don't have to turn your basement into a bike shop, either. A good basic tool kit doesn't cost thousands of dollars, and it fits in a small tool-box. And many of these gadgets can also help you hang pictures, assemble bookcases, and maybe even build your own suspension bridge. Or maybe not.

Some of the tools are bike-specific and should be bought through a bike shop. The rest can be bought at a hardware store or home center. In general, spending a little extra for quality tools is worth it — Stanley and Sears Craftsman both make fine, reasonably priced ones, whereas Snap-On, which doesn't sell in stores but instead brings its trucks to professional mechanics, is considered the *creme de la creme*.

The tools are listed in approximate order of importance, and if you already own some of these tools, go ahead and spend the extra money on beer. By the way, some of the following tools are shown in Figure 11-1.

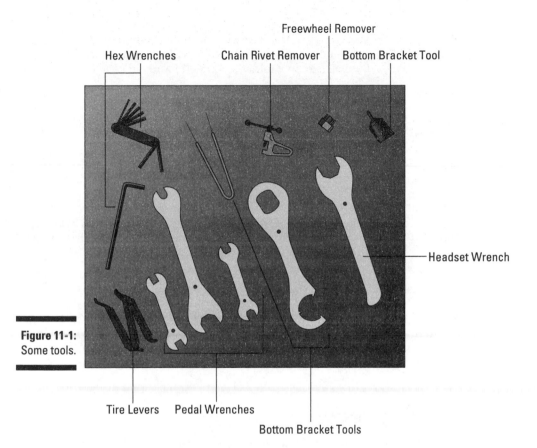

Freewheel Remover

Hex Wrenches   Chain Rivet Remover   Bottom Bracket Tool

Headset Wrench

Figure 11-1:
Some tools.

Tire Levers   Pedal Wrenches

Bottom Bracket Tools

A set of good screwdrivers

Get a number one and number two Phillips and a medium-sized flat-bladed screwdriver for adjusting derailleurs and brake levers. How do you tell if you're looking at a *good* screwdriver? Don't look at the pretty handle, the way most people do. Look at the business end. The Phillips head should be precisely machined with no rough edges, and the edge of a flat-bladed screwdriver should be smooth and even a little sharp.

A set of metric hex wrenches

Almost all the important adjustments on a bike have hex (Allen) fittings — you can identify them by the little six-sided hole in the center of the bolt. This is a good thing, because hex bolts are almost impossible to strip (as you can with a screwdriver) or round off (as you can with a wrench) unless of course you try to use a non-metric hex wrench to loosen a metric bolt. And the wrenches (or *keys*) are light and compact enough to carry along with you. You have two basic alternatives for dealing with hex bolts. Bike shops sell a neat little tool that has about eight hex keys that fold into a handle like a pocketknife. Or you can go to the hardware store and buy a set of individual L-shaped Allen keys. I personally prefer the individual keys, which fit better in tight spaces, but I also keep a foldable wrench handy in case I misplace my 5-mm.

A set of metric open-end wrenches

These wrenches are important for all the bolts on your bike that don't use Allen connectors. Typically, you can buy these in a set, which contains wrenches that range from about 6 mm–13 mm in one-millimeter increments. Each individual wrench handles two sizes of bolts. Again, look at the business end of the tools. They should be smooth, precisely machined, and substantial enough that they won't twist or bend when you need to unstick a frozen nut.

A metric socket set

A socket wrench, which ratchets back and forth so that you don't have to constantly reposition the wrench on the bolt, is a nice luxury. It won't completely obviate the need for your open-ended wrenches for tight places, but it does make most jobs faster while lessening the risk of rounding off a bolt.

A pair of pliers

A medium-size pair of pliers with nice grippy jaws is great for pulling cables and the like. One caveat: If you try to make it stand in for a wrench, your bolts will be rounder than a pumpkin pie. And the money you tried to save by not buying a wrench will go directly to your friendly neighborhood bicycle mechanic.

A pump

You say you've got a frame pump? That's great for emergencies, but if you put it to full-time use you'll do one of the following:

- ✔ Break the pump
- ✔ Snap off the valve
- ✔ End up like a pitcher — on the disabled list with a sore shoulder

You need a big floor pump, too. It'll make your life much easier.

Find one that's tall (so you don't have to bend over) with a big comfortable handle and a sturdy base. A pressure gauge that goes up to at least 100 pounds per square inch (psi) is also essential, so avoid pumps that might only be good for pumping up basketballs. Make sure that you get one that's compatible with the kind of valves your tires have. (Schraeder valves are short and stubby like the ones on your car tires, and Presta valves are thinner and shaped a little like the Empire State Building.)

A set of three tire levers

You use these to pry the bead of your tire off the rim when you're changing a flat. I like the plastic ones; they're lighter and somewhat less likely to put a pinch flat in your tube.

A tire patch kit

Ready for a checklist?

- ✔ A little piece of chalk or crayon to mark the hole
- ✔ Some sandpaper or an emery board to rough up the tube so the patch sticks
- ✔ Glue to stick the patch on
- ✔ Some tire patches
- ✔ A little gold star to stick on your shirt to tell the world you successfully completed the repair

A chain rivet remover

Though it looks like some kind of medieval torture device in miniature, a chain rivet remover merely removes the rivets that hold your chain together so you can replace a broken link or remove the chain for cleaning. Mountain bikers might consider buying two: a small one to fit in a saddle bag and a larger one with a handle for home use.

A pair of cable cutters

You need this tool for cutting the ends of cable and cable housing cleanly so they don't fray. Make sure they're big enough for sufficient leverage and sharp enough to cut cleanly. And finding a pair with a lifetime warranty — Sears Craftsman sells one — isn't a bad idea so you can return them when they get dull or nicked up.

Grease and chain lube

These items aren't exactly tools, but they truly are essential. Grease prevents corrosion on metal-to-metal interfaces (like the seat post and the seat tube). Chain lube is perfect for lubricating cables and, you guessed it, chains.

More cool tools

That's it for the real essentials. But if you're going to go beyond doing minor adjustments and maintenance, here are a few specialized items.

- ✔ **A repair stand:** This mechanic's helper makes life easier because it raises the bike and its components to a chiropractor-approved level. Of course, it also keeps the wheels off the ground, which is essential for drivetrain adjustments.

- ✔ **A spoke wrench:** Used for tightening spoke nipples, it's essential for wheel truing and spoke replacement.

- ✔ **A pedal wrench:** It's long for leverage, relatively thin to fit into the gap between the crank and the pedal, and angled to help loosen the left-handed threads on left-side pedals.

- ✔ **A crank extractor:** Though most crank sets can be removed with an Allen wrench, some of the cranks on older bikes need a dedicated crank puller. If you try to remove a crank without it, you'll probably have to dial up your bike shop for advice, which would make you, bada boom, a crank caller.

- ✔ **A freewheel cassette remover:** Pretty much the same idea as the crank extractor, minus the bad joke. You also need a chain whip — a short length of chain attached to a handle — to complete the job.

- ✔ **Cone wrenches:** To properly adjust the bearings on a hub after an over-haul, you need a pair of these thinner-than-Kate-Moss wrenches (and a good deal of patience).

- ✔ **A third hand:** This tool is basically a big spring that squeezes your brake pads against the rim so you don't have to.

The Take-It-With-You Tool Kit

The only thing more important than having a good tool kit at home is having a good tool kit to carry with you on the bike. When you're carrying it with you, you obviously have to walk the fine line between packing so light you're eliminating essentials and carrying the kitchen sink. Here's a list of basic tools that'll pack up small and fit neatly into a saddlebag.

Mr. Fixit: My pump don't blow

This situation sounds like the first line of a blues song, but it's not really all that dire. First, unscrew the cap on the top of the pump body. This step enables you to remove the handle assembly entirely. Opposite the handle, you should find a cup-shaped porous washer. Chances are it'll be shrunken and dry, which is why it isn't making a good seal with the pump body. To make your pump work as good as new, get a little dab of grease — about half a toothbrush-full — and work it into the leather. Now that the leather is softened up, carefully spread the washer so that it opens up like one of those time-lapse photos of a flower blooming. Replace the handle assembly into the pump body, trying to squish the washer as little as possible in the process. Now try pumping. Congrats. You've restored the seal to the pump. A fully inflated tire is just some muscle power away.

- **Hex (Allen) wrenches:** Take a couple of essential Allen wrenches: a 5 mm and a 6 mm. These are the ones that adjust your seat binder bolt and your stem.

- **A chain rivet tool:** This tool is optional for road riders, but mountain bikers had better bring one or risk that long walk home. A number of companies make small all-in-one tools that include a small chain tool, a small screwdriver blade, and a couple of Allen keys. They're no substitute for a good set of full-size tools for your home shop, but they can save valuable ounces in your traveling tool kit.

- **A frame pump:** Not only should you carry it, but you should also use it every once in a while so that you'll know it's working when you need it. A CO_2 tire inflator is smaller, but it's not very good at inflating a tube partially, a must for roadside flat repairs.

- **A spare tube:** A patch kit's smaller, but it won't handle every puncture, it's useless in the rain, and besides, who wants to be fooling with little patches on the side of the road or trail? So just bring along a spare tube. Make sure it's folded properly, with the valve in the center so it can't rip or puncture the tube. Mountain bikers prone to pinch flats may want to consider packing a second, just in case.

If you do suffer a flat, make sure you remove the punctured tube from your bag as soon as you get home. If you don't, you're likely to forget about it until your next flat when, surprise, you yank a pre-punctured tube from your bag.

- **Three lightweight tire levers:** They should be small and light enough to fit in your saddlebag, but big enough to do the job.

- **A dollar in change:** No matter how well prepared you are, every now and then you'll encounter some problem that you just can't fix. In that case, you'll be glad you can call your spouse or a friend — or even a cab — to come and pick you and your bike up.

Righty tighty

Do you have trouble figuring out which way to turn a screw or a bolt to loosen it? My wife Sally did, at least until she learned this little rhyme while she was crewing on a sailboat: Righty tighty, lefty loosy. If the wrench is at the 9 o'clock position, you move the handle from left to right to tighten it. And vice versa (if the wrench is at the 3 o'clock position, you move it from right to left) to loosen the bolt. Got it?

It worked great for her, but it only confuses me. I tend to think of the bolt like a clock, and I turn it clockwise to tighten it, counter-clockwise to loosen it. Remember that a few places on the bike — notably the left-side pedal — have left-handed threads (because forward rotation tends to unscrew conventional threads), which means that in those special circumstances, you have to reverse these directions.

Cable Guidance

You've probably noticed by now that your bike has more cable than Ted Turner. So how would you like to find out how these cables work? Good. It's very elegant, actually. The system has two parts. The *cable* is made of tightly wound strands of wire with some kind of cable stop, usually a ball, on one end. And the *housing* is a flexible metal tube, usually covered with some sort of vinyl coating.

Now it's show and tell time. Here's an exercise that can help you become more familiar with cables. Get a length of cable and insert one end into the housing all the way until it pokes out the other end. Pull on the ball end with one hand while holding the housing in the other. What happens? The other end of the cable moves. Okay, so it's not nuclear physics, but stay with me here.

To make this cable actually do something on the bike, you have to anchor one end of the cable to the moveable part (which substitutes for your pulling hand in the previous example) of a shift or brake lever. You then anchor the housing to a non-moveable part of the lever (taking the place of your holding hand), called a cable stop. Much the same thing happens at the other end — the cable is attached to a moving part of the derailleur or brake and the housing is anchored by a cable stop.

What happens when you move the lever? The cable moves and the housing stays still, which causes the derailleur to shift or the brake to close. Sure, there are a few extras — springs that return the brakes to an open position when you release the lever, tension adjusters that hold the shift lever against the spring in the derailleur — but it's really that simple.

Now that you're armed with all this theory, what do you do with it? In practice, the performance of the system depends on keeping the friction to a minimum. In order to keep your bike in tip-top shape, you need to keep your cables straight, well groomed, and lubricated.

Straight

Have the test cable handy? First, keep the housing straight and do the push-pull thing. Pretty easy, huh? Now bend the housing to a 90-degree angle. It takes a lot more effort, right? Try relaxing the housing into an arc. Better, no? In a perfect world, every cable run would be straight. But this isn't a perfect world. However, you can do your part by making sure that when your cables do have to bend, they do so in graceful curves rather than nasty pinches. And you need to make sure that there's enough slack in the housing to allow the handlebars to turn.

Well groomed

If you look carefully at the cable, you'll notice that it's made up of a bunch of tiny wires wrapped really tightly. As long as all those strands stay in line, it's fine. But when one starts fraying, the whole cable gets so frizzy it becomes a hairdresser's worst nightmare — and a mechanic's worst nightmare, too, because

- ✔ Frizzed-up cables don't glide very well inside the housing.
- ✔ Sliding the cable through the little hole or slot in the derailleur or the brake becomes all but impossible.
- ✔ Those little bits of cable frizz are as spiny as a sea urchin.

As any hairdresser can tell you, avoiding split ends in the first place is better than trying to repair them. The way to avoid the cable-frizz problem altogether is through proper cable cutting. First, you need a pair of sharp cable cutters. When you cut the cable to length, you want to do it on an angle, which makes it easier to thread the cable into the housing cleanly. Some particularly fastidious mechanics actually crimp a cable end or even solder the strands together after the cable's installed to keep it from unraveling. You can tell who they are because they don't have any Band-Aids on their fingers.

And lubricated

To make a cable really glide, you need to reduce the friction to the absolute minimum. That requires lubrication. A bike-specific lube like Tri Flo is the right stuff for this job. Some mechanics even use wax — just draw the cable through that green apple-scented candle — with good results. Just don't use grease. It attracts dirt, which can gum up the works.

Tool Rules

Don't you wish that you were a born mechanic? All good mechanics share certain traits, but it's not so much a matter of picking your parents as developing good work habits. Here are a few ways you can start on the road to becoming a full-fledged tool fool.

Be observant

In *Into Thin Air,* author Jon Krakauer tells that when he was climbing Mt. Everest he almost subconsciously made a little mental picture of the landscape, noting landmarks and approximating distances, because he knew that this information would come in handy to keep from getting lost on the way down. And when he returned to camp only an hour before a deadly storm hit, he realized that this old climber's habit probably saved his life.

Although the stakes aren't quite as high, good mechanics do the same thing before they begin disassembling something, and you should follow their example. Before you get out a screwdriver or a wrench, take a really good look at what you're working on. Try to memorize how it looks and how the parts fit together. Be specific. Does the cable wrap around the top or the bottom? Does the bolt go on the right and the nut on the left, or vice versa? Take notes or even snap a Polaroid if you need to. When you're ready to put it back together, you'll be happy that you did.

Be realistic

If you've never touched a wrench before, don't go disassembling your bottom bracket. Start with small jobs like fixing a flat or changing brake pads. And don't be too proud to ask a local bike shop for help.

Be orderly

Bike parts tend to disassemble like those multicolored stacking rings that 1-year-olds love. So take a cue from little Ethan: Take parts off one at a time and then lay them out in the order in which they came off — and the order in which you'll put them back. Also take note of their orientation and lay all the parts face up. But don't put them in your mouth, okay?

It's duct soup

Here's an old mechanic's adage: If it can't be fixed with duct tape, then it ain't worth fixing. I may not go that far, but I have repaired everything from broken spokes to ripped shorts with some of nature's sticky miracle wrap. But you don't want to carry a roll on the bike, do you? Instead, wrap some duct tape — oh, a couple or three feet should suffice — around one end of your pump. It weighs almost nothing and you'll forget that it's there until you're out on the road and run into something that needs to be fixed. Zip ties, which can be purchased at most electronic stores, serve a similar function and can be stashed in your saddle bag.

Be neat

Lay out a blanket or a towel under your work area. Metal parts like washers and ball bearings bounce on concrete floors, and Murphy's Law dictates that anything that can roll under the furnace will. If they fall on the blanket, they'll just go *plop,* and you can reach down and pick it up instead of scurrying around on all fours.

Be methodical

The existence of Jerry Springer and Beanie Babies to the contrary, this is a logical universe. So if, despite your best efforts, you try to reassemble something and it doesn't seem like it's fitting together right, then it's probably not. Don't force it. Treat it like a jigsaw puzzle. Find the right part and then keep turning it until it falls right into place. If it came apart, it'll go back together.

But not too methodical

There are times, especially when disassembling a component, when brute force is the solution. Bolts freeze, seat posts seize, rust happens. So after you're absolutely positively sure that you're doing the right thing, the next alternative is do it harder. Use some spray lube. Put a pipe over the wrench handle for leverage. Under sufficient duress, some have even used a hammer.

The results will usually be a loosened bolt. But sometimes — and consider this a disclaimer — the result will be a stripped bolt, a cracked frame, busted knuckles, or worse. Brute force is a powerful thing. Use it wisely.

Chapter 12

Gearing Up: Demystifying the Drivetrain

In This Chapter

▶ Getting to know the components

▶ Fixing minor drivetrain problems

▶ Discovering what you shouldn't try to fix

▶ Cleaning, lubing, and replacing the chain

▶ Searching for strange noises

I relax by taking my bicycle apart and putting it back together again.
— Michelle Pfeiffer

"*H*i, my name is Allen, and I'm a gearaphobic."

It used to be the kind of admission that you made reluctantly, mumbled, under your breath, looking at the floor. It was something that you could only share with someone else who's also transmissionally challenged. It was enough to make you want to find a support group.

But I'm here to tell you that you don't have to be embarrassed anymore. The truth is that with its Rube Goldberg vibe, a bicycle's drivetrain can freak out even people who can program their own VCRs. Cables, chains, cogs, *grease.* It's almost enough to make you take up jogging. Almost.

But fear not. Your bicycle's drivetrain may have five times as many gears as your car, but the principles are actually pretty simple, and all the parts are right there in the open for you to see and work on. And remember that the drivetrain's purpose is nothing less than noble — allowing you to get the best from your bike's engine; that is, you.

In this chapter, I describe in detail how your chain gets from one shift to the next. I talk about the most neglected component on your bike and how to take care of it, demonstrate how to troubleshoot and repair some basic drive-train problems, go over some basic maintenance that'll keep problems from cropping up in the future, and even give you some hints on locating the source of that funny, annoying little noise. As an added bonus, I recount the greatest moment in the history of bike repair.

How Do Your Gears Work?

Got your thinking cap on? Good. Now sit down in front of your bike, because what I'm about to describe makes much more sense with some visual aids. Those arms attached to your pedals are called the *crank set,* and I'd like you to pay special attention to those two or three chain rings attached to it. Now shift your attention (Get it? *Shift.*) to your rear wheel. There, you'll find a *freewheel* — a set of between five and nine cogs of different sizes. You'll notice that your chain connects the chain rings and freewheel cogs. The size of both the cogs and the chain rings are expressed in terms of the number of teeth around their perimeter — a 32-tooth cog is larger than a 28-tooth cog. The ratio of the size of the chain ring and the size of the cog determines how far the rear wheel turns for each turn of the chain ring.

What you need to know is that moving the chain to a smaller chain ring while staying on the same cog gives you a lower gear and makes it easier to pedal. Conversely, shifting to a larger chain ring gives you a higher gear and makes it harder to pedal. In the rear, the effect is opposite. Shifting to a larger cog in the back (while staying on the same chain ring) gives you a lower gear. Shifting to a smaller cog gives you a higher gear. Got it? There'll be a quiz later, right about the time you get to the first hill.

Here's where the fun begins. How do you move the chain from chain ring to chain ring, or cog to cog? That's what your derailleurs are for, those complex looking things with the cables attached. You've got a front and a rear derailleur, but while they look very different, they essentially do the same thing: push or pull the chain from cog to cog or chain ring to chain ring, which changes the gear ratio I talked about a minute ago. Some bike mechanics refer to this as a chain reaction. (Ba-da-boom!) Most do not.

The part of the derailleur that the chain is threaded through is called the cage. On the front derailleur, the cage is essentially two plates just slightly wider than the chain, bolted together. The rear derailleur cage has two little wheels on the rear derailleur — called the *pulleys* — that the chain is threaded through. Attached to the cages on either derailleur are strong springs that move the derailleur cages in or out. When you move your shift lever, it tightens or slackens the cable, which moves the cage by either pulling directly on the cage, or allowing the spring to push it back. And of course, where the cage goes, the chain follows. And Newtonian physics being what it is, it's much easier to redirect the chain while it's moving than when it's stationary. Which is why, on a derailleur-equipped bike, you should only shift while you're pedaling.

Which of course begs a question. How come there isn't a lot of slack in the chain every time you shift? It's because there's another spring in the rear derailleur that allows the cage to pivot up and down as well as in and out. This spring essentially takes up the slack when you shift to a smaller cog. Pretty neat, huh?

It's a relatively simple and elegant system that hasn't changed very much in the last 50 years. But bike manufacturers have continually refined the system, and today's derailleurs work better and more easily than ever. Thanks in large part to the mountain bike revolution, they shift without protest over wider freewheels and chain rings and work without protest in the funkiest conditions. Once upon a time, executing a clean shift required the precision and finesse of Yo-Yo Ma bowing a legato passage of Brahms' Cello Sonata in E Minor — well, maybe not *that* much finesse, but you get the point. Today's klutzproof indexing derailleurs have definite stops for each gear and shift with a reassuring click. Ain't progress wonderful?

Fixing the Rear Derailleur

But progress or no progress, every now and then your derailleurs don't work the way you'd like them to.

Adjusting cable tension

The most common problem with derailleurs is cable tension. Indexing derailleurs depend on cable tension to shift accurately. The problem is that cables stretch minutely with each shift, and before long, your bike doesn't shift like it used to. Here's the solution:

1. **Click your rear derailleur shift lever until all the slack is out of the cable, which should move the chain onto the smallest cog.**

2. **Shift to the second cog.**

   If the chain moves sluggishly or not at all, you need to increase the tension on the cable. If the chain overshifts the second cog, you need to loosen the cable by turning the adjustment barrel clockwise.

3. **Find the adjustment barrel.**

It's either on the lever where it meets the cable housing, on the derailleur body where it meets the cable housing, or both. If you have two, use the one on the derailleur first.

4. **To tighten the cable, turn the adjuster counterclockwise.**

   If you max out the cable adjusters before the derailleur's shifting properly, then the cable has too much slack to shift properly, and you need to tighten up the cable itself. First loosen the cable adjusters. Then find the anchor bolt that clamps the cable to the derailleur body. Loosen the bolt and pull the cable tight, using pliers if necessary. Then re-tighten the bolt securely so that the cable doesn't pull out of the anchor bolt, being careful not to strip the bolt.

Adjusting limit screws

On the derailleur, there are two screws that limit how far the derailleur moves with each shift (see Figure 12-1). If these screws are out of adjustment, the derailleur will shift too much or not enough. If adjusting the cable tension (covered in the preceding section) doesn't help, or if the bike is misshifting drastically, it's time to adjust the rear derailleur limit screws.

When adjusting the screws, start with a quarter turn, and keep track of how much and which way you've turned them so that you can undo the last step if you turn the wrong screw or turn it too far. Remember that if you turn the adjustment screws too far, you'll send the chain flying off into the spokes or the chainstay, so turn the cranks gingerly when working with these screws.

Not sure which screw to turn or what direction to turn it in? Here are some simple solutions to common problems:

Problem: The rear derailleur won't shift the chain onto the smallest cog.

Solution: Loosen the high gear adjustment screw.

Problem: The rear derailleur won't shift the chain onto the largest cog.

Solution: Loosen the low gear adjustment screw.

Problem: The rear derailleur throws the chain when you're trying to shift onto the largest cog.

Solution: Tighten the low gear limit screw.

Problem: The rear derailleur throws the chain when you're trying to shift onto the smallest cog.

Solution: Tighten the high gear adjustment screw.

Figure 12-1:
The two adjustment screws on a doraillour.

Fixing the Front Derailleur

The front derailleur looks quite different from the rear derailleur, but it operates in much the same way. Here's are some brief troubleshooting tips:

Problem: The derailleur shifts sluggishly or not at all.

Solution: With the chain on the inner chain ring, eliminate any excess slack in the cable by turning the adjustment barrel counterclockwise or by loosening the anchor bolt, pulling the cable tight, and retightening the bolt.

Problem: The derailleur throws the chain when shifting in the big chain ring.

Solution: Tighten the high gear adjustment screw, found on the large chain ring side of the derailleur, a quarter turn.

Problem: The derailleur throws the chain when shifting to the small chain ring.

Solution: Tighten the low gear adjustment screw, found on the small chain ring side of the derailleur, a quarter turn.

Don't Touch That

While I encourage a hands-on approach to bike mechanics, there are limits. And one of the keys to being a successful mechanic is knowing which jobs you should and shouldn't tackle. Here are three components that you shouldn't take apart if you have any hope of getting them back together.

Indexed shift levers

While old style non-indexed shift levers didn't have anything more than a couple of washers inside, modern indexed shifters, whether they're push buttons or Grip-Shift style, are different animals. They've got dozens of tiny parts. Mess with them beyond just adjusting the tension or changing the cable and you'll probably end up carrying a box full of parts to your bike shop (where they'll probably tell you you're better off just buying a new set).

Freewheels and freehubs

You know that little ratcheting sound your bike makes when it's coasting. It's the result of dozens of tiny pawls and fine gear teeth inside meshing just so. Watchmakers are daunted, and you should be too.

A little history

Sometimes necessity is the mother of invention. In cycling's earliest days, riders had to make do with two-speed bikes. There was one sprocket on each side of the rear wheel, and they had to actually remove the wheel and flip it around in order to change gears. On November 11, 1927, a young Italian racer, Tullio Campagnolo was climbing the snow-covered Croce D'Aune pass, when he stopped to change gears. However, the wingnuts that held the wheel on were frozen, and his hands were too cold to budge them. At that moment, cycling legend has it, he muttered a sentence that would change the world of cycling forever: "Bisogno cambia qualcossa de drio," or in English, "Something must change at the rear." Campagnolo lost the race, but he scored a more important victory that day. He returned to his workshop and began working on not one but two innovations that would revolutionize the sport: the invention of the quick release hub and the refinement of the derailleur. And the company that bears Tullio's name soon became, and continues to be, one of the largest and most prestigious manufacturers of bicycle components in the world.

Internally geared hubs

The hub on your three speed bike may look simple from the outside, but that benign exterior houses an array of precision parts that makes your car's transmission look like a Lego set. Bike shops generally won't even touch one. Use it until it breaks (the one on my errand bike has lasted more than 30 years) and then replace it.

Chain, Chain, Chain

Your chain is the Rodney Dangerfield of bicycle components. A chain is made of literally hundreds of precision-machined parts — pins, plates, and rollers — all working in concert to help transform your energy into forward motion. And yet the only time you think about yours is when it gets some grease on the sleeve of your new jersey.

The other thing they say about chains is true: They're only as strong as their weakest link. And nothing will slow you down quicker than a broken chain. (For the specifics of chain repair, see Chapter 14.) That's why it's important to treat your chain better. There are three steps to good chain maintenance: cleaning, lubing, and replacing.

Cleaning the chain

These steps will make your chain clean enough to eat off of:

1. **Take your bike outside and spray degreaser (a mild solvent sold in bike shops) on the chain, the derailleur, the cogs, and the chain rings.**

2. **Loosen serious gunk by cleaning the chain and the cogs with a rag or, better yet, a stiff bristled brush.**

3. **Let the bike sit for 20 minutes or so to let the degreaser do its work.**

4. **Hose down the drivetrain with water, being careful not to spray directly at the bottom bracket or the hubs.**

5. **Shake off excess water by dropping the bike from a height of six inches or so.**

Lubricating the chain

After you clean your chain, you have to lube it. Just follow these steps.

1. **Turn the cranks slowly, and drip some lubricant onto each link of the chain.**

It's best to use a lubricant specially formulated for bike drivetrains.

Regular oil doesn't have enough viscosity, spray lubricants like WD-40 evaporate too quickly, and grease attracts dirt, which defeats the whole purpose of this exercise.

2. **Wipe down the chain to remove the excess lubricant.**

Be careful of overlubing the chain, because excess lubricant can get thrown off the chain and find its way to your rims and brake pads where it can sabotage your braking performance.

Replacing Your Chain

Despite your best efforts, your chain will wear. What happens is that as the individual small parts wear, it'll stretch. And once that happens, it doesn't mesh very well with the cogs and the freewheel anymore. As it wears, it also begins to lose its lateral stiffness.

The negative consequences of chain wear are twofold. First, it won't spin smoothly because the chain and the teeth of the cogs and chain rings aren't meshing properly. And it won't shift crisply because some of the motion of the derailleur is absorbed by the lateral flex of the chain. But even more important, a worn chain will start wearing out the other more expensive parts of your drivetrain: your chain rings, your freewheel, and your derailleur pulleys.

So if your ride a lot, plan on replacing your chain every few thousand miles. If you don't ride very much, it's still wise to replace your chain every spring.

Spending a few extra dollars for a quality chain is a good investment. Keep in mind that since chain lengths vary from bike to bike, your new chain will likely be longer than you need. Use your old chain to determine the length of your new one, and then remove an appropriate number of links. (For step-by-step instructions on how to remove links and reattach them, see Chapter 14.)

Getting Your Bearings

Your bike is full of bearings. Your hubs have them, your headset has them, your bottom bracket has them, and your pedals have them. But the good news is that most newer bikes have sealed cartridge bearings, which don't have to be overhauled. You should just clean your bike periodically so that dirt doesn't work its way inside the seal, and avoid submerging the bearings in water. If you've got an older bike with non-sealed bearings, these need to be cleaned and regreased about once a year. Your bicycle shop can do this (some shops even run off-season specials), or if you're feeling intrepid, you can buy a tube of grease, a few of the specialized tools you'll need, and a more comprehensive bike repair book, such as *The Bicycle Repair Book* by Robert Van der Plas, Leonard Zinn's *Zinn and the Art of Mountain Bike Maintenance* or *Barnett's Manual* by John Barnett and overhaul away.

In Search of Strange Noises

There are two kinds of people in this world. People who are bugged by little noises in the machines that populate their lives and people who aren't. I'm one of the former. My brother-in-law is the latter.

I constantly bring my car over and say, "You know, there's this odd little squeal when you turn really sharply to the right when it's raining."

And he says, "Is the car still running?"

"Yeah."

"Then don't worry about it."

What he knows is that little squeaks can be very hard to track down, and more often than not, they're not an indicator of anything that's seriously wrong. What I know is that they still bug me.

So when my bike starts chirping at me, I try to play bike detective, the two-wheeled equivalent of Inspector Poirot — or is it Clouseau? Does it happen only when I pedal? That eliminates the hubs and the brakes. (They'd still make noise when you coast.) Does it still happen when the bike's on the workstand? If it does, that lets out any number of collateral causes — from the handlebars to the seat. Then I zero in on the drivetrain. Does it seem like it's coming from the front — the chain rings, the pedals, or maybe the front derailleur. Or the rear — where the rear derailleur or the freewheel is the likely culprit. At that point, I get out a can of spray lubricant and start lubing the pivot points, and I get out a wrench to make sure all the bolts are tight.

Still no luck? At that point, I'm left with two options:

- ✔ **A.** Take it to a bike shop.
- ✔ **B.** Be more like my brother-in-law.

In this case, I generally choose B.

Chapter 13

These Are the Brakes: How to Stop Right and Roll Better

● ●

In This Chapter

▶ Troubleshooting your brakes

▶ Repairing and adjusting your brakes

▶ Keeping your tires in good shape

▶ Making sure your wheels are straight

● ●

*W*hat's worse than a bike that won't go? A bike that won't stop. Ba-da-boom. Or for that matter, although it doesn't lend itself quite as well to a punch line, a bike with wheels that wobble and thump when you ride it.

But seriously, folks. While they may not be quite as sexy and mysterious as your derailleurs, wheels and brakes that are out of adjustment cannot only make riding less fun, they can make it downright unsafe. The two most important safety skills are being able to ride in a straight line and being able to stop quickly and predictably. If your wheels are out of true and your brakes are only sort-of adjusted, then you're basically an unguided missile.

And face it, these components do an awful lot with very little. Your wheels weigh only three pounds each, but they can support hundreds of pounds of your weight and absorb thousands of pounds of force when you forget to slow down for that pothole. As for your brakes, they generate enough friction from four little pieces of rubber to haul your bike to a stop from speeds of up to 30 mph. All in all, pretty impressive.

In this chapter, I talk about how to do routine maintenance on your brakes, wheels, and tires. I discuss how your brakes work and how you can make them work better. How to get the wobble out of your wheels. An easy way to customize the ride of your bike in 30 seconds or less. The fine art of patching an inner tube. And why some people think the bicycle wheel is a work of art.

Brakes: An Overview

All cable-operated bicycle brakes work pretty much the same way. The cable is attached to the brake arms and the lever. Squeezing the lever increases the tension on the cable, causing the brake pads to squeeze against the rim, causing the bike to slow or stop. There are, however, three variations on this theme:

- ✔ **Long-arm brakes,** found on most new mountain bikes and many hybrids, feature two long, pivoting brake arms. A stop for the cable housing is located on one arm, while the cable core continues horizontally (like the bottom of an upside-down U) to the other brake arm, where it is anchored.

- ✔ **Cantilever brakes,** found on some older mountain bikes and many hybrids, feature two shorter pivoting arms, which are connected by a transverse cable. The brake cable housing terminates in a cable stop near the headset or the seat stays. Bolted to the end of the main cable core is a small clip that attaches to the short transverse cable. The whole cable assembly resembles an upside-down Y.

- ✔ **Caliper brakes,** found on road bikes, feature a pair of interlocking arms, the upper of which has a cable housing stop, and the lower of which has an attachment point for the cable core.

Troubleshooting Your Brakes

Good braking is a little like a game of telephone. You know, that party game where someone whispers a message in your ear and you do the same to the person next to you. The whole joke is how things get lost in the translation. Same for your brakes. If there's any slack in the system — cables that are loose, pads that are too far from the rims — the message ("Stop this bike now!") gets diluted, and before long, you're squeezing the brake levers but the bike isn't stopping. Not a good situation.

The other major brake problem, which is admittedly not quite so serious, has the opposite problem: The pad rubs against the rim. The downside is that some of your precious pedaling energy is going toward wearing out your brake pads prematurely instead of moving you down the road. There are better ways to burn more calories on your ride.

So if your brakes aren't stopping quite the way they were intended to, it's time for a little troubleshooting.

While brake adjustments are well within the capabilities of any competent amateur mechanic, it's important that they be done correctly, or you could face serious injury if parts fall off or your bike doesn't stop when it's supposed to. If you're not sure about how to proceed with a repair on your

Braking in the wet

Want to hear an enigma wrapped up in a conundrum wrapped up in an old Power Bar wrapper? You know that brake performance suffers in the wet because there's just not very much friction between the rim and the brake pad. But yet, says Steve Morrissey, chief mechanic for USA Cycling, your brake pads wear far more in the wet. Why? The rain throws up a lot of gritty debris, which doesn't grip your rim very well, but eats up your brake pads like John Goodman at an all-you-can-eat buffet.

brakes, or if you're not sure you've done it correctly, consult your local bike shop to have them fix the problem (ask them if you can watch), or have the shop check your work before riding the bike.

The rims

Most people don't often think about it this way, but your rims are part of your braking system — the two-wheeled equivalent of the brake rotors in your car's disc brakes. First spin the wheel gently. If the brake pads drag or rub on one side on certain parts of the rotation but not others, it's a sign that your wheels are out of true. You'll have to solve this problem before you can get your brakes working properly, so flip to the section on wheel truing, later in this chapter. Then give the rim surface itself a once over. The rim should be clean and the braking surface smooth. If there's grease on the rim, you can clean it off with a solvent, but be careful not to get the solvent on the tires, and wipe it off thoroughly.

The pads

Are the pads worn? On the part that contacts the rim, most pads have three or four little nubs or some other pattern that looks a little like the tread on a car tire. If they're smooth, chances are they're worn out and you'll have to replace them.

Then feel the surface of the pad. It should have roughly the consistency of a pencil eraser. If the whole pad feels pretty soft but the braking surface is glazed — usually the result of a few high-pressure stops — you can restore the pad's braking performance by removing the glaze with a light swipe of a file or sandpaper.

And while you're at it, check for small particles of metal or rock that may be embedded in the pad, and pry them out with a screwdriver or an awl. If the whole pad feels like a brownie that's been unwrapped for a week, it's time for new pads.

If the pads themselves seem fine, check their adjustment. Squeeze the brake lever and see where the brake pads contact the rim. They should hit the side of the rim flush. They shouldn't hang off the bottom, and they certainly shouldn't hit too high on the rim, where they can wear out the casing of your tire and cause a blowout.

On a really well-adjusted set of brakes, you should just be able to slip a credit card between the brake pads and the rims. A gap of two credit cards is acceptable. More than that, you need to adjust the cable tension, which is discussed later in the chapter.

The levers and cables

Squeeze the brake lever. Can you squeeze it all the way to the handlebars or the grips? If you can, you'll need to increase the cable tension, as outlined below. Is it hard to squeeze? Does the lever not snap back cleanly when you release them? Then it's probably the cable that's the culprit. If you've got cantilever or long-arm brakes, you can double-check this problem easily by releasing the transverse cable. If the cable still feels balky even with nothing attached to it, try lubing it. Or better still, you can replace both the cable and the housing. If that doesn't improve the situation, it's probably time to take the bike to the shop.

Fixing Common Brake Problems

The following sections cover how to make common brake repairs and adjustments.

Adjusting pads that are too far from the rims

Here's the way to adjust your brake pads:

1. **Locate the barrel adjuster for your brakes.**

   You'll find it either near where the cable comes out of the brake lever, or where the cable meets the brake arm or tranverse cable.

2. **Turn the adjuster counterclockwise.**

3. **Check the alignment of the brake pads again.**

   If you've hit the magic gold-card gap, you're, well, golden. (But don't just keep turning the adjuster until it falls out.) If the adjuster maxes out before you get to that point, you need to tighten the cable (covered in the next section).

Tightening the brake cable

Here's how you tighten the cable:

1. **Loosen the cable adjuster until it's a turn or so away from fully loosened.**

2. **Get your third hand brake tool (it's essentially a large spring clamp, and it's described in more detail in Chapter 11) and use it to squeeze the pads to the rim.**

   If you don't have one, you can use your hands.

3. **Undo the anchor bolt at the brake arm (on long-arm or sidepull brakes) or on the cable hanger (on cantilever brakes).**

   On cantilever brakes, leave the transverse cable itself alone.

4. **Pull all the slack out of the cable, using pliers if necessary.**

5. **Retighen the anchor bolt securely.**

6. **Release the Third Hand tool.**

   Your brakes should be within gold card parameters by now.

If the pads are still a little far from the rims, tighten the cable adjuster by turning it counterclockwise. If the pads are rubbing against the rim, back off the cable adjuster slightly by turning it clockwise.

Installing and lubricating a cable

When you inspect the cable and the housing, if you notice that the cable is frayed or the housing is old, brittle, or damaged, you should replace them.

You install a new cable this way:

1. **Wipe the cable with a light coating of chain lubricant, being careful not to get any on the rims or brake pads.**

2. **Thread the new cable through the housing, and then hook the ferrule onto the brake lever.**

   Be sure the cable ferrule is completely seated at the lever. If it's not, it could pull out under breaking and cause brake failure. On some cables, there are ferrules at both ends, so look at your old cable to determine which kind of ferrule is right for your brakes. If you have to cut off an extra ferrule, make sure not to fray the cable when you cut it, which can make it difficult, if not impossible to thread it through the housing.

3. **Thread the cable through the anchor bolt, cut it to length with a pair of cable cutters, and tighten the cable as described in the preceding section.**

Taming the wild pigs

Do you have wild pigs on your bike? That's mountain bike slang for brakes that squeal in a porcine way every time you stop. It's easy to handle. You need to make sure your brakes are toed in. This means that the front of the pad hits the rim a fraction of a millimeter before the rear. Most cantilever brakes have an adjustment that allows you to pivot the brakes in the horizontal plane. If yours doesn't, you can quiet your brakes by filing a small amount from the rear of the pads. We're talking the width of a sheet of paper here. If you overfile the pad or caliper, you'll reduce the effectiveness of your brakes.

If you're also replacing the cable housing, cut it to length using the old housing as a template.

Installing new pads

If you need to install new brake pads, follow this procedure:

1. **Open the quick release on the brakes, or detach the transverse cable on cantilever or long-arm brakes.**

2. **Remove the old pads one at a time and replace them with new ones, noting the arrangement of bolts and washers.**

3. **If the brakes are basically in good adjustment, use a pencil to mark the brake arm for pad height or the post of the pad itself for depth (on cantilevers) so that you'll have a starting point for aligning the pads.**

4. **Tighten the fixing bolts finger tight for the moment.**

5. **Squeeze the calipers using your hand or a Third Hand Tool, to check the alignment of the pad on the rim.**

   The pad should hit the rim completely flush on both sides, neither dropping off the inside of the rim nor riding up onto the tire. If it's not aligned properly, adjust it with the Third Hand still in place, sliding the pad up or down, or twisting it in a vertical axis as necessary.

6. **Tighten all the fixing bolts for the pads securely and then double-check the pad alignment.**

7. **Adjust the cable as described earlier in "Tightening the brake cable."**

Your Tires

Your tires bear a lot of responsibility. After all, they're the only part of your bike that actually comes in contact with the road. They also determine a lot about the way your bike rides. This section covers how to dial in your tire pressures and how to deal with that annoying problem of a tube that won't hold any pressure at all.

Blown out of proportion: The real deal behind tire pressure

Is your bike riding rough? Is it rolling slow? There's an easy way to adjust the ride of your bike, and all you need is a tire pump with a pressure gauge and some elbow grease. And best of all, you can make a change, and if you don't like it, you can put it back the way it was in 15 seconds.

Sure, your tire is stamped with a recommended pressure on the sidewall. This is largely to keep people from riding on a tire that's flat as a pancake or blowing a tire off the rim by doubling the recommended tire pressure. You'll also notice that the recommended pressures are generally expressed as a range. Somewhere in the middle of that range — generally between 35 and 55 pounds per square inch (psi) for mountain bike tires and between 80 and 100 psi for road bike tires — is a good starting point. And then you can fine-tune your ride by increasing or decreasing your tire pressure.

On the road, it's relatively simple:

- Lower pressures = smoother ride
- Higher pressures = lower rolling resistance

Off road, those two factors still hold true, but there are two additional variables:

- More tire pressure = fewer pinch flats
- Less tire pressure = better traction

There is one other variable: your weight. The air in your tires essentially supports your weight, so if you weigh 200 pounds, you need more pressure in your tires than someone who weighs 120.

So decide what you need more of — a faster ride or a plusher one — and try increasing or decreasing your tire pressure accordingly in five-pound increments. And don't be afraid to experiment.

Under pressure at the Olympics

Track racers at the Olympics are under a lot of pressure — and on top of a lot of pressure, too. For important events, mechanics pump their tires to pressures of up to 260 pounds — fully three times as much pressure as a conventional road bike tire, and six times as much as a mountain bike tire. And they don't use just plain air. They fill the tires with nitrous oxide, the anesthetic gas favored by dentists and Grateful Dead fans. The reason? The gas is lighter than air, and when a gold medal is on the line, every fraction of an ounce counts. The downside? These tires are way beyond "rock hard," and even the slightest abrasion to the tire casing can cause a catastrophic puncture. Catastrophic? The sound is basically like a shotgun, and the punctured tire couldn't be more useless if it had a slug in it.

A softer tire can turn a rough-riding bike into a plush machine, and a harder tire can make any bike roll faster.

Women often ride overinflated tires because they often have their husbands or boyfriends pump them up, and the well-meaning but unthinking guys pump as if they were pumping for themselves, not for someone 50 pounds lighter.

 How do you know if you've got the right pressure? Lean on the tire. If you press your hand on the top of the tire, you should be able to flatten it out a little. On a mountain bike, you should see it bulge a decent amount. On a road bike, it'll only bulge a little.

 Remember that tires will leak at a rate of a few pounds per week. If you don't ride your bike for a while, be sure to check your tire pressure. Cornering hard on a soft tire is an easy way to fall.

Patching a tube

I'm assuming that you've removed the tube from the tire. If you haven't, see "Fixing a flat" in Chapter 14. You need a patch kit for the following steps:

1. **Inflate the tube lightly, with about five pounds of pressure.**

2. **Hold the tube to your lips and feel where the air is escaping.**

   If you can't feel the hole this way, try immersing the tube in water (to look for air bubbles).

3. **Put your finger on the hole.**

4. **Mark the hole with chalk.**

5. **Scuff the tube lightly with some sandpaper or an emery board in the area around the hole.**

6. **Find a patch that's the right size for the hole.**

7. **If you have a self-adhesive patch, peel the backing and then press it firmly onto the tube.**

   If the patch isn't self-adhesive, apply some glue to the tube and press the patch on firmly and allow it to dry for a few minutes.

8. **Inflate the tube gently and check that it's holding air.**

9. **Re-install the tube in the tire as in Chapter 14.**

Be True: Dewobbling Your Wheels

Wheels are not like Weebles. They should not wobble. And if they do, *you* might fall down. That's why it's important to keep your spokes evenly tensioned and your wheel true — that is, round and straight from side to side.

A rim is round and true to start with, but it's spoke tension that keeps it that way. The theory is that each spoke is exerting an equal pull on the rim. And wobbles happen when that equilibrium is broken. If one spoke loosens up, the tighter spokes on the opposite side pull the rim in that direction. And in a larger sense, a group of looser spokes on one side of the wheel will make the rim something less than completely round.

How do you know if a spoke is tight or loose? Pluck it. Good wheel builders are almost like piano tuners. No, they don't carry tuning forks, but they can tell if a wheel is tensioned evenly by plucking spokes and listening for the pitch. The higher the pitch, the tighter the spoke. The lower the pitch, the looser.

(There's an exception to these general rules. In order to make room for your freewheel, your rear wheel is *dished.* This means that the two sides of your rear wheel have different length spokes and different tensions. What this means is that you can use the pitch method to compare spokes on the same side of the rear wheel, but not on the opposite side. It also means that adjacent spokes have different tensions.)

If you suspect that your wheel is out of true, try these steps:

1. **Put the wheel in the dropout and use the brake pad to determine where the side-to-side wobble is.**

2. **Mark the "high spots" with a magic marker.**

3. **Look at the area where the marks are. You'll likely find a loose spoke or spokes on the opposite side.**

4. **Tighten the loose spoke a quarter of a turn by turning the spoke nipple counterclockwise as viewed from above.**

5. **Check to see if the wobble's gotten better.**

   If it's better but not quite right, give the offending spoke another quarter turn.

   If the wobble is still really really bad, loosen the spokes on the opposite side of the of the loose spoke by an eighth of a turn each, turning the spoke nipple clockwise.

If you've made your wheel worse, you should bring it to your friendly neighborhood bike shop before you reach the point of no return. You should also head to the bike shop if the wheel has a dent or a flat spot or is simply out of round. These problems are much more complex, and if you attempt to fix them, your likely to make them worse instead of better.

Is it art yet?

Your bicycle wheel is a work of art. If you don't believe me, will you believe the Museum of Modern Art? Just around the corner from Van Gogh's *The Starry Night* and across the way from Picasso's *Les Demoiselles d'Avignon* stands Marcel Duchamp's *The Bicycle Wheel*, considered one of the most important works of sculpture of the 20th Century. It's a stool with a bicycle fork and a wheel (but no tire) stuck, into the seat. Duchamp, one of the leading exponents of the Dadaist movement, revolutionized the art world by eschewing "technique" and introducing the concept of found art. The original version of *The Bicycle Wheel,* which dates to 1913, was destroyed and the one from the Museum of Modern Art is a 1953 replica.

Chapter 14

Roadside Repair Guide

. . . .

In This Chapter

▶ Removing and replacing your wheels

▶ Fixing a flat the easy way

▶ Dealing with four other common emergency repairs

. . . .

The long walk home. Every rider dreads it. You're 2 or 5 or 20 miles from your front door and because of one mechanical thing or another, your bike has declared in no uncertain terms that it's not going to carry you another inch. Now what do you do?

Well, you could start pushing. Or you could decide that now's as good a time as any to become a bike mechanic. No, you may not be Mr. Derailleurhead, but you have two hands, a brain, and hopefully a few tools. And necessity, after all, is the mother of invention, and even a slow but triumphant ride home beats a slow, dejected walk.

That's where this chapter comes in. With a couple of tools, a little advance preparation, and some ingenuity, you can repair most common on-the-road problems. So in these pages, I walk through how to diagnose your problem, how to fix it well enough to get home, and what to do when you get back home to fix it permanently. And as an added bonus, I include some preventative maintenance tips that'll help you avoid these problems in the first place.

Removing and Replacing Your Wheels

If there's one thing you really need to know, it's how to take off a wheel and put it back on. Not only do you need to know how to do it to fix a flat tire or repair a spoke, but it's also a necessity for performing that most rudimentary of bike repair moves — putting the bike in the car and driving it to the bike shop. Don't worry, it's actually very simple, but follow the directions carefully, because having your wheel fall off while you're riding is a very bad thing.

Removing the front wheel

Start out by pulling off the front wheel, because it's a little simpler.

1. **Release the brakes.**

   If your brakes are adjusted properly, you'll probably have to release the brakes before you remove the wheel because the tire won't quite clear the brake pads. If you have cantilever or V-brakes, the kind found on most mountain bikes and many hybrids, release the brake by squeezing the top end of the brake arm and then unhooking one end of the transverse cable from the caliper (the other side is bolted on). If you have caliper brakes, which are found on most road bikes, look for a quick-release lever on the caliper near where the cable is secured. If you can't figure out how to release the brake, as a last resort you can let the air out of your tire and reinflate it once it's back on.

2. **Open the quick release or unscrew the axle nuts.**

   The quick release is the small lever on one side of the hub. Pull it out so that it's parallel to the axle. This loosens the cam mechanism that holds the hub into the *dropouts* (the part of the fork that holds the wheel). Unscrew the nut on the opposite side of the axle to clear the wheel retention tabs. Then pull the wheel out of the dropout.

   If your bike doesn't have quick release hubs, you have to unscrew the axle nuts that hold the wheel to the dropout by using an open-end or adjustable wrench.

Replacing the front wheel

1. **Align the wheel.**

   Place the wheel on the fork, aligning the axle carefully so it's fully seated in both dropouts.

2. **Adjust the tension.**

   With the quick-release lever open screw in the nut on the opposite side of the skewer until it's just slightly tight (see Figure 14-1).

3. **Close the quick release.**

   Close the quick release by pressing the lever with the heel of your hand. It should take significant amount of pressure to close it. How much? The lever should leave an imprint on your palm. If it closes too easily, screw in the nut a little more. If, despite your best Arnold Schwarznegger impression, you can't close the lever so that it's completely perpendicular to the axle, then back the nut off a little, maybe a quarter of a turn, until you can press the lever all the way in. When you're done, the quick release lever should be parallel to the fork blade to prevent it from snagging on road or trail debris.

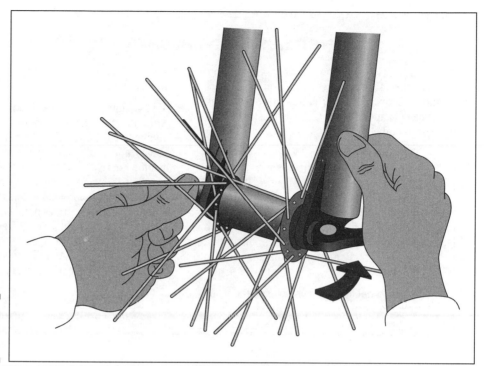

Figure 14-1:
Replacing a
front wheel.

(On some suspension forks, the forkblades are so fat that you can't close the quick release all the way with the lever parallel to the fork. In this case, close it parallel to the ground pointing backward.)

If you have hubs without quick release, tighten the axle nuts securely, alternating a turn on one side with a turn on the other until they're both very tight.

Removing the rear wheel

On the rear, the drill is similar, but a few additional steps are necessary. When removing the rear wheel, you have to contend with the chain.

1. **Shift to the smallest cog.**

   Before you start to take the wheel off, make sure that the chain is on the smallest freewheel cog. (It slackens the chain.)

2. **Clear the chain.**

   After you loosen the wheel as you would on the front (see the previous section), you need to clear the chain by pulling the rear derailleur to the rear — it pivots at the place where it attaches to the bike.

Three tips that can save your life

If your front wheel comes off while you're riding, you could face a very serious injury: a skull fracture, a broken neck, or worse. Here are three basic but important tips that could just save your skin someday:

✔ Even though it may look like one, the quick release is not a wingnut. You can't just keep turning it until it's tight. An incorrectly closed quick release may hold while you're pushing your bike, but the wheel won't stay on while you're riding. The lever must be pressed closed completely, as described earlier in this chapter, or it is not going to hold the wheel.

✔ If you're not sure that you closed the quick release correctly, take the bike to a bike shop and have someone there check your work. Most shops will gladly do this for free.

✔ Always tighten the quick release as if you were about to ride. It happens all the time: Someone will pull a bike off a car in the driveway and lazily slap on the wheel with insufficient force on the quick release. The next time they ride, they may not remember to retighten it. A corollary to this rule is that if someone else may have handled your bike (like a friend who unloaded it from the car for you), check that the quick release is closed all the way. And check your quick release before every ride, just to be safe.

3. **Remove the wheel.**

   Finally, pull the wheel downward and forward to remove it from the dropout, moving the chain out of the way if necessary.

Replacing the rear wheel

1. **Align the cogs and the chain.**

   Make sure the freewheel side of the wheel is on the side of the bike with the derailleur.

2. **Seat the chain.**

   Pull the rear derailleur back so that the chain seats itself on the freewheel. If the chain isn't cooperating, put it on the cog yourself.

3. **Guide the wheel into the dropout.**

   Push the wheel as far back into the dropout as you can. Then close the quick release or tighten the axle nuts.

4. **Check your work.**

   Is the wheel clear of the chainstay on both sides? Is it centered between the brake pads? If it is, then pat yourself on the back. If not, then the wheel probably isn't seated correctly in the dropout.

The Top Five Roadside Problems and How to Fix Them

This is the moment you've been waiting for. The advice for the following five situations can save you from a long walk home.

A flat

Symptom: You're riding down the road and you hear *pssssssst* and then *thump, thump, thump, thump.*

Roadside Rx:

1. **Stop riding immediately.**

   Aside from not being very much fun, riding with a punctured inner tube is an easy way to ruin the tire or damage the rim, two conditions that can leave you little choice but to start hoofing it.

2. **Look at the outside of the tire to determine what caused the flat.**

   If a nail or a piece of glass is embedded in the tire, remove it now before it gives you another flat. If you aren't able to locate anything, remember to look inside the tire after you remove it from the rim. If the puncture happened right after you hit a big bump, you probably suffered a *pinch flat,* caused by pinching the tube between the rim and the ground.

3. **Remove the tire.**

   If any air still remains in the tire, let it out by depressing the center of the valve. (If you have a Presta valve — the long skinny kind — you have to unscrew the locknut first.) Your tire has a wire bead which holds it onto the rim, and in order to get access to the tube, you have to remove the tire. Get out your tire levers. Hook one end of the first lever under the bead and use it to pry a section of the tire up and over the rim. Do the same with the next tire lever about six inches away from the first (see Figure 14-2). Ditto with the third. By now you should have enough of the tire off that you can slide one of the levers around the rest of the rim until the bead is completely off on one side.

4. **Determine the cause.**

   If you haven't been able to figure out what put the hole in your tube, do some detective work before you proceed.

   Examine the old tube and see if you can locate the puncture. If you can't see it, try pumping up the tube slightly. You should be able to feel the *hisssss.* Then locate the corresponding area (mounting the tire label over the valve makes this easier) on the tire and feel the inside of the casing.

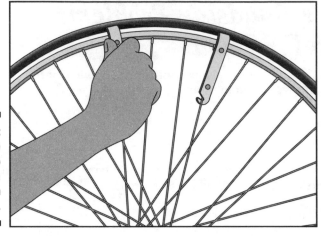

Figure 14-2:
Using tire
levers to
remove a
tire from
a rim.

If the tire doesn't seem to be the culprit, look at the rim. Is the rim strip in place? Is a spoke protruding? If you don't find the cause now, you're likely to be repeating this process a mile down the road.

5. **Install the new tube.**

   Now put in the new tube — you do have one in your saddlebag, right? The trick here is being careful that you don't pinch the tube between the tire and the rim while you're putting it in. Putting a little air in the tube will make this easier. Seat the valve stem in the valve hole in the rim and tuck the tube into the tire as deeply as possible. Then, starting opposite the valve, remount the tire onto the rim, pushing the bead up and over the rim with your thumbs. You can use your tire levers if manual dexterity alone isn't working, but be careful: Using tire levers increases the chance of an accidental pinch flat.

6. **Seat the tire.**

   Check that the bead of the tire is fully seated all around the rim and the tube isn't protruding.

7. **Begin to slowly pump up the tire.**

   Stop and look at the bead all the way around. If the tube or the tire is improperly seated at any point, it may "bubble" and force the tire off the rim. If you ignore a bubble, you'll eventually be treated to a violent explosion, so any suspicious bubbling has to be dealt with before you continue pumping. Deflate the tube and get it seated better in the tire. Also, a tilted valve stem is the sign of a bad job. If the stem isn't straight, deflate the tube and work on seating it correctly before resuming inflation.

8. **Pump up the tire to its recommended pressure, and you're on your way.**

When you get home: If you found the source of the puncture and replaced the tube with a new one, your job is pretty much done. You should patch the punctured tube (see Chapter 13) or buy a new one so you'll be prepared for your next flat.

Preventative maintenance: Buy a tube that's pre-filled with Slime or some other sealant. It's essentially a gooey liquid that contains fibers that can patch most holes temporarily. A typical debris puncture — such as from glass or a nail — that would normally result in a flat results in the loss of maybe five pounds of pressure. So you're ready to toss your spare tube, right? Not so fast. First, sealants make the tube heavier, so unless you're especially prone to flats, you might want to think twice. Also, sealants aren't effective on pinch flats (which are typically too large to be sealed that way) or holes from protruding spokes (centrifugal force pushes the glop to the outside of the tire). And you do have to be vigilant about inspecting your tires and checking their pressure lest a sealed puncture turn into a slow leak that turns into a damaged rim.

Why carry a tube instead of a patch kit? Steve Morrissey, chief mechanic for USA Cycling, knows that most punctures happen in the rain, and it's more than just Murphy's Law at work. "The rain just pushes the debris to the shoulder of the road," he says. And the weather not only makes your repair wetter, it makes it harder, too. "It's virtually impossible to patch a tube when it's wet, so don't even try. Just pop in a new tube instead."

How to think like a mechanic

If this were one of those books about how to improve your management skills in six easy steps, this would be the part where I'd start talking about thinking "in the box" and "outside the box." Come to think of it, I'll do that anyway. Are you ready for the two traits of effective bike mechanics?

✔ In the box thinking: When faced with an on-the-road problem, a good mechanic first focuses on analyzing the situation thoroughly and methodically. What exactly is wrong? Do I have the tools that I need? Are any of the parts actually broken? What can I remember from that chapter in *Bicycling For Dummies* about how to do this repair?

✔ Outside the box thinking: After you've analyzed the situation, taken your inventory, summoned all your stored knowledge, and still haven't fixed your bike, then it's time for a little improvisation. Use a dime as a screwdriver. Use a piece of duct tape to repair a broken spoke. Use a house key to dig a nail out of your tire. Use a dollar bill or a PowerBar wrapper to fix a slashed tire casing. The power of human ingenuity is almost boundless. After all, if the Professor on Gilligan's Island could build a radio out of coconuts, you can fix your bike with a twist-tie.

A broken spoke

Symptom: While riding, you hear a *ping* and then *clink, clink, clink.*

Roadside Rx: Stop riding. If you don't, the spoke will get tangled in the frame, and you'll face a much bigger mess.

1. **Remove both pieces of the broken spoke, if possible.**

   To take off the piece on the rim side, remove the tire and tube from that section (see the previous section, "A flat") and push the spoke through the hole in the rim. At the hub side of the spoke, push the spoke back through the hole in the hub. If the broken spoke is on the freewheel side of the rear hub — and it usually is — you probably won't be able to access the hole in the hub to remove this piece. In that case, you need to wrap the spoke around the adjacent spokes so that it doesn't get tangled in the gear train and use a small piece of duct tape or a zip tie to secure it.

2. **Give the wheel a spin.**

   Chances are, you'll see a significant side-to-side wobble in the rim. Get out your spoke wrench. To help pull the wheel back into line, you need to loosen the spokes on either side of the now-empty spoke hole. Turn the spoke nipple clockwise — from right to left if you're facing the wheel — a quarter turn to loosen the spokes (see Figure 14-3). Keep track of how much you loosen these spokes — that'll come in handy when you're making a complete repair later on. Don't loosen the spokes more than half a turn or you'll begin to compromise the strength of the wheel. Playing with the spoke tension should help fix the wobble situation, but you won't eliminate it completely. If the rim is rubbing against the brake pads, loosen up the cable adjuster on your brakes to give your pads more clearance — a task covered in Chapter 13.

3. **Ride home very gingerly.**

   A wheel with a broken spoke is a little like a chair with three legs. You can use it in a pinch, it but if you lean on it hard, it's likely to collapse completely. Make sure your tires are fully inflated, ride slowly, avoid bumps, and if you do encounter rough pavement, ease the burden on your wheels by moving your pedals parallel to the ground, lifting yourself off the saddle, and letting the bike move beneath you.

When you get home: Don't ride the bike again without replacing the spoke. Bring the broken spoke to a bike shop to make sure you get an exact replacement. Thread the new spoke exactly like the rest of the spokes on the wheel, being sure to pass it under an adjacent spoke before it gets to the rim. Remember those spokes that you loosened? Tighten them back up just as much as you loosened them. Then snug up the new spoke until the tension is

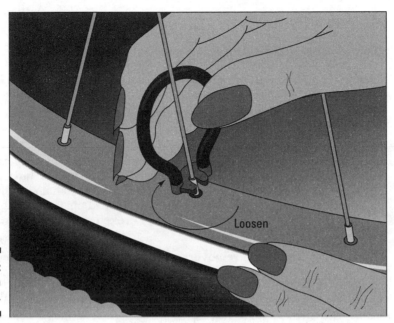

Figure 14-3:
Loosening a
spoke.

Loosen

the same as on the rest of the wheel. Spin the wheel, using a brake pad as the guide. Ideally, the rim should be both round and relatively wobble-free. If it's not, then see Chapter 13 for more about wheel truing. If you decide to leave the respoking job to your friendly neighborhood bike shop, remember to tell the mechanic about the spokes you loosened. If this is the second time that you've broken spokes on the wheel, it's only a matter of time until it happens again, so consider getting the wheel rebuilt with new spokes and a new rim.

Preventative maintenance: Broken spokes don't just happen. Except in cases of severe trauma — read *massive pothole attack* — a broken spoke is usually the result one or more loose spokes somewhere else on the wheel. Check your wheels for loose spokes periodically — just pluck them and listen for a much lower pitch — and you'll keep your spoke replacement to a minimum.

Time and effort-wise, there's not much difference between removing a broken spoke and replacing it. That's why Steve Morrissey, chief mechanic for USA Cycling, always carries a couple of spare spokes, a practice he started on his first transcontinental tour. "I carry a couple of each length and duct tape them to my right chainstay." Each length? On the rear wheel, the drive side and non-drive side spokes are different lengths, and the front-wheel spokes, which are the same on each side of the wheel, may be a different length altogether. Spare spokes are a must for long-distance touring (where you want to do the best roadside repair that you can) or serious off-road riding (where broken spokes are more common), but recreational riders can make do with one-size-fits-all Kevlar replacement spokes, available at your local bike shop.

A thrown or broken chain

Symptom: You pedal, and, well, nothing happens.

Roadside Rx: If you feel the chain disengage, stop pedaling. If you keep pedaling, you'll only make things worse. A thrown or broken chain is usually the result of putting the chain under stress, such as on a long climb.

1. **Examine your drivetrain.**

   If the chain is dangling around your bottom bracket like the latest creation of some post-industrial jewelry designer, then you have the dreaded chain suck. Proceed to Step 3. Ditto if the chain is jammed between the freewheel and the spokes. If the chain is dangling with two ends, congratulations; you've actually broken the chain. Continue to Step 2.

2. **Get that chain rivet remover (see Figure 14-4) out of your tool kit.**

   Your goal is to remove the broken links and reattach the good ends. First keep the chain threaded through the front derailleur, but drop it off the small chain ring to the inside. This should put enough slack in the chain to allow you to work easily. To reassemble the chain together, you need to have an outer plate with a rivet attached and an inner roller ready to accept the rivet. You may have to remove another link to get to that point. The key in using a chain rivet remover is to push the pin out only as far as you need to — about ⅝ of the way out is usually far enough. When the rivet is protruding, bend the link back and forth and try to work it free. Then give the chain tool a quarter turn and do it again. Repeat the process until the link is free. If you push the link all the way out, it's almost impossible to replace, and you'll just have to move on to the next link. Align the holes in both links and carefully drive the pin back in. The rivet should be just short of being flush with the plate — take a peek at an adjacent link to see how it should look. Flex the link by moving the chain up and down to make sure that it's loose and proceed to Step 3.

3. **Reinstall the chain.**

   If it's wedged between the chain ring and the chainstay, pull it out gingerly while turning the crank just enough to get it free. Then grab the rear derailleur with your left hand — assuming that you're facing the drive side of the bike — and pivot the derailleur to the front. This position should give you enough slack in the chain to loop it back over the chain ring. Now you're ready to ride.

When you get home: If this was basically an isolated incident, just check the chain over and reinstall any missing links. If you've broken your chain several times, think about replacing it.

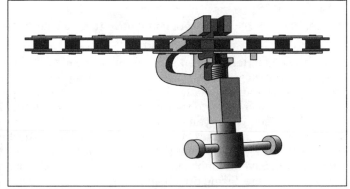

Figure 14-4:
The chain
rivet
remover.

Preventative maintenance: If broken or thrown chains become a persistent problem, you may have a front derailleur that's bent or out of adjustment (see Chapter 12), worn chain rings or cogs, or a very bad chainline (see your bike shop). Chain suck and chain breakage are special problems for mountain bikers. One solution, if not a cure, is mounting an anti-chain suck device, a precisely machined plate that helps keeps the chain on the straight and narrow.

Although your slightly-shorter-than-before chain should get you home fine, it does have its limitations. "If you take links out, avoid using the big chain ring and the big cog," says Steve Morrissey, chief mechanic of USA Cycling. If you don't? Chains don't stretch well, nor do rear derailleurs, and the result could be a catastrophic failure.

A bent rear derailleur

Symptoms: You've fallen on the drive side of your bike or gotten a stick wedged in your drivetrain, and, well, something doesn't look or shift quite right.

Roadside Rx:

1. **Look at the bike from the rear.**

   If the derailleur cage or the mounting hanger isn't perpendicular to the ground, you probably bent the derailleur. Continue to Step 2. If the derailleur is severely bent or any of its parts are missing or broken, skip to Step 3.

2. **Bend the derailleur back.**

   Try to pull the derailleur/hanger back into alignment with your hands, using slow, even pressure and holding on to the seatstay for support. Bend it a little and then check it again from the rear so that you don't move it too far in the other direction.

3. **Do a gear bypass.**

   If the derailleur is really broken, you'll have to do a gear bypass.

   Essentially you convert a bicycle with 24 non-functional speeds into a bike with one functional speed. First, remove the chain from the bike. Then put the chain around your middle chain ring (or your smaller chain ring if you have a double chain ring setup). Then wrap the chain around one of the middle cogs of your freewheel, completely bypassing the rear derailleur. When you join the ends of the chain, you'll encounter a significant amount of slack. You need to remove the extra links and reattach the ends. (See the previous section for tips on using the chain rivet remover.) Save them because you need to reattach those links when you get home. Sizing the chain properly is very important because you won't have the pulleys and the springs in the derailleur to take up the slack.

4. **Check your work.**

   Turn the pedals gently and make sure that the derailleur isn't hitting the spokes. Now pedal home carefully, and keep your shifting to a minimum.

   A major caveat: If you've bypassed the rear derailleur, don't under any circumstances use your front derailleur. All it'll do is dump your chain off and probably break it, which means you may be walking home after all.

When you get home: If the derailleur is broken, you either need to replace the broken parts or, more likely, just replace the whole thing. If the hanger is bent, having a mechanic look at it is a good idea in order to make sure that it's perfectly straight and that there are no cracks in the dropout.

A tacoed wheel

Symptom: *Bump, kerthump, kerthump, kerthump, graunnnch.* You hit a big bump and your wheel isn't just a little out of true (see the broken spoke repair earlier in this chapter); instead, it looks like something off the menu at Taco Bell.

Roadside Rx:

1. **Examine the wheel.**

   First make sure that the rim isn't broken.

   Once you've determined that your wheel is really, really bent, imagine that you're Homer Simpson pretending he's a bicycle mechanic. "Doh. Dirty, stinking, wheel taco. Hmmmm, taco." If the wheel is so bent that it's unrideable, but the rim is intact, you can often straighten it enough to ride home in the way that Homer would, through sheer brute force.

2. **Find the place where the wheel's bulging out and mark it.**

3. **Turn the wheel over and smash the side of the rim on a hard, flat spot on the ground.**

   Smash it hard but precisely, as shown in Figure 14-5. Check to see how much progress you've made. Continue doing this until the wheel is reasonably straight. You can actually get the wheel reasonably true using this method. You may have to open a quick release or loosen the cable tension in your brakes to keep the wheel from rubbing. Keep in mind that this is a last-resort measure, not a replacement for normal truing with a spoke wrench.

4. **Ride home gingerly.**

   Believe me, you don't want to add any salsa to your taco.

   When you get home: You need to inspect the rim and see if it's damaged or flat-spotted. Odds are it's relatively trashed. Consider having the wheel rebuilt with a new rim and new spokes.

After the fall: A post-crash checklist

How can you tell if a bicyclist is really hurt after a fall? If he's not asking, "Hey, man, is my bike okay? Is it? Is it?", you should start to worry.

But seriously, if you've had a crash and you've determined that your physical, corporal being is basically okay, you can turn your attention to your bike. (Of course, if you're in an accident involving a motor vehicle, your next move should be to file a police report.) Essentially, this checklist is a modification of the pre-ride inspection that I discuss in Chapter 8.

First, give the frame a once-over. Look at the fork and make sure both fork blades aren't bent and that there are no cracks in the frame joints. In a head-on collision, pay special attention to the area where the head tube meets the top tube and the down tube. If the head tube is bulged, or there's a crack in the paint, you have a broken frame and you shouldn't ride the bike. Check the whole frame for significant dents. If you have any doubts about the structural integrity of the frame, stay off it.

You're also likely to notice that the handlebars are facing one way and the front wheel is facing another. This problem actually isn't a big deal. You can fix it by approaching the bike from the front, holding the front wheel between your legs, and twisting the handlebars. Voilà.

Now look at the handlebars themselves. Give them a good yank to test their integrity. If they're partially broken and they fail while you're riding, another crash is in the cards. Be especially careful if you're on a road bike. The bars could be broken underneath the handlebar tape.

Then check the wheels and drivetrain. Examine the wheels for flat spots and trueness. Check the pedals to make sure they're not bent. Then spin the cranks to make sure that they didn't bend so that they're rubbing on the frame. Check for bent derailleurs as I explain in the section covering roadside problems.

Figure 14-5:
Bang the
wheel
against the
ground
until it's
reasonably
straight.

Part IV

Having Fun with Your Bike

In this part . . .

I talk about all of the fun things you can do with your bike. From teaching kids to ride, to joining a cycling group, to biking off-road, to commuting, I offer tips and tricks that will help you get the most out of your bike.

Chapter 15

Riding with Kids

• •

In This Chapter

▶ Riding with a child on your bike

▶ Shopping for a kid's bike

▶ Teaching children to ride

▶ Riding safely with kids

▶ Planning rides for little riders

• •

Kids love bikes. Even more than Tomb Raider III. Even more than Leonardo DiCaprio. Even more than chocolate pudding.

Why? Because they get to go fast, pretend, and explore — even if it's just the deep, dark reaches of the other side of the cul-de-sac. And they understand that their first ride around the block is a big step. A step toward freedom. A step toward independence. A step toward "Hey, Dad, can I borrow the car keys?"

Okay, so that's what's in it for them, but what's in it for you? Well, one of the best things about bicycling is that it's a family activity. It's a chance for you to spend a little quality time with your kids while telling them you're just having fun. When your children see you riding, they'll be that much more motivated to do likewise. They'll find out that bicycling is not like Barbie or Power Rangers — you never outgrow it. And maybe they'll even think you're kinda cool.

This chapter discusses how to ride safely with a small child as a passenger. I also cover how to buy a children's bike, how to teach your child to ride, the pros and cons of training wheels, and how you can have fun riding together. And, most importantly, how to keep your kids safe on their bikes.

Kids as Passengers

Little kids love bikes, too. They love to tag along and sit on the back. The view is way better than the stroller. A rear-mounted child carrier (shown in Figure 15-1) is a great way to bring your kids along for the ride, but keep these important safety considerations in mind.

Figure 15-1:
A rear-mounted child carrier.

Check it over

Make sure that the carrier is securely mounted at the dropouts when you first install it, and check the security of the mount before every ride. Also check the plastic for stress cracks and check that buckles and straps on the restraint system are working properly.

Dress them right

Remember that little children are much more susceptible to the cold than you are. And while you're pedaling, they're just sitting there. So dress them in one more layer than you'd use in a stroller in similar weather. But no baby blankets — they can get caught in the spokes or the drivetrain and cause a fall.

Keep them safe

Although most carriers are designed with this priority in mind, make sure that your child can't reach any moving parts on the bike, specifically the tires or the spokes. Make sure that any stationary parts of the bike that the child may be able to reach are free of sharp edges. And, of course, properly fitted helmets for both of you are absolutely mandatory.

Riding a bike with a child on it is like riding a bike that's fully loaded for camping — you're carrying around a significant amount of extra weight, which means that you need to allow extra time for stopping. You also need to corner carefully and conservatively and think twice about descending that big hill. You need to be that much more disciplined when starting off from a full stop — downshifting, moving the cranks to an optimal position — lest you have a potentially serious low-speed tumble. And, unlike most other loads, carriers put the child high enough to raise the bike's center of gravity, thereby decreasing stability. And unlike a camping load, your child is likely to wiggle. Obviously, you should encourage your children to sit still and enjoy the scenery. But on the other hand, don't expect that they'll always remember that, and be prepared for the sudden balance shifts that happen when they don't.

Keep them occupied

A happy child is generally not a wiggly child. Interacting with your child while you're riding is important — point out things that you pass or just sing "Little Bunny Foo Foo." Bringing toys along is generally not a good idea, because as sure as Barney is big and purple, they'll drop the toy, causing a U-turn at best and an accident at worst. And remember to keep the ride short to keep the fidgeting to a minimum.

Trailers and Tandems

If you're serious about riding with your child, consider a trailer, like the one shown in Figure 15-2. They may look unwieldy, but they are actually very stable and affect the handling of the bike less than a frame-mounted child carrier. A trailer is also a great alternative if you want to take along more than one kid at once, and many models can also be converted to a jogging stroller when you're not using them on a bike.

Another option for larger kids is a *bolt-on tandem*. It's essentially the rear two-thirds of a kid's bike that bolts onto the back of your bike. Your child can help you pedal while you do the steering and navigating. You're also providing most of the balance, but your child should have at least some experience on a two-wheeler before going tandeming.

Helmets: Setting an example

I see this all the time: A parent rides down my street with a child in a bike seat. The kid, of course, is wearing a helmet. Mom or Dad, of course, is not. I'm going to forget for a moment what kind of example this is setting for the child and look at this issue in a more practical way.

To say that a kid's head is worth more than yours is looking at things in a very narrow way. A friend of mine once suggested that as a parent, your first responsibility is to stay alive. And I see a certain brutal logic here. You can't provide for your kid, you can't teach your kid, you can't set an example for your kid, and you can't love your kid if you're dead. Wearing a helmet significantly reduces your chances of suffering a fatal or debilitating injury while you're riding your bike. Case closed.

And if you *still* don't care about your own head, then think about the example you're setting for your child. Kids want to act like grown-ups. If they see that the grown-ups around them don't wear bike helmets, they'll ditch theirs just as soon as they're old enough to ride out of your sight. So wear your helmet. It's the right thing to do.

Figure 15-2: A bike-mounted stroller.

Buying a Kid's Bike

Think about buying a kid's bike the way you think about buying kids' shoes. Yes, it's true that kids grow fast, and they're likely to outgrow a bike or a pair of sneakers before they fall apart. But you don't cheap out on shoes. You look for good arch support and a solid heel counter. In much the same way, you want a bike that's going to be rugged, safe, and fun to ride, and getting a bike with those qualities is usually worth spending a little extra. Look for the same things you'd look for on an adult bike:

- ✔ Clean welded joints
- ✔ Bearings on the pedals, hubs, and bottom bracket that spin easily
- ✔ Brakes that works effectively
- ✔ Relatively light weight
- ✔ A comfortable seat

Figure 15-3 shows a neat little kids' bike.

Figure 15-3:
A bike that
any kid
could love.

Photo courtesy of Trek.

It's also tempting to try to buy a bike that's a little too big, figuring your child will grow into it. Not a good idea. A correctly fitted bike is just as crucial as correctly fitted shoes. You don't buy your kids little Nikes that are two sizes too big, do you? Bikes that are too big are hard to control, which means not only that they're not much fun, but also that they can be downright dangerous. On the other hand, a bike that's slightly too small poses fewer safety problems as long as the saddle and bars aren't raised too high.

How do you know if your child's bike fits? You size a child's bike not much differently than you size an adult bike. The child should have adequate standover clearance. You should see at least an inch of clearance over the top tube when the child straddles the bike. If this is the child's first bike, you should be able to lower the seat enough that they can touch the ground with their feet while sitting on the seat. And, of course, don't leave the store without purchasing a properly fitted helmet. For older children (pre-teen and up), bike sizing methods are the same as for adults.

Bike bonding

When children like their bikes, they ride more. They're less likely to leave them in the driveway or push them off the deck just to see what would happen. To help your kids bond with their bikes, try these suggestions.

- ✔ After you've narrowed the selection down to a couple of bikes, let your child participate in the final decision, especially if it just involves a color choice.
- ✔ Let them buy accessories. A horn, streamers, or a speedometer can make a bike feel more like their own.
- ✔ Help them decorate their bikes. Stickers are a great way for kids to personalize their wheels and their helmets.

The responsibility game

Think of your kid's bike as a pet that doesn't have to be housebroken. A bike can provide an opportunity for a child to learn little lessons in responsibility.

Here are a few suggestions.

- ✔ Make bike cleaning a part of their chores.
- ✔ Get your children a set of tools and have them help you do routine maintenance.
- ✔ Buy your children a lock and make them responsible for locking up the bike.
- ✔ Hang a helmet hook and put them in charge of hanging their helmets back up.

Training wheels

Training wheels are a subject of some controversy among parents. Like pacifiers and Teletubbie videos, some swear by them and others swear at them.

The pros

Training wheels allow children, especially younger children, to ride unsupervised and to explore balance, steering, and braking on their own.

The cons

Training wheels can also become a crutch. Even when your child no longer needs the physical support that training wheels provide, he or she may grow to depend on them psychologically.

Using them right

Training wheels aren't outriggers. After a brief four-wheels-on-the-ground orientation period, they should be adjusted high enough — about two or three inches off the ground — so that they'll keep the child from falling over while at the same time encouraging the child to find the bike's balance point.

Teaching Your Child to Ride

One of my favorite *Calvin and Hobbes* cartoons shows Calvin learning to ride a bike. Calvin's father is spewing a barrage of directions. "The trick to balancing is to have a little forward momentum," he instructs. The normally fearless Calvin, on the other hand, is perched on the seat in mortal terror, unable to focus on anything but the catastrophic crash he's sure is about to happen. "You'll let go and the bike will launch me into the ionosphere!" The moral of the story? To be a good teacher you have to be able to think like a kid.

Riding a bike may seem simple to you. But to a five-year-old, the prospect of staying up without training wheels or without you holding on may seem like magic. And when faced with having to rely on something they can't see or feel, they're liable to panic. The result? The bike falls, and a self-fulfilling prophecy begins.

These two keys are crucial to teaching complex tasks effectively: setting up an environment in which learning can happen and dividing the task up into manageable chunks. Here's how to do both.

Making learning fun

Kids learn. They do it almost automatically. They almost can't help themselves.

That's why, despite my teachers' best efforts to bore me to death, I left grammar school knowing long division and how to conjugate a sentence. But kids learn better when they're engaged and challenged and inspired and loved. So when you're teaching your child to ride, or anything else for that matter, your most important assignment is to provide a supportive, nurturing, and fun environment. Do that and the learning takes care of itself.

How old is old enough?

The answer to the when-should-I-start-them question really depends on your child. It's a function of their muscular strength, their coordina- tion, their attention span, and, of course, their own motivation. Kids who really want to ride because their friends or siblings do will undoubtedly find a way, whereas a kid who'd really rather be playing video games will find a way to zone out. Physically, most kids can learn to ride by the time they're five or six, but the learning process is quicker when they're bugging you for some bike time instead of you bugging them.

Be encouraging

Encourage your kids when they do something right. Encourage them when they fall. Encourage them when they get up after they fall.

Encourage them for looking cool on the bike. Encourage them for just trying. Kids may try to act indifferent, but they thrive on praise.

Set achievable goals

Nothing ensures success like success. And the larger goal of riding a bike can be broken into lots of smaller goals that can be achieved almost immediately. Make your kids a bet over whether they can pedal ten times in a row without stopping. Or make one turn without toppling. Or just sit on the bike while you count to 20. Remember that kids have a short attention span. If ten minutes have passed without some kind of success, you set the bar too high to start with.

Make it fun

Kids are basically fun machines. Given the chance, they'll make even the most boring task into a barrel of laughs. So if you can manage to keep your own stress level down and resist the temptation to turn into a schoolmarm, they'll find a way to get everyone chuckling.

Allow experimentation

They're going to be riding, not you. So you need to allow them to find the solution to the problem of pedaling, steering, and staying upright at the same time. Don't bombard them with a constant barrage of advice. An occasional tip is more than enough. Remember, they learned to walk and talk without your kibitzing. They can learn this, too.

Finding a place to start

There are plenty of places that are ideal for a first lesson:

- ✔ A driveway (away from the street)
- ✔ A parking lot (when it's empty)
- ✔ A lawn (if it's smooth)
- ✔ The sidewalk (if it's not crowded)
- ✔ A park or bike path (if it's dog and skater free)

Needless to say, the street is not a good place to teach kids. Even if your street is all but deserted, your kids might get the message that riding in the street is okay, and the next thing you know, they're pedaling over to a main road.

Holding on

Before you can start the learning process, you have to learn to support your child the right way. Grab the back of the saddle in such a way that you can let go quickly if you have to, and don't hold onto the handlebars (see Figure 15-4). Run alongside the child, being careful to stay out of the way of the pedals. Remember, with all but the smallest kids, you're there to help keep them from toppling over, not to hold them up. As you feel the child gaining balance, loosen your grip and let centrifugal force take over.

Figure 15-4:
Supporting
a child
on a bike.

Breaking it down

An exercise physiologist could tell you that riding a bike requires the integration of a series of interrelated skill sets. Or your mom could tell you that you have to walk before you run. So to make the learning process both simpler and easier, I break riding down into its component parts and give you some ways to let your kids work on these skills while they think they're just playing a game.

Posture

Most kids can figure out how to sit on a bike from watching you. But what they don't understand is the necessity of keeping their eyes on the road. The Beanie Babies sticker on the top tube is much more exciting. So before you set your kids in motion, have them practice looking where they're going.

Make it a game: Play a low-speed game of red light–green light with you rolling the bike gently and a third person being the traffic signal. Or have the friend hold up flash cards or fingers to count or anything else that will keep the kids from looking at their feet or the handlebars.

Pedaling

Your kids probably already know how to do this from pedaling their Big Wheels or their tricycles. But they probably don't understand the causal connection between pedaling continuously and staying upright or the balance problems that can be caused by a foot flying off the pedals.

Make it a game: Tell them to pretend that they have gooey glue on the bottom of their shoes and their feet are simply stuck to the pedals. And remember to tell them that the glue only comes unstuck when they stop.

Steering

Kids need to learn how to steer gently. A big lock-to-lock steering motion that they may have used on a tricycle will probably send them tumbling on the ground if they try it on their bikes.

Make it a game: Set up a little course marked with something flat and non-threatening like coffee can lids. Have your child steer down the pathway you've set up. And include a nice gentle turnaround at the end.

Balance

Your kids will develop balance before they even realize it. I remember my first moment of solo bicycling. Dad was running alongside of me. He let go. I peeked around, realized he wasn't holding on anymore, and just kept going. You can help your kids find their natural balance point by having them focus on riding in a straight line and keeping their movements quiet.

Make it a game: Play tightrope or balance beam. Find or make a straight narrow lane — between a foot and two feet wide — and have your child ride on it quietly and precisely the way a tightrope artist or a gymnast would.

Braking

Braking is likely to be a foreign concept to your kid — with a tricycle, stopping is mostly a matter of dragging your feet on the ground. Before they're ready to solo, show them how the brakes work and encourage them to experiment, braking both hard and gently.

Make it a game: Playing a slightly faster version of red light–green light is a good way to introduce the concept. Then have them work on their depth perception. In this game, they have to stop before they get to the white line you draw in the driveway or a particular crack in the sidewalk. As they get more advanced, have them try to get as close to the line as they can without going over it.

Kids and Safety

Kids are not simply little adults. They see the world differently and they respond to it differently. And a lot of the very same characteristics that make them so delightful to be around can cause big safety problems when they're on a bike.

A child's eye view of the road

Here are a few things to keep in mind when choosing how and where your kids ride. Kids who may have the bike handling skills to ride on the street — they can ride in a straight line, turn confidently, and even keep pace with traffic — may lack the judgement to do so safely. If you're educating older children, see the bike safety guidelines outlined in Chapter 8.

Kids don't understand cause and effect

Younger kids don't understand that they'll get hurt if they get hit by a car. Or they may think they'll just get the same kind of booboo that they get when they fall at the playground — one that requires nothing more serious than a day-glow Band-Aid and a hug from Mommy.

Kids have tunnel vision

Little children haven't developed peripheral vision. They can also be confused about the source or even the direction of sounds, like a siren or a car horn. Finally, they also don't judge their own speed or the speed of oncoming traffic well.

Boys and safety

According to the U.S. Department of Transportation, 173 children under the age of 12 were killed in bicycle accidents in 1997 nationwide. Shockingly, 143, or 83 percent, of the victims were boys. Any number of factors could contribute to this significant gender split, from the possibility that boys ride their bikes more than girls to the fact that they may be more likely to take physical risks or may be less likely to wear helmets. But whatever the reason, the bottom line is that parents of boys have a special obligation to teach them about safe cycling.

Kids fantasize

They often mix fantasy with reality, and they may think that they have super powers that can keep a car from hitting them or that beeping their horn at a car or a solid object is an effective substitute for stopping.

Kids depend on others

In the same way that they depend on you to watch out for them at home, kids often expect drivers to watch out for them. They don't understand that to a motorist they can be almost invisible.

Kids are impatient

They're often unwilling to wait at a traffic light or a stop sign. They're also easily distracted, and they often turn their attention to something they see or even something they're just thinking about and stop paying attention to where they're going.

Riding with Your Kids

You know the old saying: The family that rides together . . . um, stays together.

Well, you get the idea. What could be better? Rolling along with your kids, you beaming ear to ear. How about *them* beaming ear to ear? Remember, you're the adult and you have to be the tour director. If they have fun, they'll want to do it again. If they're bored or frustrated, they may run straight back to the TV. Here are a few things you should look for when planning a family ride.

Helmet laws

As of January, 1999, 15 states had "age specific" helmet laws: Alabama, California, Connecticut, Delaware, Florida, Georgia, Maryland, Massachusetts, New Jersey, New York, Oregon, Pennsylvania, Rhode Island, Tennessee, and West Virginia. Many municipalities also have helmet laws, so check with your local law enforcement agency.

✔ **Low traffic:** Little kids have enough trouble keeping their bikes upright without having to worry about dodging Subarus. Stick to side streets, and pick not only a low-traffic route but a low-traffic time. A lazy Sunday afternoon makes for a safer and less-stressful ride than a Saturday morning abuzz with moms shuttling the kids to soccer practice and dads hurrying back from the home center.

✔ **A fun destination:** Just think like a kid. Where do they bug you to go? The ice cream shop, the pizza parlor, the pet shop, or the park are all perfect.

✔ **A short distance:** Five miles may seem like a warmup to you. To a six-year-old, it can seem like the Battaan Death March.

✔ **A reasonable pace:** Again, kids have short legs and their bikes have small wheels. And they won't have fun if they have to keep shouting "Hey, wait up!"

Who is your kids' role model? No matter how much they may say they want to be like Mike or Sporty Spice, they're much more likely to take their cues from you, which means that your riding also sets an example. Do you stop at traffic signals? Do you give a hand signal before making a turn? In short, you'd better child-proof your riding or you'll see your kids making the same mistakes you make.

And remember that kids are the future. Learning good riding habits now will make them better drivers a decade from now and maybe even turn them into lifetime cyclists.

Chapter 16

Joining In: The Joys of Social Cycling

In This Chapter

▶ Riding with a partner

▶ Riding with a club

▶ Participating in charity rides

▶ Biking on vacation

▶ Discovering the art of biking in groups

*I*n my opinion, simple math doesn't cut it in the bicycle world. If one bicycle is a good thing, then by my reckoning, two is a lot more than twice as good. That is, of course, assuming that another person is riding it.

Riding with a friend, a club, a tour, or an organized ride is a great way to get off the couch on those days when inertia rules. It's a great way to meet people. It's a great way to push your limits. It can even be a way to do a good deed while getting a good workout.

But how do you get started in the world of social cycling? That's where this chapter comes in. I talk about all the different ways of finding someone to ride with; the pros and cons of different kinds of group rides, both formal and informal; how to join cycling clubs; how to finance a charity ride; and how to book a bicycling vacation. And I even show you how to ride safely and courteously in a group.

Partnering Up

You remember when you were a kid and you'd just go over to your friend's house and say, "Hey, wanna go ride bikes?" Well, although nothing else in your life seems quite that simple anymore, riding a bike can be. All you have to do is get a biking buddy — someone with a similar schedule. Someone who can keep up with you and vice versa. Someone who makes you laugh, who makes you think, who makes you want to ride an extra mile. Someone who's as much of a regular buddy as a bike buddy.

The pros

Well, first and foremost is the motivation factor. Hopefully, your buddy calls and says "Hey, let's go for a ride" at least as often as you do likewise. With someone to prod you, you'll probably ride twice as often as you would have if left to your own devices. And unlike bigger group outings, which usually have to be planned in advance, a buddy ride can happen on the spur of the moment. A phone call and a change of clothes later, you're out the door and on the road. This setup is like when you were a kid, only better, because now you know how truly valuable these get-up-and-go moments really are.

The cons

Can you say *codependency?* I knew you could. About the only downside to having a regular cycling buddy is the possibility of ending up in a rut. You want to avoid connecting the whole idea of riding so much to one person that you don't ride with anyone else or go off and ride by yourself.

The cure

Try to expand your circle of buddies. Make plans to take some group rides, too. Ride on your own when the spirit moves you. And don't sweat it so much — I won't tell Oprah if you don't.

Getting hooked up

Start your buddy search by looking around your house. No takers? How about the speed dial on your phone? Still not working? How about your address book? I'm using the term *buddy* in the broadest possible way.

A bike buddy can be your spouse, your son or daughter, a neighbor, a work friend, someone you met at the gym, or someone who's already a buddy of some other kind. The idea is not to limit yourself. Anybody who rides — or may want to — is a potential candidate.

And sometimes you don't *find* a bike buddy, you *make* one. Know someone who wishes they could get out of the house more, get a little more exercise, or just get out and play a little? Then you've found a bike buddy in the making. A little encouragement, a little prodding, and maybe a copy of *Bicycling For Dummies,* and they'll be on their way. In truth, putting a buddy on a bike in the first place is often easier than trying to make a buddy out of someone who already bikes.

Club Rides

Joining a club. Bet you haven't done that since tenth grade. Though you won't earn any extracurricular activity points for joining a cycling club, there are plenty of really good reasons to do so. Mostly, you'll find the more-the-merrier factor at work when lots of people gather together for the same reason: turning the pedals. But often the most rewarding moments of belonging to a club come when you're hanging around the parking lot before or after a ride. Forget about those awkward pauses — you have an arsenal of instant icebreakers. "Is that a new bike?" "Have you ever ridden out on Hidden Valley Road?" "Can you recommend a good mechanic?" Anybody wearing a helmet becomes an instant acquaintance. And maybe, before long, a friend.

The pros

If you're the kind of person who needs a schedule, then a cycling club is perfect. Most clubs have regularly scheduled rides that you can pencil into your Filofax. And clubs can add structure to not only your week, but also your season. The shorter, slower rides in the early spring get longer as the days do, leading up to a 50-miler perhaps or even a multi-day tour.

Joining a club is also a great way to expand your cycling horizons. You can find clubs for just about any special interest you can think of, such as mountain biking, racing, touring, and tandems.

The cons

By their nature, clubs have a hierarchy, or at least a structure. There's work to do, priorities to be set, plans to be made. And often people can get a little wrapped up in the question of who's doing what, who's not doing what they're supposed to, and who's in charge. Remember all those kids who wanted to be president when they grew up? For most of them, president of the Wannaride Cycling Club is the closest they'll come.

The cure

Be *in* the club but not *of* it. Do your fair share, check your ego at the door, and leave the politics to the senators. The object, after all, is to get out and ride.

Getting hooked up

How do you find a club? Ask around. The local bike shop is a good place to start. You can also check out the community calendar section of the local newspaper. Or search the Web. Most clubs welcome new members, even complete beginners. Even so, when you're talking to the ride organizer, be honest about your ability. Whether they do it formally or informally, most clubs offer rides at different paces. So if you make it clear up front that you're new to the sport, the club rep will steer you to the slower, shorter rides.

Charity Rides

The wind at your back. The sun on your shoulders. Money in the pockets of people who need it. What could be better? More and more charities are using bike rides as a way to raise money and consciousness.

Goal-setting

Even if you agree that riding your bike is the most fun you can have that doesn't involve a half pound of bittersweet chocolate, sometimes the sheer joy of turning the pedals isn't quite enough to get you out the back door. To keep riding high on your list of priorities, you need something to look forward to and something you can brag about when you're done. In other words, you need a goal. The goal you set can be as lofty as completing a *century* — that's 100 miles in a day — or as modest as making it up that long hill down the road from you. A goal provides the motivation to ride when the rest of your life intrudes and a way to measure your progress when you're sitting back and taking inventory. So figure out what you want to do, cycling-wise; write it on your mental to-do list right next to "Pick up the dry cleaning"; and look at each ride as a little step toward reaching that objective.

And here's a little secret. Scientists have determined, in the way that scientists do, that your brain has a single pleasure pathway and all sorts of different kinds of stimuli cruise on it, which means that reaching a goal (or just feeling like you're making progress) releases the same kind of feel-good chemicals that make exercising and eating chocolate so rewarding. This fact therefore provides the motivation to find some more motivation, right? Right? Pardon me while I go out for a ride and try to make sense of all that.

The AIDS ride, The Tour de Cure sponsored by the American Diabetes Association, the MS-150 rides to support multiple sclerosis research, and the American Lung Association's transcontinental Big Ride, are just a few of the nation's biggest charity events, but they're far from being the only ones.

The pros

Putting aside the good-deed-for-the-day factor, a charity ride can be a very tempting proposition, even if you're a misanthrope. Large rides get official considerations that small rides can only dream about. Sometimes roads are closed off entirely or at least have police posted at busy intersections. Technical support — that is, someone to fix your bike if it breaks — is often available, as are food and water stops. And you'll probably get a neat T-shirt, too.

The cons

Well, it's not exactly a negative, but the sponsors of these rides view them as a serious fundraising opportunity. The idea is that you go around to your friends and neighbors and ask them to pledge a dime or a quarter or a dollar a mile. If you do one or two rides a year, requesting pledges isn't a problem. If you do more than that, though, you may get to the point where people start turning off the porch light when you walk up the front steps.

The cure

Take the donating duties upon yourself. Put your own name at the top of the donor sheet, and a nice healthy amount next to it, enough to cover all or most of your obligation. After all, you're riding for a worthy cause. And your donation is tax deductible.

Getting hooked up

Again, try the usual suspects: your local bike shop, the Web, an area bike club, signs in the laundromat. But get your information well in advance: Most of these events involve a good bit of riding — anywhere from 25 to more than 100 miles in a day — so you're not only going to need time to collect pledges, you'll probably need a little time to get in shape, too. And because big rides equal big crowds (at least for the first few miles), you should practice riding in a group.

Bicycling Vacations

Is there a better way to escape than on your bicycle? A two-wheeled vacation can provide such an escape: just you, your bike, and nothing to do but ride. Although you can certainly plan your own cycling vacation with nothing more than a map and a credit card — I cover this in more detail in Chapter 19 — more and more riders are letting a touring company do the legwork for them. The locations can range from Death Valley (no, this isn't a joke) to the rolling hills of Vermont to the mountains of the Alps. Themes can range from gonzo mountain biking to mellow eat-and-ride gourmet getaways to literally following the path of the famed Tour de France bike race. The choice, as they say, is yours.

The pros

If you have the kind of life in which you can find time for everything but having fun, then a cycling vacation is a perfect antidote. You do nothing but ride all day — whether it's from inn to inn on winding country roads or on challenging singletrack loops. But don't think that you're going to boot camp. Most cycling vacations feature certain indulgences. Rides are fully supported, with everything from mechanics to make sure your bike stays in tip-top shape to *sag wagons* that follow the pack to deal with equipment failures or failures of the flesh. And the accommodations often reflect a certain casual elegance, with antique-filled rooms and dinners that start with foie gras and scale the gastronomic heights from there.

The cons

That said, a cycling vacation isn't like lying on a beach. It takes commitment. A commitment to advance planning. A commitment of funds. A commitment to conditioning so that you can ride all day every day for the duration. Even a commitment to packing up your bike so that the airline can ship it.

The cure

Save up and shape up. Most cycling vacations are less expensive than a cruise or going to Disney World. And the prospect of spending seven consecutive days in the saddle can motivate you to get out on your bike in the weeks and months beforehand, which is not a bad thing at all.

TIP

Ask first, book later

Keep in mind that starting a bicycle tour company doesn't take much. An ad in a magazine, a colorful brochure, an 800 number, and you're on your way. Most tour companies are well-meaning and reputable, but some sweat the details a little better than others. So with that in mind, you need to do a little bit of homework about where you're thinking of spending your hard-earned money and vacation time.

Here are a few of the questions you should ask before plunking down your plastic.

- ✔ How long have you been planning tours?
- ✔ What's your cancellation policy?
- ✔ Do you provide airport transfers?
- ✔ What kind of insurance you have?
- ✔ How many miles a day will we be riding? How fast?
- ✔ How large are the groups and who leads them?
- ✔ What kind of evening activities are available?

- ✔ What are the accommodations like?
- ✔ If you book double occupancy, can you pair up singles?
- ✔ Do you make provisions for special diets, such as vegetarian?
- ✔ Do you rent bikes? Do you have mechanics available in case my bike breaks?
- ✔ What if I want or need to skip a day?
- ✔ What's the weather like at that time of the year?

No, there are no "right" answers to these questions. What you want is a sense of whether this tour matches up well with your priorities. What's more likely to freak you out — a dinner that's a half-hour late or a ride that's an hour short? An unmade bed or an un-trued wheel? And beyond that, you want a certain level of preparedness laced with honesty. For example, no tour company can guarantee good weather. What you really want is the sense that they've planned for the contingency.

Getting hooked up

Cycling magazines like *Bike* and *Bicycling,* as well as general outdoors magazines like *Outside* and *Men's Journal,* run stories about cycling vacations, generally in the late winter and early spring. Not coincidentally, these same publications also run advertisements from companies that run such vacations. Word of mouth also works well. Ask your riding friends or fellow club members about cycling trips.

Riding in a Group

No, this isn't a matter for Miss Manners, but a certain etiquette is involved in riding in a group. A lot of it is common sense and common courtesy, but a few basic techniques are involved in riding well with others.

Following the rules

Here are some do's and don'ts for cycling together in perfect harmony.

Do ride predictably

Leave the improvisation to Wynton Marsalis. Your goal on a bike is to ride in a way that makes it easy for your riding partners (not to mention UPS trucks) to anticipate what you're going to do next. Ride in a straight line. Keep your pace consistent. Don't slam on your brakes.

Don't ride side by side

Bikes weren't built for conversation. More to the point, most roads weren't built with one bicycle in mind, much less two. Follow this scenario: You're riding beside your partner and she has to swerve suddenly to avoid a pot-hole or a car door. Chances are she'll swerve, you won't, and you'll both go down. If you do find a road shoulder or a bike path that's especially wide, leave a gap of at least four feet to minimize the possibility of bike-to-bike contact.

Do use hand signals

Unless you ride with Dionne Warwick and her friends, odds are that your riding partners aren't psychic. So it's your responsibility to communicate and pay attention. Each rider in a group has the responsibility to give hand signals whenever he or she is slowing down or making a turn. (See Chapter 8.) Pointing out road hazards — potholes, railroad tracks, broken glass, or dead skunks on the side of the road — to the riders behind is also mandatory. A finger pointed to the ground is the standard signal that you ought to steer around something. But be careful that you don't swerve while you're giving hand signals.

Don't overlap wheels

Just like Buicks, bicycles have blind spots. And overlapping wheels — riding with your front wheel next to the rear wheel of the rider in front of you — is the worst of all possible worlds. You're not getting any of the social benefits of riding side by side, and you're incurring even more risk, especially if the lead rider doesn't know you're sitting back there. If you touch wheels with another rider, you'll fall at least and do a somersault at worst. Even in a pace-line you should leave at least a couple of feet between your front tire and the lead rider's rear.

Do pay attention

Riding in a group is great fun. But it's not an excuse to take a mental vacation and spend your time staring at your friend's new jersey instead of watching the road, the traffic, and the other riders. You'll have plenty of time for schmoozing after the ride's over.

The fine art of riding in a paceline

Two or more riders can ride further and faster than a single rider alone if the first rider breaks the wind for the others behind. Racers and serious riders ride in a *paceline*. The lead rider takes the lead for, say, 30 seconds or a few hundred yards, with the other riders following in formation directly behind. He or she then pulls aside and gradually slides to the back of the line, letting the next rider in the line take a "pull" at the front. Essentially the whole thing looks a little like a train, with each rider taking a turn being Thomas the Tank Engine.

When it works, a paceline is a thing of beauty. It's also a great way to let riders of different levels of fitness ride together — the strong riders take longer or more frequent pulls while the weaker riders ride in their wake.

You can also adapt the paceline to the prevailing conditions. When there's a crosswind, riders stagger the paceline laterally — it's called an *echelon* — so that they're not directly behind each other, but a foot or two to the right. This technique helps create a buffer zone of calm air. Be careful, however, not to move into the flow of traffic.

Generally, pacelines work best with a small group of no more than about five riders. This way the line can stay compact — an important consideration in traffic — and the choreography doesn't have to be as complex as the Rockettes.

If you've never ridden in a paceline before, make sure that you tell your partners so. They'll be happy to show you the ropes (and if they're not, go find someone else to ride with). They'll also give you a little extra space until you get the hang of it.

When you're riding in a paceline, you have to ride a little harder when you're at the front to maintain the same speed as the other riders. If you don't adjust, you'll slow the group. But if you push too hard, you may leave the folks behind you going faster than they would like. How do you maintain this delicate balance? Use a cycle computer to help you maintain a constant speed. They're discussed in more detail in Chapter 5.

Mountain biking in groups

Group mountain bike rides are a lot of fun and share some of the benefits of group road rides, with some extra bonuses too. For one thing, mountain bikers tend to stop, rest, and enjoy the scenery. These stops provide an opportunity for the fast riders to wait for the slower riders to catch up. And because mountain bikers don't ride in tight bunches, they don't have to worry as much about pack-riding etiquette as road riders do.

Chapter 17

Happy Trails: The Many Faces of Mountain Biking

In This Chapter

▶ The start of something big

▶ Mountain biking's many genres

▶ Happy trails

I've seen mountain bike rides transform people — not just their bodies, but their way of thinking. Their spirit.

— Charlie Cunningham

Have you ever noticed that only about, oh, maybe 5 percent of the world is paved? It's that simple observation that's at the core of mountain biking's appeal. Mountain biking is about exploring the other 95 percent — or at least the part of it that's covered with less than six inches of water.

Mountain biking is also mostly about plain, pure, unadulterated fun. Whereas the rest of the cycling world is focused on things like getting from place to place, getting fit, or getting to the finish line first, mountain bikers make no bones about their agenda: Go out and have a blast. Get dirty. Get sweaty. Even get a little lost. And that injection of attitude has made cycling better for everyone who turns a pedal.

In this chapter I talk about how mountain biking got started; the hows and wheres of off-road riding; how to coexist peacefully with other trail users; how the technical improvements that got their start in the fat tire universe have trickled down to all two-wheelers; and how good citizenship, both on and off the bike, can ensure that you'll have a place to ride for years to come. But most of all, this chapter is about discovering why so many riders believe that the fun begins where the pavement ends.

In the Beginning . . .

Like everything important — the birth of a nation, the beginning of the universe, the invention of baseball — mountain biking has a creation myth, too.

The story of mountain biking's origins goes back to in the mid-1970s. A few Northern California racers, including Gary Fisher, Joe Breeze, and Charlie Kelly, got bored with logging miles on the road, and instead took some beaten-up balloon-tire Schwinns and started bashing them around on the trails and fire roads of Marin County with silly grins on their faces. They told two friends, who told two friends, and within a couple of years a sport was born. Within a few more years, mountain biking was hotter than five-alarm chili.

And while, unlike the Abner-Doubleday-invented-baseball myth, this tale is largely true, the reality is a little more complex.

People have been riding bikes off road, well, as long as there have been bikes. In Europe, racers put knobby tires on their road bikes every winter and ride *cyclocross* — little loops that include on-road, off-road, so-funky-you-gotta-carry-your-bike sections. And beginning in the early 1970s, little boys rugged-ized their Choppers and Stingrays for riding on dirt and catching air, and BMX — bicycle motocross — was born. In fact, some of mountain biking's early heroes, most notably former world champion John Tomac, got their start in BMX. In short, the idea of mixing bicycles and dirt has been in the air for a while.

But whatever the truth about how mountain biking started, once mountain bikes began showing up in bike shops, the sheer thrill of riding off road brought a niche sport into the mainstream. After all, 16 million mountain bikers can't be wrong.

The Wheres and Hows

Where do people ride mountain bikes? Well, if you can imagine it, someone's tried to ride a mountain bike there: Mount Everest; Death Valley; Nome, Alaska; over the top — as in up the bumper and down the hood — of a Los Angeles traffic jam.

Don't be fooled by the name *mountain bike*. Fat-tire bikes aren't made only for the hills, they're at home almost anywhere. An early, and now all-but-forgotten designation — the all-terrain bike — is really a more descriptive term. Here's a rundown of the different ways and different places that people have fun on their mountain bikes.

Cross-country

Cross-country is the meat-and-potatoes — as opposed to the macaroni and cheese, or risotto and white truffles — of the mountain bike world. It basically means finding a trail and taking a couple of hours to ride a long loop, or maybe an out-and-back route. The trail can be mellow, it can be intense, it can be just about anything but paved. Cross-country is also the jumping-off point for all of the sport's other genres, and the place where just about every newbie gets his or her feet wet.

Where to do it

Ever wonder where your tax money goes? Well, at least some of it maintains mountain biking trails. Most off-road riding is done on public lands, whether they're local, county, state, or national parks or preserves. And if you want to get a mountain biker excited just say "Singletrack." *Singletrack* is really just a gearhead word for a hiking trail, but it's the kind of ride that most mountain bikers live for. The setting is the woods, either dense and dark or open and sparse. The surface can be anything from hard-packed dirt, to gravel, to pointy softball-sized rocks colloquially known as chicken heads, to mud, to leafy forest debris. The trails are usually pretty narrow and somewhat technical — full of things like big rocks, downed trees, steep climbs, dropoffs, and switchbacks that can conspire to make you get off your bike or make you want to give yourself a high five when you don't have to.

The other popular cross-country venue is a fire road — an open, unpaved road that often connects sections of singletrack. Here the riding's faster and more furious, and the emphasis turns to the cardiovascular side of the sport, with a little dust thrown in for good measure.

What's the thrill?

A great cross-country ride is a study in contrasts. During the mellow parts, it's as peaceful as can be, just getting back to nature and hanging out with the woodland creatures. During the gnarly parts, it can be an adrenaline jolt that puts Space Mountain to shame. If you doubt that it's intensely physical, take your pulse at the top of a long, steep climb. But it's also like a game of three-dimensional speed chess — the difference between riding a tough section cleanly and having to get off and hike is often as much a matter of quick thinking as good riding. Is cross-country all things to all riders? Maybe not, but it's pretty darn close.

Cross-country racing

It may sound like a Borscht Belt joke, but most mountain bike racing is a lot like cross-country riding, only faster. Unlike road racing, which is worlds apart from regular riding, cross-country mountain bike racing is really just kind of a regular ride on steroids (figuratively, of course).

Where it's done

Most race courses are pretty similar to the trails recreational riders frequent — hilly singletrack and fire roads. The field tends to string out pretty quickly, so drafting and team tactics just don't enter into these races. And in the end, you're not racing against other riders so much as you're racing against yourself.

What's the thrill?

Some call it masochism. Your heart's pounding and the rest of you is getting pounded. But standing at the starting line with a bunch of other riders and someone with a stopwatch is the best way to find out just how fast and just how tough you really are. There's a lot to be said for the satisfaction of passing someone when you're both wondering how you're going to make it to the finish line. Then there's the satisfaction of actually crossing the finish line; and of course the satisfaction of a cold swig of post-race Gatorade.

Downhill

Get a bike that owes as much to Evel Kneivel as to Eddy Merckx. Point your bike downhill. Now get to the bottom as fast as you can. That, in a nutshell, is downhill, mountain biking's outrageous waltz with gravity.

Where to ride

Anywhere there's a hill. Most downhillers simply fixate on the gravity-driven portion of regular cross-country rides, choosing trails based on their thrill potential and choosing their bikes based on their ability to handle big bumps at high speeds.

But have you ever wondered what ski areas do in the summer? Well, up until the advent of mountain biking, the answer was "Not much." Now when the weather gets warm, many ski areas open their lifts and trails to mountain bikers looking for downhill thrills. You can take a chairlift to the top, ride to the bottom, and then do it again. The combination of on-demand uphill transportation coupled with trails designed with high-speed recreation in mind, and the absence of other trail users, make ski resorts perfect for downhilling, two-wheel style.

What's the thrill?

Speed thrills. Downhilling is all about adrenaline straight up. You may not reach speeds that could earn you a ticket on the interstate, like pro downhillers like Leigh Donovan and Shaun Palmer, but you certainly feel like you are. And no matter how fast you go, you have the understanding that if you read the line better, relax on the bike more, and screw up a little additional courage, you can go faster next time. Can you say "instant gratification?" I knew you could.

Just say "Thanks"

Even if you never drop a wheel off the pavement, you owe mountain bikers a debt of gratitude. Why? The demands of off-road riding spurred improvements that have made all bikes much better.

Riding off road is simply more demanding of a bike than riding on pavement. A machine has to be more rugged, the controls have to be easier to use, and it has to be able to cover terrain that would have even sport-utility vehicles making U-turns.

Fingertip shifting is a mountain bike-inspired innovation. Wide range gearing? Before the dawn of the fat tire era, most bikes had only 12 speeds that didn't shift well under duress. Lots of other features that have become common in the bike world at large, from TIG-welded frames to threadless headsets to suspension seatposts, got their start on mountain bikes.

Backcountry

Imagine bike touring taken to its logical extreme. Forget about county roads and 7-Elevens. It's just you, the trail, and whatever you can carry with you. Mountain biking's back-to-nature contingent melds a backpacker's into-the-woods aesthetic with the practical advantages of riding a bike — you can simply cover more ground than you can on foot.

Where to ride

The short answer is anywhere that the nearest paved road is half a day away. Because mountain bikes are less nimble than hiking boots, trail choices are somewhat restricted compared to hiking. And, of course, mountain biking is prohibited or restricted in many federal, state, and local wilderness areas.

What's the thrill?

Thoreau said it best. "Nature is full of genius, full of the divinity." There's nothing more inspiring than being smack dab in the middle of an Ansel Adams landscape. But it's more than just the view, there's something refreshing, and more than a little humbling about being out in the wilderness, miles away from the nearest car, the nearest fax machine, the nearest Burger King. And because nature can be as unforgiving as it is beautiful, a backcountry bike trip is an exercise in self-reliance of the kind that would have made the poet of Walden Woods proud.

Fit for the Trail

Turning the pedals is turning the pedals, right? Well, yes and no. It's true that cardiovascular fitness is the basis of all forms of cycling, which is why so many top riders, from John Tomac to Ruthie Matthes to Alison Dunlap, have made a quick and easy transition from road to dirt or vice versa. In fact, most mountain bike racers do most of their training on the road. And even those riders who stick with one discipline do some cross training to smooth out their pedal strokes or improve their bike handling.

That said, mountain biking does require a broader spectrum of athletic skills than road biking. Wheelies, *bunny hops* — jumps over small obstacles — and just squeezing the brake levers places more emphasis on upper body strength. And because of uneven trail surfaces, mountain biking places a higher premium on balance.

"You can't control the terrain," says David Farmer, coach of world champions like John Tomac and Juli Furtado. He emphasizes balance so much that he actually puts his athletes on a low balance beam. He has them start by simply walking across, heel to toe, both forward and backward, and as they gain agility, he ups the ante by adding lunges and hand weights to the mix. Farmer also emphasizes cross training. Any sport that enhances your balance — skiing, skateboarding, in-line skating, ballet — helps you be that much more nimble on your bike.

As for the upper body work, Farmer says, "I like them to start off with a broad spectrum of exercises — biceps curls, leg extensions, wrist and forearm extensions, and flexions. Then I like them to move on to squats, dips, and chin-ups." The progression is from simple exercises that isolate a single joint in one plane of movement to more complex exercises that involve several muscle groups, and more accurately mimic the demands of the trail.

Trail Access

There's a problem with being the new kid on the block: finding a place to play. And that's what mountain bikers have been up against since the sport's beginnings. The trails that mountain bikers want to use have been used by hikers and equestrians for decades, and just like two-year-olds in the sandbox, they're often unwilling to share.

Let me tell you a story. The best place to ride near where I live is called South Mountain Reservation in South Orange, New Jersey. It's part of the Essex County Park system, the oldest county park system in the U.S. And sometime around the turn of the century, the County Freeholders passed a resolution declaring that South Mountain would be off-limits to vehicular traffic. This was designed to keep those newfangled horseless carriages away, but technically, the ban included bicycles. For the better part of a century, nobody paid all that much attention — hikers hiked, horses trotted, mountain bikers rode, and cars stayed on the pavement — until a few riders became aware of the lame-duck ban and petitioned the board to get rid of it entirely.

The result? A number of local hikers found out about this and argued that not only should the bike ban stay in force, but it should be actively enforced. They claimed — erroneously — that mountain bikers were responsible for serious erosion, trail congestion, just about everything short of global warming. The freeholders ultimately sided with the hikers and closed South Mountain to riders.

The problem, of course, is that this decision backfired on all levels. Only responsible riders were deterred by the ban — the few riders who rode too fast and otherwise ignored the rules of the trail weren't stopped by a few signs. The trails in the park continued to be neglected, despite the fact that the mountain bikers had volunteered to help with upkeep in exchange for lifting the ban. And this trail closing just outside the New York metropolitan area — where riders are many and trails are few — set up a domino effect: The displaced mountain bikers flocked to other nearby trails, which caused increased congestion and even some grumblings about further trail closings.

The moral of this story? That mountain biking is not a right, it's a privilege that can be taken away. And if you want to keep riding, you better ride responsibly, because non-riders will judge all mountain bikers by your actions.

Another lesson to be learned is to get involved — join clubs, meet with land managers, talk to your public officials, and last but not least, educate your fellow mountain bikers about trail safety and etiquette. In the end, mountain biking isn't just an active sport, it's an activist sport.

IMBA's Rules of the Trail

A mountain bike doesn't do you much good if you don't have a place to ride it. That's why you should know about the IMBA (International Mountain Bicycling Association), mountain biking's main trail advocacy group. Its functions include lobbying governmental bodies, providing support for grassroots efforts to build and maintain trails, and disseminating information about impending trail closures. Perhaps their most enduring accomplishment comes in the form of rider education. Here are IMBA's Rules of the Trail. All responsible riders follow them at all times. You should too.

1. Ride on open trails only

Respect trail and road closures (ask if you're not sure), avoid possible trespass on private land, obtain permits or other authorization as may be required. Federal and State Wilderness areas are closed to cycling. The way you ride will influence trail management decisions and policies.

2. Leave no trace

Be sensitive to the dirt beneath you. Even on open (legal) trails, you should not ride under conditions where you will leave evidence of your passing, such as on certain soils after a rain. Recognize different types of soils and trail construction; practice low-impact cycling. This also means staying on existing trails and not creating new ones. Don't cut switchbacks. Be sure to pack out at least as much as you pack in.

3. Control your bicycle

Inattention for even a second can cause problems. Obey all bicycle speed regulations and recommendations.

4. Always yield trail

Make known your approach well in advance. A friendly greeting or bell is considerate and works well; don't startle others. Show your respect when passing by slowing to a walking pace or even stopping. Anticipate other trail users around corners or in blind spots.

5. Never spook animals

All animals are startled by an unannounced approach, a sudden movement, or a loud noise. This can be dangerous for you, others, and the animals. Give animals extra room and time to adjust to you. When passing horses use special care and follow directions from the horseback riders (ask if uncertain). Running cattle and disturbing wildlife is a serious offense. Leave gates as you found them, or as marked.

6. Plan ahead

Know your equipment, your ability, and the area in which you are riding — and prepare accordingly. Be self-sufficient at all times, keep your equipment in good repair, and carry necessary supplies for changes in weather or other conditions. A well-executed trip is a satisfaction to you and not a burden or offense to others. Always wear a helmet and appropriate safety gear.

Trail maintenance

Let's get one thing straight: Trails weren't put there by the Supreme Being of your choice. They were cut by human beings just like you and me.

Every time anyone uses a trail, even in a responsible manner — whether it's a mountain biker, a hiker, or a horse — an incremental amount of damage is done to the trail. And with entropy being what it is, there's nature's tendency to revert back to the pre-trails state: Trees topple, leaves fall, undergrowth grows back. Then there are other unnatural forces, such as erosion caused by riders who make their own shortcuts around the harder parts of the trail.

The solution? Get out and do your share. The IMBA has a recommendation it calls 20-20-20: $20 to join your local mountain biking club, $20 to join the IMBA, and 20 hours of volunteer work per year. Many mountain bike clubs get out a few times a season and have a trail maintenance day. In cooperation with the local land managers, they go out and build water bars, repair erosion damage, and close off those little detours. It only takes a few hours and it's actually fun. Give back — it's the right thing to do.

Sensitive when wet

You don't have to be a soil geologist to understand that trails are most susceptible to erosion when they're wet. Which is why it's good common sense to avoid sensitive trails early in the season when melting snow leaves standing water on the trail, and immediately after a heavy rain. If you're leaving a muddy tire print, you shouldn't be riding there. Taking a detour to a less sensitive trail, with better drainage or a rockier road surface, is one important way to help out on the crucial task of trail maintenance without so much as lifting a shovel.

Chapter 18

Riding Off-Road: A Mountain Biking Primer

● ●

In This Chapter

▶ Absorbing the shocks

▶ Looking where you're going

▶ Practicing your moves

▶ Climbing every mountain (and coming back down)

▶ Popping wheelies and bunny hopping

▶ Riding safely

● ●

So you want to be a mountain biker. You've seen the Mountain Dew ads and the magazine covers and you're intrigued. And to be honest, you're a little intimidated, too.

Well, don't be. Let's just keep this between you and me, but mountain biking is an extreme sport: Extremely peaceful, extremely relaxing, extremely back to nature. For most of us, mountain biking isn't about heart-stopping descents and catching big air on bumps and qualifying for the next X-Games. It's about getting out into the woods and riding your bike in a place where you're more likely to run into a deer than a Dodge.

And mountain biking is not all that hard. The basic road riding skills like pedaling, climbing, and cornering that I cover in Part II are necessary for skillful riding off-road, too. Much of the rest simply comes with a little saddle time. But there are a few new techniques to master, and a few new wrinkles in old standbys.

Most roads don't offer much in the way of technical challenge — after all they were designed with Pintos and tractor trailers in mind. But mountain biking trails were originally designed to be traversed by hikers and horses, both in their way more agile than bikes. But the technical challenges — how do I tackle this section? — are part of the fun of mountain biking.

In this chapter, I tell you what you need to know to get started off-road: how to become a human shock absorber on uneven road surfaces; how to maintain traction when the going gets slippery; how to descend safely; how to leap small obstacles in a single bound; and most of all, how to have fun and be safe while you're doing it.

Be a Human Shock Absorber

The first thing you notice about riding off-road is that it's, well, bumpy. So, it's a no-brainer that one of the basics of better off-road riding is learning to use your bike and your body to smooth out the ride.

Your arms as springs

The road to a plush ride begins with your arms, specifically your elbows. Try this experiment: Stand with your arms straight in front of your, elbows locked and have someone give your hands a shove. Bonk. Pretty severe impact, eh? And not only did your arms move, your back did too, and you probably even had to take a step backward to keep from getting knocked over.

Now relax your arms, bend your elbows, and repeat the exercise. What happens? Not much. Your elbows just bend a little more, and it's a piece of cake to absorb the impact.

Which strategy do you think is going to work better when you're riding your bike over a big rock? Right. If your elbows are bent, as the front wheel rolls over the front side of the rock, your elbows naturally flex a little more to absorb the impact. And when the impact is over, they straighten back out (but not completely), which has the effect of pushing your front wheel back onto terra firma. As long as you stay loose, this all happens so quickly you hardly have a chance to think about it even if you wanted to. Pretty neat, huh?

Sometimes, especially when the bumps get a little bigger or you get going a little too fast, you can end up in this weird rigor-mortisy kind of position in which your elbows are bent, but your muscles are still tight. To keep your sinewy shock absorbers working, focus on relaxing your hands and keeping your grip on the handlebars loose. Don't worry, you still have plenty of control over the bike. Loosening your grip also relaxes the muscles in your arms and shoulders, leaving your arms available to soak up the bumps.

Your legs as springs

Now, you want to get your non-hydraulic shock absorbers going at the other end of the bike. The key, as you may have figured out, is keeping your legs

Suspension supplement

A suspension fork or a fully suspended bike can only do so much. "But I paid good money for my suspension bike," you say. "Why should I have to do all the work?" Having shocks may make your ride a little faster and a little cushier — it may even mean that you can spend a little more time with your butt in the saddle — but it does not mean that you can be just a passenger. Maintaining an athletic, flexed-and-ready position makes it easier to adjust your balance when the terrain throws you a curve ball. And staying quiet and relaxed helps the suspension do its work.

---

flexed. "How do I do this and keep pedaling?" you ask. Well that's sort of a trick question. Of course, your legs *are* flexed while you're pedaling, which does help absorb the bumps. But the next step to a smoother ride is to pedal, not *out* of the saddle, so much as *off* it. Pretend that your saddle is a $286,000 Chippendale chair. Sit on it gingerly. You may even lift your butt off the saddle, oh, maybe a quarter-inch. That's enough to allow the bike to move a little underneath you, so you, your butt, and everything attached to it don't take a lot of punishment.

On really rocky or rough sections, all bets are off, though. Stop pedaling, and move your cranks to the 3 and 9 o'clock positions. Now, move your butt a few inches off the seat but still right over it, bend your knees, bend your elbows and let the bike do the rumba beneath you while you float relatively shock-free above it all.

The key to riding over rough terrain is being loose and relaxed — which isn't as easy as it sounds. The natural tendency when you're in a tough spot — or on a rough trail — is to tense up as though you're bracing for something. If you give in to that instinct, you'll probably be bracing for a crash. So in a strange Zen-like way, your mission is to fight the impulse to fight the bike. Without too much interference from you, the bike will stay upright, continue rolling, and find the path of least resistance. Trying to over-steer the bike, or manhandle it, only makes matters worse. In short, the less you do, the better off you are. Don't you wish your whole life were like that?

The Eyes Have It

"Look where you're going." If you had a dollar for every time your mother said that, you wouldn't envy Bill Gates quite so much. But it turns out that, as usual, your mother was right. There's a definite causal link between where you're looking and where you end up.

That's one of the things that Alison Dunlap, an Olympic road racer turned professional mountain biker, discovered when she took to the trail. "Don't look down at the trail, look 10 or 15 feet ahead," she advises. "When you stare at that rock, you're going to hit it." And while this seems like simple, sound advice, the next time you're out, take note of where you're really looking. Are you peeking at your handlebars? Your front tire? That tree root you're about to go over? It's natural, especially when you're feeling intimidated by the circumstances, to try to restrict your field of vision. The world seems less scary that way. But if you're right on top of an obstacle, it's way too late to do anything about it. You need to look a few feet — and a few seconds — ahead. When you're riding down a rutted trail at 15 miles an hour, the present is the past and the future is the present.

While most beginners think that being a better mountain biker is all about riding the toughest, gnarliest parts of a trail, the experts know different. The best riders have an uncanny ability to find the easiest path. The secret is training yourself to look not at the obstacles ahead, but the spaces in between them. Do that and you'll instinctively steer around the impediments. But don't be too hard on yourself — even the pros catch themselves looking down. As Dunlap says, "It's such an easy thing to do and such an easy thing to forget."

Practice, Practice, Practice

One thing you have to say about golfers — they may dress funny, but they're not afraid to practice. They hit balls on the driving range. They take practice swings on the tee. They take practice swings in the bathroom. Mountain bikers can learn a thing or two from them.

Most riders just go out and ride and then ride some more. If they come to an obstacle on the trail, they either improvise a way to get over it, or they get off and walk around it.

But there's something to be said for just plain practice. I honed my basic mountain biking skills in a city park on a mound of red clay maybe 5 feet tall and 15 feet wide that sat on the side of a baseball diamond. Again and again, day after day, I'd ride up the steep side and down the shallow side or vice versa. I'd ride the off-camber route around the side. I'd catch air, finesse the brakes, climb seated, climb standing, practice dropping off the back of the saddle. Some days, it'd be muddy and traction would be at a premium, other days it'd be hard as asphalt and as rutty as a prairie dog's backyard. And while I must have looked a little silly, it was a great, um, crash course in bike handling. Because I didn't have to worry about keeping up with anyone or following the trail, or even getting tired or out of breath, I was able to concentrate completely on how my body positions affected the handling of the bike.

You can do the same thing. Find your own little hill. Build a small obstacle course in your backyard. Put in a little practice time. And pretty soon your riding will be as smooth and picturesque as your golf swing. Or maybe even more so.

Uphill Battles: A Quick Guide to Climbing

The good news: Off-road climbing is more than a matter of sheer horsepower. The bad news: Off-road climbing is more than a matter of sheer horsepower. "On the road it's almost all legs," says Alison Dunlap, Olympic road cyclist turned professional mountain biker. "On a mountain bike, it's a matter of trying to figure out if you've got enough traction." Not only are you fighting gravity, but because of the loose dirt and gravel, you have to contend with friction, or the lack thereof.

Don't misunderstand. Good road climbing techniques and strategies like the ones outlined in Chapter 7 are invaluable off road. It's just that the extreme steepness and variable surfaces make off-road climbing even more of a challenge, so much so that even the strongest riders occasionally have to get off and hoof it.

There are two basic approaches to off-road climbing — seated, and out of the saddle. Each technique is appropriate for different conditions and can be used in combination. Generally, seated climbing is best for longer hills and slippery conditions where traction is at a premium. Out-of-the-saddle climbing is good for quick charges up short hills in a slightly higher gear and as a change up in the middle of a long, slow grind.

Seated climbing

The key to strong seated climbing is good body position. Cindy Whitehead, a former racer and member of the Mountain Bike Hall of Fame who now teaches mountain bike skill camps, suggests bending deeply at the elbows and thinking about pressing your chest toward the top tube. This flexed position allows you to enlist your powerful gluteus muscles in your pedaling.

Still slipping? "If you're losing traction, move your hips backs," Whitehead suggests. However, if you get your hips too far back on a very steep hill, your front wheel has a tendency to lift. To counteract this pop-a-wheelie syndrome, keep your hips where they are and move your *shoulders* down even further. That should bring your front wheel back to Planet Earth.

If, after all that, you're *still* having traction problems it may not be you: It might be your bike. To test this, put the palm of your hand on your tire and press. You should be able to flatten the tire at least a little. If you can't, you're riding with too much tire pressure. This problem is especially common for female riders whose husbands or boyfriends pump up their tires and unconsciously pump in enough air pressure for a 200-pound guy instead of a 120-pound woman.

Out-of-the-saddle climbing

When that long, steep hill begins to look like the Lhotse Face on Mount Everest, smart riders get out of the saddle (see Figure 18-1). Standing in the pedals not only gives you a psychological break, it lets you recover physically by enlisting different muscle groups. *If* you do it right.

"A lot of my riders climb like they're on a Stairmaster," says Whitehead. "Their body weight is doing most of the work." Needless to say, this stomp-stomp-stomp style of climbing is inefficient. Instead, Whitehead suggests actively rocking the bike side-to-side, using the bar ends for leverage. This motion gets the strong muscles of your shoulders and your chest into the action, and allows you to push a bigger gear, which means getting to the top faster.

Figure 18-1:
Getting out of the saddle to climb.

Getting back on

What do you do when you've spun out on a climb? Unless the terrain is atrocious or you're totally toasted, try to get back on the bike. To get restarted on a hill, you have to straddle the bike, grab the bars, and put a forward pedal in the 2 o'clock position so that you can get a good push on the first downstroke. You ideally will power the rear wheel, get yourself situated on the saddle, and get your other foot onto the other pedal when it comes around — all in one motion. It takes practice, but it's a good skill to have because no matter how strong you are, you are not going to make it up every climb without interruption. There's no shame in walking, though.

Downhill Fast: The Fine Art of Descending

Yes, Virginia, there is such a thing as too much of a good thing. Gravity, for instance. Even former world downhill champion Leigh Donovan confesses, "I get very scared on steep descents." But she doesn't let her bike know that, and suggests that you don't either. "Once you freeze up, it's a disaster waiting to happen." The most important aspect of descending is good body position. To keep from going over the handlebars, you want to move your center of gravity as far back as possible. On a very steep descent, you should actually drop your butt off the back of the saddle and leave it hovering just over your back tire, as shown in Figure 18-2.

The other key to descending successfully is using your brakes effectively. You need to be able to squeeze your brakes hard enough to *almost* lock them up. The balance between the front and rear brakes is crucial, too. Concentrate about 70 percent of your braking effort on the rear brake. If you do lock up the rear, you'll just skid a little. If you lock up the front, you'll probably do a face plant. It goes without saying that you should practice your braking technique on level ground before you hit the hill that the locals call the Widowmaker.

Next, it's time to get your brain in gear by thinking positive thoughts. Donovan builds her confidence by visualizing a safe and clean descent before she even starts, a tactic that helped her clean the toughest section of a downhill in Breckenridge, Colorado in 1997, only two days after a training crash landed her in the hospital.

When your moment of truth arrives and you're at that big hill, Donovan suggests a thinking-person's approach. Roll up to a steep drop-off slowly. You should already have your butt behind the seat and both hands on the brakes before you reach the lip. Once you're committed, you need to maintain that flexed body position, look down the trail, and pick out the line with the fewest obstacles.

Figure 18-2:
The right
way to
descend
a hill.

Common sense is part of the equation too. Donovan often scouts a steep drop by walking it and watching the lines that other riders take. And even then she sometimes dismounts if the karma isn't right. "I don't want to get hurt," she says. "A lot of times, I'll go out and walk a section." And you should too.

Water Crossings

You're riding off road and all of a sudden you discover a small stream running quite inconveniently across the trail. Do you:

a. Turn around and wait for the end of monsoon season.

b. Build an ark.

c. Ride right through it.

If you went for answer c, you win yourself a free all-expense paid cruise to the other side. Riding through water requires mostly an attitude adjustment, and following these steps:

1. **Speed up before you hit the water.**

   Don't worry about carrying too much speed — the water will slow you down, and you don't want to have to get off in the middle and wade.

2. **Keep your pedals horizontal.**

   You don't want to pedal through the puddle because a submerged obstacle could snag your crank.

3. **Steer away from the dark spots.**

   That's where the water is deepest.

4. **Remember to pre-soak those mud stains before you toss your cycling clothes into the washer.**

Overcoming Obstacles

Do you wish you could get over that log in the middle of the trail without dismounting? The first move you need to learn is the *wheelie*.

You may be ashamed to admit it, but you probably learned to pop a wheelie on your Ross Apollo Racer when you were in fourth grade. I'm sure you remember the "popping" part, because it's pretty descriptive of the move: You simply straighten your elbows and pull the handlebars sharply toward you, while shifting your weight backward slightly.

Make the motion sudden and explosive, with plenty of "pop." This should get your front wheel at least a few inches off the ground, and your rear wheel will just follow the lead of the front.

A wheelie can help you clear small obstacles — downed limbs and medium-size rocks — and as an added bonus, it can also help you ride up a curb without turning your wheel into something out of a Salvador Dali painting. On big obstacles, however, the rear wheel might just slam into the obstacle instead of rolling over it. That's where the next move comes into play.

When you get the wheelie down, you can then progress to the *bunny hop,* a move that literally vaults you up and over an obstacle (see Figure 18-3). When Mountain Bike Hall of Fame member Cindy Whitehead teaches this basic off-road skill in her clinics, the class looks like let's-do-the-bunny-hop time at a wedding reception. "I have people get off the bike and actually jump," says Whitehead. Once that training exercise is done, she has her students transfer that action to the bike. "You want to crouch like a little bunny," she says. "You should get so low you feel like your back is parallel to the ground." Just before you get to the object you're jumping over, spring up and simultaneously lift the front wheel of the bike by pulling up on your handlebars. At the same time, lift the rear of the bike by pulling up with your feet — toe clips or clipless pedals make this much easier. Absorb the landing by returning to that coiled rabbit-esque position. Speed is your ally when hopping so try your first bounds on a gentle downhill. Naturally, until you've got it nailed, pick a smooth approach and a very small obstacle, like a small stick or a pile of leaves. And when you do it correctly, reward yourself with a carrot for lunch.

Figure 18-3:
The
Bunny hop.

A Guide to Trail Safety

All things considered, mountain biking is basically just as safe as riding on the road. But it does pose different kinds of hazards. The good news is that you don't have to worry about cars. The bad news is that you do have to worry more about running into obstacles and just plain falling over.

Because you're on a deserted trail instead of a busy street, you have to think more like a backpacker than a taxi driver: What if you get lost? What if you get injured? What if your bike breaks down? To help keep you safe on the trail, here are a few simple Dos and Don'ts, that, along with good common sense, can help make sure that every ride is an uneventful one.

Do leave early

Remember, it gets dark earlier in the woods — all those trees block the sun, don't you know. And once it gets dark, it gets very dark. So if you leave late, a small mishap — getting lost, or having a small mechanical problem — can leave you stumbling the woods, which are dark and deep, and maybe not so lovely if you're supposed to be home for dinner.

Don't ride alone

In a perfect world, you'd always ride in threes. In an emergency, that leaves one rider to stay with the victim and the other to go off and get help. The reality is that this isn't always possible. If you're riding a heavily trafficked two-mile loop in your local park, then it's probably okay to ride alone. But if you're venturing deep into the backcountry — and depending on the terrain, five miles can qualify as deep — or exploring a place you've never been to, you should think twice before going solo. A good litmus test is to ask yourself "What would I do if I fell and broke my collarbone?" If you don't have a good answer, you should probably wait until you can bring a friend or two.

Do carry tools

And know how to use them. At the minimum you should pack a few hex wrenches, a chain rivet tool, a pump, a spare tube, and a patch kit. And read Chapter 14.

Don't cut off your options

Always give yourself the option of backtracking. Going down a hill that's too steep to climb back up is one of the best ways — especially in a mountainous area — to get yourself seriously lost.

Do leave word

Just as if you were going off on a camping trip, it's important to let someone know where you're going on your ride, who you're going with, and when you expect to be back. If something does happen, rescuers can start searching for you sooner, and be more likely to find you in a hurry. If you don't tell a friend or at least leave a note, your friends just might think you're on a business trip to Cincinnati, while you're trying to set up a bivouac under a big spruce tree, in the dark, with a Hefty bag for a tent.

Do take emergency supplies

Essentially, you should be prepared to spend the night. That means taking matches in a waterproof container, an extra layer of clothes, something to keep you dry if it rains — a large plastic bag will do in a pinch, but a metalized space blanket is better — a knife, a first aid kit, and extra food and water.

Don't panic

Search and rescuers understand that most of the time it's not one single mistake that gets someone into serious trouble in the wilderness. It's what you do after you're a little lost that determines whether you'll just be a little late or the subject of a Movie of the Week. It's all too easy to freak out about your situation and start making a series of silly and potentially serious errors. Common brain-lock blunders include wandering off without taking note of landmarks and getting yourself even more lost in the process; trying to find a shortcut by bushwhacking off the trail; forgetting to pace yourself and take breaks for rest, food, and water; and waiting until it's pitch dark to make camp, when it's clear that you have to stay out overnight. If you find yourself lost or stranded, remember that your brain is your most valuable survival tool. Use it.

Don't zone out

Yes, the scenery can be pretty, but you're likely to come across all kinds of large and small dangers on the trail, from horses to hunters to unexpected drop-offs to poison ivy and poison oak. So ask other riders about what to expect in your area and find out how to protect yourself.

Lyme disease

There are a few things that mountain bikers have to worry about that roadies don't. One of them is tick-borne diseases. The ticks that carry the disease hang out in woods where they can find hosts — deer, mice, and occasionally mountain bikers. In 1997, there were cases of Lyme reported in 45 of the 48 states in the Continental United States. Ticks are most active in the spring, but they can and do bite all year long.

Plan a three-pronged strategy to protect yourself:

✔ Wear an insect repellant containing permethrin or DEET on all exposed skin.

✔ Wear protective clothing — long pants with cuffs that tuck into your socks and a long-sleeved shirt — preferably in light colors so that ticks are easier to see.

✔ Do a post-ride tick inspection when you get home. This is especially important because deer ticks generally don't infect the host until they've been attached for between 36 and 48 hours.

Deer ticks are sneaky little buggers. They're tiny, not much bigger than the period at the end of this sentence. And they tend to hide in out of the way places, like the back of the knees, the groin, and the nape of the neck. For this reason, it's smart (and maybe even fun) to enlist a friend to assist in your post-ride tick inspection.

Finally, be on the lookout for symptoms of Lyme disease. A large, red, often ring-like rash that appears within a week or two of the bite is the first and most prominent symptom, but it's not apparent in all cases. Unfortunately, the rest of the symptoms — fatigue, low-grade fever, headache, sore throat, swollen lymph nodes, and joint pain — are typical of many other diseases, including the flu. That's the reason that many cases go undiagnosed and untreated for long periods of time. If you exhibit these symptoms, be sure to tell your doctor that you mountain bike, and if the symptoms persist, ask to be tested for Lyme. If it's caught in its early stages, Lyme disease can be treated easily and effectively with antibiotics. Left untreated, Lyme can be very serious, with complications including arthritis, heart problems, and neurological damage.

The good news is that the FDA recently approved a three-stage vaccine which has proven 90 percent effective in preventing Lyme disease infection in people under 65 years old.

Chapter 19

Hitting the Road: The Wonderful World of Bike Touring

· ·

In This Chapter

▶ Getting prepared

▶ Picking a partner

▶ Finding a route

▶ Packing your gear

▶ Riding a loaded bike

· ·

> *It is by riding a bicycle that you learn the contours of a country best, since you have to sweat up them and coast down them.*
> — Ernest Hemingway

Have you ever thought of your bicycle as a two-wheeled Winnebago? No, it's not really that far-fetched. Like an RV, your bike can get you from place to place and serve as the home base for a really fun vacation. Granted, you have to leave the electric-powered cooler and the waffle iron at home, but your bike's other advantages should more than make up for those small inconveniences.

Traveling under your own power is very satisfying, and covering four times as much ground as you could on foot is equally satisfying. It's also a great way to really see the country. When you're rolling along at oh, 15 miles an hour, you get to soak up all the things that you miss when you're zooming past at 65 encased in an air-conditioned steel cocoon: the mating song of a lonesome whippoorwill, the barnyard dog trying to get the cow's attention, the sweet aroma of someone's backyard barbecue.

And riding a fully-loaded bicycle is enough of a novelty that you'll attract the right kind of attention. People will stop and make small talk, wondering where you're from, where you're going, and how long it's going to take. In the process, they'll tell you about the covered bridge down the road a piece that was featured in a Ford ad, the International Thimble Museum over in Jackson, and Mabel's World Famous ice cream shoppe just off Main Street. They may let you pitch your tent in their back yard or even sleep on their sofa.

In this chapter, I talk about planning a tour — and how much to leave unplanned. I discuss what to bring, what to leave home, and how to pack it all. I explain the fine art of riding a fully loaded bicycle. And ultimately, I show you how to live out of your panniers without feeling like you're roughing it.

Preparing for Your Tour

Understand this fact about bicycle touring: If something goes wrong, you can't pick up the phone and yell at your travel agent. Every successful tour begins with homework — on the phone, on the Web, and at your friendly neighborhood bike shop. Good planning and thorough preparation won't guarantee that every mile is as idyllic as an Evian ad, but it'll help you avoid most big, nasty surprises.

But it's not all grunt work. Before you start nailing down the details, your tour is just a tabula rasa — you and your bike on some vague road somewhere. But after you pick a destination, map out a route, and start acquiring the gear that'll help make it all possible, you begin to flesh out the details and the whole experience begins to come to life. What follows are some no-nonsense guidelines for taking your bike tour from dream to reality.

Be clear

What do you want to get out of your vacation? The best part of a bike tour is that it's as flexible as Gumby. Is your idea of fun roughing it — sleeping on the bare ground, eating freeze-dried food, and purifying your own water? Or do you find credit-card touring more appealing (in which you provide your own transportation, but after you're done riding, you sit down to a four-course meal and then go upstairs to sleep under a down comforter)? Or somewhere in between? A bike tour may not be the easiest vacation, but if you're honest with yourself while you're planning, it can be exactly what you want it to be.

Be realistic

Psychologists can tell you about a phase in child development called *magical thinking* — if little Zoe imagines that Clifford the Big Red Dog will come and help her pick up her toys, then she fully expects that he will.

Although this stage usually ends by the age of four, it can often recur in adults when they're picking a destination for a bike tour. They say, "Well, I did 83 miles on that long club ride two years ago. So if I ride 83 miles a day for five days, that's 415 miles, and hey, Montreal is only 430 miles from here, and Quebec City's only a little farther . . . " The logic may be sound, but the underlying assumptions are faulty. If you did 83 miles once on a perfect (but very long) day on an unloaded bike with plenty of rest before and after, isn't thinking that you can do that every day for a week kind of ridiculous?

Here's a better way. Figure out how much you can reasonably ride in a day. How does 40 miles sound? That distance translates into three to four hours of riding (factoring in a couple of stops) on a fully loaded bike. And say you want to take a six-day vacation. Multiply 40 miles by *five* days. That equals 200 miles.

Why five days? I'm purposely figuring in an extra day to play with. This way, if there's a monsoon, you can hang out in the B&B instead of riding through the rain. Or you can just slow your pace a little and sleep in one morning or take a long lunch. Believe me, you'll be grateful to have a little slack in your schedule. (Of course, it also helps to be fit before you start. For tips on training, see Chapter 10.)

And although these calculations seem to limit your options, understand one thing. Purists may call it cheating, but you don't have to start from your front door. Nothing says that yourself can't put your bike on top of your car and drive 50 or 100 miles to give yourself a head start. Then just park your car — preferably not in a tow-away zone — and ride away. (Do, however, remember where you left it.)

When you pick your destination and sketch out your route, remember that this isn't an airline trip. Ending up someplace that you've always wanted to go would be nice. But if your dream destination is surrounded by miles of busy highways and seedy strip malls, heading somewhere else via the scenic route may be nicer. On a bike trip, getting there isn't half the fun, it's more like 90 percent.

Be flexible

If you wanted to stick to an itinerary, you would have taken a bus tour, right? The whole idea of bike touring is that you have the option of following your fancy. That's why I stress the importance of good planning. It eliminates as many of the bad surprises as possible so that you have the option of embracing the good surprises. If you're just charmed by a little town and you'd love to spend an extra night, then just do it. Want to take the long way around and stop for a picnic by the lake? Go for it. The whole idea isn't to maximize your mileage or the number of sights you see, but to have as much fun as possible.

Be prepared: Your route

After you figure out where to go, you need to make sure you get there. Your first order of business is to get some maps. However, the kind of road maps you get from the gas station won't cut it. On those maps, landmarks are 20 miles apart, and you certainly don't want to wait that long to find out you've made a wrong turn. You probably need two sets of maps. Your first line of defense is a regional map that shows county roads and local streets. The second is a topographic map, which lets you know when two towns 20 miles apart also have 2,000 feet of climbing between them.

When you have your maps in hand, spread them out on your kitchen table and start plotting a route. Stay away from the major highways. Most are closed to bicycle traffic, and even if they aren't, riding isn't much fun with tractor trailers zooming by your ear at 75 miles an hour. Instead, look for the secondary roads that people used to take before the interstates. They're easy to find on a map and usually well marked, and they're both prettier and less heavily traveled.

Checking one of the many regional bike touring guidebooks or calling a bike shop in the area should also help you target bike-friendly roads.

You need to break the route up into manageable chunks and figure out where you're going to spend each night. If you plan to go from inn to inn, collect phone numbers and maybe even make reservations. If you're camping, mark off the campsites in the area. You don't have to have every mile and every minute planned, but if 60 hilly miles lie between your projected Night Two and Night Three destinations, you want to know that before you head out.

Be prepared: Your gear

Unless you own a racing bike or a high-zoot full-suspension mountain bike, neither of which have much carrying capacity, the bike you already have should be a fine companion for your tour. But before you go, you need to make sure that your bike is in tip-top shape. Either do a complete overhaul — lube the drivetrain, true the wheels, replace the cables and brake pads, and spring for a new set of tires if you need them — or bring it to your local bike shop and have them do the work. (For a complete rundown on bike maintenance, see Chapters 11–14.) But make sure you take your freshly tuned bike for a shakedown ride before you head out. Finding out that your headset's loose 15 miles into your first day is a real bummer.

You should also consider buying new tires for the occasion. If you have a road bike, you want the fattest 700c tires that will fit on your frame and fork. They will protect your rims and cushion the ride. If you have a mountain bike, ditch the knobbies (unless you're on an off-road tour) and get medium width (1.25- to 1.5-inch) road tires, which roll much more easily.

And double-check your camping gear, if you're going that route. Pitch your tent to make sure it's not torn or mildewed or missing any parts, and apply some seam-sealer while you're at it. Air out your sleeping bag so you don't end up sleeping in something that smells like your hall closet. Give your stove a trial run. If you have a problem, best you should find out in your backyard.

Buying Bags

Low, close, and *rigid* are the three guiding principles of packing a bike. The goal is to affect the bike's handling as little as possible, and the way to accomplish that is to keep the load below the bike's center of gravity. The kind of bags that accomplish this are called *panniers* (see Figure 19-1). They mount securely on a rack and straddle your front or rear wheel, where the majority of the weight should be concentrated. But you'll also need a handle-bar bag (also in Figure 19-1) or a saddle bag which allows quick access to food, maps, sunscreen and other items you'll need while you're on the road. When you're considering which bags to buy, look at them the way you'd look at a backpack. Is the fabric tough, light, and at least water resistant? Are the seams strong? Are the zippers sturdy and easy to use?

Figure 19-1: A bike equipped with pan- niers and a handle- bar bag.

Transforming your bike into a packhorse starts with a good rack. The kind of light-duty racks that work fine for carrying *The New York Times* from the store probably aren't up to snuff when you're hauling 30 pounds. Stiff welded steel or aluminum racks with a good mounting system are the best choice. Try mounting the bags on the racks before you buy them to make sure they work well together. All the flaps and straps should stay well clear of the spokes and the drivetrain, and there should be enough clearance that your heel doesn't hit the bag while you're pedaling. Figure 19-2 shows a bike with as much stuff as you can expect to carry.

Figure 19-2:
A fully
loaded bike.

Touring Together

Though you can go it alone, bike touring is really best done in pairs. Bringing someone along offers both tangible and intangible advantages. On the one hand, there are any number of things that you can share — from a tube of toothpaste to a camp stove. This means that each of you can carry less weight. Two riders are also more aerodynamic than one. By drafting, you can conserve energy by taking turns breaking the wind. (See Chapter 16 for more about the fine art of riding together.) And while it's sad to have to say it, traveling in pairs is probably safer, especially for women.

Then you have the less practical, but no less important aspects of touring with a companion. You have someone to whom you can point out that old Plymouth Duster just like the one you learned to drive on. You have someone to high five when you get to the top of that big hill. You have someone to corroborate your great story about the moose and the squirrel. Small groups can also be workable, but in general, the more people you have along, the more time you spend making decisions and reconciling different agendas. Democracy is a great way to run a country, but it's often less than ideal on a bike tour.

Here are a few things you want to consider when picking a partner for your tour.

Equal ability

If one of you wants to ride 17 miles an hour and the other can only ride 10, well, you can see that you're going to have a problem. However, if one rider is only slightly stronger, you can work around that. She can carry a heavier load or spend more time at the front breaking the wind.

Similar attitude

Being on the same page philosophically is probably even more important. Though your friend who updates her fully-cross-referenced and annotated to-do list three times a day might be great to have around when you're organizing a dinner party for 20, she may not be the ideal bike touring partner. Nor, perhaps, is the friend whose apartment always looks like it's been ransacked. Unless of course you want to spend an hour every morning looking for the deodorant.

A sense of humor

You don't have to bring along Jerry Seinfeld, but no matter how thoroughly you plan and how well you prepare, you're going to encounter some trying moments on your tours, such as when you realize you took a right when you should have taken a left. Ten miles back. Or you realize that you forgot a ground cloth for your tent. Or it rains for the third straight day. Having someone who'll laugh about these things *with* you instead of kvetching *at* you can mean the difference between grinning and bearing it and wishing you had booked a cruise instead.

Packing

If you overpack on a business trip, you may have to fumble around for some quarters to rent one of those little carts in the airport. If you overpack on a bike tour, you'll pay for your bad decision-making with every pedal stroke. Smart packing means striking a balance between packing as little as possible in order to keep weight down and making sure to bring everything that you need.

Wardrobe

When it comes to clothes, get out everything you think you'll need and then bring half of it. Concentrate on being practical. Bring clothes that can be layered together when it gets cold. Choose dark colors so you can spend more time riding and less time doing laundry. Although the fashion police may protest, ditch the cotton. High-performance synthetics like polypropylene and polyester fleece are more versatile because they wick sweat, launder easily, and dry quickly in case you're caught in a rainstorm. Wool has many of the same advantages, but unlike synthetics, it doesn't retain odors, so it can be worn day after day. And don't skimp when packing the shorts. You need a fresh, laundered pair every day. Finally, if you're concerned about such things, make sure that everything color-coordinates well enough that you won't be embarrassed to wear things together.

Miscellaneous equipment

After your clothes are packed, leave some room for the miscellany that can help salvage a trip in times of need.

- A roll of duct tape
- A needle and thread
- A Swiss Army knife
- A few large garbage bags
- A few Ziploc bags
- Matches in a waterproof container
- A good flashlight
- An extra battery for the flashlight
- A compass
- An extra pair of shoelaces
- A tool kit (see Chapter 11)
- A bottle of ibuprofen
- Sunscreen
- A package of zip ties

Stuff for the campers

If you're camping, you need to expand your gear selection beyond the obvious — tent, sleeping bag, ground pad, and stove. Here's a list of some essentials that could otherwise fall through the cracks.

- Extra tent stakes
- A water filtration system and/or water purification tablets
- An extra bungee cord

- ✔ Animal-proof food containers
- ✔ A sponge
- ✔ A pillowcase

Trial packing

After you assemble your items, get your panniers out and complete a trial packing. Remember to pack heavy items low and close to the bike, so they don't change the bike's center of gravity too much. Pack frequently-used items on the top. Then take a step back and analyze the process. Was it more of a challenge than a Rubik's Cube? Did you spend half an hour juggling, folding, refolding, compressing, and wrestling to close the zippers? If you did, consider whether you want to do this every morning before you can hit the road. And even if you're up for it, are the zippers on your panniers up for it, too? Now's the time to make the choice between that sweater and the fleece, between the navy tights and the black ones. Lightening your load by leaving your flashlight at home, however, is definitely not recommended.

Finally, leave a little room for a couple of small splurge items. You know better than I do what's going to make you happy. Is it a mystery novel? A portable CD player with a couple of Miles Davis discs? A bathing suit? A harmonica? A half pound of Godiva chocolate? You can't have all of the comforts of home — after all, that's what camping's all about — but you can have at least one or two.

Riding a Loaded Bike

You have to understand that if your bike is loaded with 30 pounds of gear, it's not going to handle the way it does when it's empty, no matter how well the gear is distributed. That's just physics.

So you need to take that into account when you're riding. First off, you have to be smarter with the way you use your brakes. On the one hand, you need to allow for longer stopping distances — probably at least 30 percent longer. On the other hand, the extra weight will cause your brake pads to heat up faster — especially on long downhills — causing your braking power to fade as the temperature of the pads rise. So you need to anticipate your stops and brake well in advance. And on long hills, you need to release the brakes periodically to let the pads cool.

The same goes for cornering. You need to take corners more slowly but still use good cornering technique. Turn your handlebars as little as possible and straighten out the turns by starting wide, finishing wide, and cutting the apex of the turn as close as possible.

You also have to use your gears differently. Because of the extra weight, you need to react to the terrain and shift earlier. And because it's that much harder to get the bike going from a standing stop, downshifting just before you stop at a stoplight is especially important.

On the Road

If you've been smart and thorough with your planning, the fun starts once you hit the road. To find out more about how to ride efficiently and safely, see Chapters 7 and 8. For information about how to deal with roadside repairs, see Chapter 14. And to keep yourself happy on the road, follow these three simple rules.

Start early

Save your sleeping in for the first Saturday morning after you get home. Getting an early start gives you plenty of advantages. First and foremost, it gives you that much more flexibility in your day. If you hit the road at 8:30, you'll never have to make a choice between taking a detour to that cool old lighthouse and getting to your campsite before nightfall. You also have a cushion in case you get lost or have a flat or some other kind of problem that costs you an hour. And if you're riding in the summer, you avoid the hottest part of the day.

Pace yourself

Especially at the beginning of the tour, you may be brimming with energy. That's all the more reason that you should pace yourself. If you go too hard, you'll build up lactic acid in your muscles, and you'll hardly be able to get out of bed the next morning. The same goes for micro-pacing each day's ride. Don't go too hard at the outset and schedule a rest break at least every hour — more frequently if it's hot or the conditions are especially challenging. And don't get so preoccupied with the scenery that you forget to eat and drink.

Treat yourself right

You shouldn't go for an hour without asking yourself one question — "Are we having fun yet?" If the answer is no, do something about it. If you're tired, rest. If you're hungry, eat. If you're grumpy, tell yourself a knock-knock joke. If you don't like where you are, get on the bike and ride somewhere else. Remember, you're not only the source of power on this vacation, you're the guest of honor.

Chapter 20

To There and Back: Making Your Bike a Second Car

In This Chapter

▶ Committing to using your bike more often

▶ Running errands on two wheels

▶ Commuting to work

There's something wrong with a society that drives a car to work out in a gym.

— Bill Nye, The Science Guy

The best thing about your bicycle? Unlike your golf clubs or your rowing machine, it's not a toy. It's a full-fledged honest-to-goodness vehicle, which means that you can actually use it to get around. To go places. To carry things.

I don't know about you, but I always feel more than a little guilty about hopping into my car to drive half a mile to buy a newspaper or a printer ribbon or a loaf of sourdough bread. I feel doubly guilty when I drive my car to go to the tennis court.

And I feel a lot of frustration when I'm sitting in a city traffic jam, knowing that if I were on my bike, I could've done my errand and been back home in the time it's taken me to creep three car lengths.

That's why it pays to put your bike to work, to make it a part of your daily getting-around routine. In this chapter, I talk about using your bike to run errands and commute to work or school. I also cover how to park your bike . . . and have it still be there when you get back. And I tell you what to look for in a great utility bike. In short, I talk about how you and your bike can save money, save the planet, and get a workout at the same time. Sound good? Read on.

Walking vs. Riding vs. Driving

Back where I grew up, in a small city called Bayonne, New Jersey, things were a little different. People walked. My father walked to the grocery store. My mother walked to go Christmas shopping. I walked to school. Not because we belonged to some kind of anti-car cult, but because most of the places we needed to go were within a couple of blocks of our house and parking spaces were scarce. Saving the car for long trips just seemed like the smart thing to do.

However, most of today's suburbs aren't designed for taking a stroll down to the drug store. The places you need to go aren't a few hundred yards away, but a few miles. And because many suburbs are sidewalk-free, you could end up dodging pink plastic flamingos and Little Tykes Cozy Coupes as you traipse across front lawn after front lawn after front lawn.

You don't have to be a mechanical engineer to see the inherent inefficiency in using a 3,000-pound vehicle to transport a 150-pound person a mile or two. That's where your bike comes in.

Although it won't carry 200 pounds of mulch from the garden center or take you 25 miles down the interstate to the mall, your bike is the perfect conveyance for a trip to the library or a run to the convenience store.

Taking the Plunge

How do you get started? As they say in the sneaker ads, just do it. Using your bike for short errands is more of a attitude adjustment than something you've got to start training for. Make up your mind this morning, and you can be pedaling around by this afternoon. Here are a few tips to help get you rolling in the wonderful world of two-wheeled transport.

Make a resolution

Promise yourself that once a week you'll do an errand on your bike. And then when you do it, acknowledge your accomplishment by, say, marking it off on your calendar. A gold star is always nice.

Keep your bike handy

Move your bike to an easily accessible place — in the garage, in the mud room, or on the deck instead of in the basement. If your bike's right under your nose, you're more likely to use it. Also, find a handy central stashing place for your other riding necessities. My helmet and cycling gloves sit on a shelf in my pantry, nestled happily between a bag of flour and a box of Count Chocula.

If your bike is not in tip-top condition (tires pumped, chain lubed, nuts and bolts tightened), it's not a mode of transportation. It's a handyman's project. Faced with a half-hour of tinkering before rolling out the door, you may be tempted to reach for the keys to the minivan instead. So perform regular maintenance on your bike so that it's ready when you are.

Don't rush

The ultimate goal is to save time, but when you're starting out, save your bike for those times when you have a few extra minutes. You'll be much less likely to go operatic over not finding a place to park your bike if you don't have to meet Eli at school in 20 minutes.

GEAR TALK

Putting your bike to work

To be honest, all your errand bike really needs is air in the tires. But if you find yourself using your bike regularly for commuting or running errands, you may want to think about getting a dedicated utility bike. A good errand bike has a few features that make it well suited to its purpose. It has a wire basket in the front. Or a rack in the back. It has detachable fenders and a chain guard to keep your clothes dirt and grease free. It has lights and reflectors. It has a nice cushy saddle designed expressly for riding without cycling shorts and pedals that work well with street shoes. And hopefully it has a light patina of grime to make it less attractive to bicycle thieves.

Molecules being what they are, all of these things that make a bike more utilitarian also add weight, which makes the bike less fun to ride when you're only interested in breaking a sweat and piling up the miles. Don't misunderstand me — you don't have to spend a lot on a utility bike. If you stop at a garage sale or scour the classifieds, you can pick up a used bike for less than the cost of a monthly train pass or a brake job on your second car. For more information about what to look for in a good utility bike, see the "City Bikes" section in Chapter 2.

Keep it simple

Although a bike is great for multi-tasking — cramming nine "I'll just be a minute" stops into one trip — start small for now. Eventually, you'll think nothing of carrying a five-pound bag of dog food, three library books, and your dry cleaning on your bike. But for now, a trip to the ATM should suffice.

Reward yourself

Acknowledge that you've done a good thing. You've taken one car off the road for a little while, set a good example for your kids, and burned a few calories in the process. Now do something nice for yourself. Take the long way home past the botanical garden. Sit under a tree and read a few pages of Robert Frost. Stop at Starbucks for a double latte. Call up a friend you haven't talked to in a while and tell her about your ride. Go ahead, you deserve it.

Getting to Work: Commuting on Your Bike

It's no exaggeration that for many of us the trip to work is about as much fun as a trip to the dentist. You're either squished like a sardine into a commuter bus or train or sitting in bumper-to-bumper traffic while the radio traffic report drones on about light to moderate volume. The whole mess is enough to make you look forward to a shot of Novocain.

What if your commute could actually make getting there more than half the fun? That's where your bike comes in. If you work within 15 miles of your home, your bike can transport you from your doorstep to your cubicle in less than an hour. And not only are you multi-tasking — getting your aerobic exercise for the day while you make your way — you'll probably arrive at that Monday morning staff meeting in a much better mood.

The first step is finding the right route. The interstate you usually drive on isn't particularly bicycle-friendly. But that interstate wasn't always there, so get a local street map and find some of those local roads that can get you from here to there.

Then wait for one of those perfect April mornings when staying inside seems like a crime. Instead of reaching for your car keys, grab your bike. Of course, you don't want to do this on the morning you have a 9:00 meeting with the senior vice president. Or when you think you may be working late. The ride home is a lot more pleasant during daylight.

Is your commute a multi-stage ordeal in which the first leg of the journey involves hopping into the car for a short drive to the train station or the bus stop? Your bicycle can be a perfect "station car." Just strap your briefcase to the back and go. When you get there, just lock the bike to a railing, get on the train, and congratulate yourself for doing your part for the environment. The only thing shrinking faster than the hole in the ozone will be that spare tire around your middle.

Dressing for success

Thank heavens for Casual Friday. And Casual Tuesday and Casual Thursday. The trend toward tie-less and dress-less dress at the office has made bike commuting that much easier. Mr. Blackwell notwithstanding, most days you can ride in your work clothes (see Figure 20-1) or work in your riding clothes, however you care to think about it. But here are a few common-sense ways to dress smart so you still look smart when you get to work.

Figure 20-1:
A well-
dressed
bike
commuter.

Dress dark

Leave your khakis for some other day — one trip through a small puddle and you look like a third-grade tie dye project. You don't have to dress like a funeral director, but choose patterns or colors that can withstand a little dirt.

Dress tailored

No, I'm not suggesting that you head off to Brooks Brothers. It's just that bicycles and flowing skirts, puffy sleeves, and bell bottom pants don't mix.

It's too easy to get loose material caught in the chain, the spokes, or the cables, both while you're riding and when you're parking your bike. The result of too much material flapping around can be a snag, a stain, or even an accident. But even if you save your caftan for another day, buy a pair of reflective pants clips — available at your friendly neighborhood bike shop. They'll help keep your bike and your wardrobe separate, the way nature intended.

Dress flexibly

Dress in layers — shirt/sweater/shell — so that you can shed a piece if you get too warm or add on if the day turns chilly. And choose garments that can stand being folded up in your bag for a little while. Linen is the cycling fabric of the '90s. The 1890s.

Dress up

Someday, you may find yourself forced to choose between dressing up for the big meeting and riding to work. How do you choose? Don't. Plenty of executives ride to work, just folding a suit and stashing a pair of pumps or wingtips in a bag, and hitting the road. Worried about wrinkles? You dress out of a suitcase for a business trip, don't you? Or even better, on a day that you're driving, bring in an extra suit to hang behind your door for just such occasions.

But of course you want to give your packing a trial run before the day of the big presentation. Nothing's worse than getting to the office and finding out that you forgot your pantyhose or left your tie on the hanger at home.

The sweat factor

But won't I smell? Personal hygiene is a legitimate concern. But look at it another way: Do you worry about the sweat factor when you're running for the bus? When you're crammed elbow-to-elbow in a jammed commuter train with broken air conditioning? If you're looking for a sweat-free commute, then start telecommuting. Now that that's out of the way, here are a couple basic stay-clean strategies to ensure that you don't offend your co-workers.

Ride slowly

Remember that your goal is getting to work, not getting a workout. If you ride slowly, you'll keep the sweat to a minimum. If you want to ride hard, save it for the way home. Your clothes are also part of the low-sweat equation. Wear things that are breathable, and don't overdress.

Freshen up

If you think about it, you can probably find a place where you can grab a quick shower between your bike and your desk. In San Francisco, for example, new offices are now required by law to provide shower facilities. If you're not that lucky, there are other alternatives. Does your company have a gym with a locker room? Is there a health club or a YMCA near your office? And if you can't find a shower stall, there's always the restroom. You can towel off, wash your face, comb your hair, reapply anti-perspirant and cologne, and change your clothes if you need to. And no one will ever know that you pedaled to work, except for the smile on your face.

Parking 101

I can't think of a bigger bummer than coming outside and finding your bike gone. And the grim reality is that a skilled thief can get through even a good lock in less than a minute. So the key to keeping your bike is finding the right parking space. Here are some survival strategies for those times you've got to leave your bike alone.

Bring your bike inside

If you're making a short stop, you can usually get away with it. I've used this strategy plenty — coupled with a sheepish smile for the cash register clerk — when I'm out on my good bike and I want to stop for a banana or bottle of Gatorade. And if you're commuting, try to leave your bicycle in your office, or maybe stash it in the copier room or a storage closet.

Find a clean, well-lighted place

If you must leave your bike outside, then the ideal is a solid bike rack or some other solid fixture in a highly trafficked area. If you work in an urban setting, park your bike on the sidewalk side of your building. If you work in an office complex, find a place as close as possible to the main entrance from the parking lot. Just remember, bike thieves are anti-social when they're working.

Avoid sketchy locales

If necessity forces you to park your bike in a place that, well, just gives you bad vibes, more drastic action is necessary. Enlist the help of a tag team lock combo — a U-lock around the frame and a cable through the wheels, saddle rails, and anything else that can be easily removed (see Figure 20-2). Try bringing your front wheel with you, which effectively eliminates the possibility of a thief using your bike as a getaway vehicle. Or pay a neighborhood kid a couple of bucks to watch your bike until you get back. And don't leave your bicycle there a minute longer than absolutely necessary.

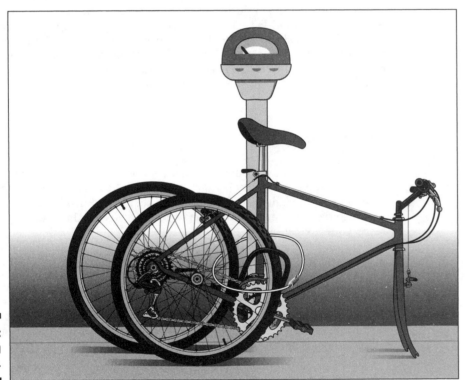

Figure 20-2:
Locking
your bike.

When the rack walks away

Freaky as the possibility may seem, it's possible to come back and find out that not only is your bike gone, but the signpost you locked it to is gone as well. A thief can loosen the sign, wait for you to park your bike, and then just slip it over the top and worry about cutting the lock later. So look at the big picture and consider not only the security of your lock, but also the security of what you're locking to. Here's a quick rundown:

Good:

- ✔ **A parking meter:** They're full of money, so they'd better be sturdy. Just make sure a thief can't lift your bike over the top.

- ✔ **A bike rack:** Just make sure it's cemented to the ground. If it's simply bolted, the rack could disappear — with your bike on it. And lock your bike to the beefiest part of the rack. The thinner tubes can be cut.

- ✔ **A utility pole:** It's not going anywhere. Just make sure your chain or cable is long enough to go all the way around it and through both your wheels.

Not so good:

- ✔ **A chain link fence:** Can be cut with anything this side of a butter knife.

- ✔ **A small tree:** If George Washington could chop it down, so can a bike thief.

- ✔ **A signpost:** Since they don't have to support anything more substantial than a stop sign, most are relatively flimsy, and they are often just bolted together.

The ultimate commuting story

Once upon a time, I used to live in Chicagoland, which as you may know has the worst winters this side of Siberia: Temperatures that stay below freezing for weeks at a time, tempered by 32-mile-an-hour northwest winds that send the wind chill plummeting below zero. Snow that turns to ice that turns to black frozen gunk. While I was living there, I met Tom Schuler, a road racer who would later go on to win the United States Professional Championships and manage a team that raced in the Tour de France. He lived in a third-story apartment five or six blocks away from me. And despite the fact that he was a professional bicycle racer — or maybe because of it — he also had a day job at a bank in the western suburbs about 15 miles away. How did he manage to be a world-class athlete and a working stiff at the same time? He rode to work. Every day. All year. All winter. Honest.

Schuler's secret? A combination of good planning and mental toughness. He set up his bike — he just used one of his old racing bikes — with fenders and a rack and lights. He had really warm gloves (the kind of electric mittens favored by ice fishermen, as I remember it), and fleecy tights and neoprene shoe covers. And he didn't leave himself any excuses. Whereas most of us would have been deterred just by having to carry the bike up and down three flights of stairs, Tom said to himself, "Hey, I ride my bike to work. And if the weather's too bad to ride, then I guess I ought to stay home." He missed exactly one day of work that winter.

Did I start riding my bike to work every day in the cold, rain, sleet, and snow? No. But I did reconsider the notion of mothballing my bike between November and March. And am I a better person for it? You'd have to ask my wife about that.

Chapter 21

Life in the Fast Lane: Bicycle Racing

● ●

In This Chapter
▶ Road racing
▶ Track racing
▶ Mountain bike racing

● ●

*W*hen was the first bike race? No one knows for sure, but it probably started about 10 minutes after the second bike was built. It's always been human nature to take a new toy and see how fast you can go on it — and whether you can go faster than your friend. The bicycle is no exception.

Because of the bike's natural efficiency, and the way it supports the rider, allowing her to pedal even when she's too exhausted to stand, bike racers are capable of remarkable feats of speed and endurance. Sprinters can reach speeds of 45 miles an hour for short distances. Track riders can cover more than 30 miles in an hour. And road racers can ride 150 miles a day at an average of over 20 mph, day after day for three weeks.

But that's not the reason why bicycle racing is one of the most popular sports in world. People the world over watch races because they're fun: fast, furious, and full of strategy. That sounds a lot more exciting than the Pro Bowler's Tour, doesn't it?

And bike racing is almost as egalitarian as bowling. While you can't waltz up and enter the Tour de France, all you need is a bike and a pair of legs to enter a cross-country mountain bike race.

Bike racing comes in three basic flavors: road racing, track racing, and mountain bike racing. Each has its own charms and its own challenges. But since they all basically consist of turning the pedals as fast as possible, it's not surprising that some racers compete in two or even all three disciplines.

Road Racing

Road racing is the most accessible kind of racing. Racers ride on public roads and on bikes that are very much like the ones you can buy in stores. Even though it's relatively unknown here in the United States, road racing ranks right up with soccer in terms of popularity throughout the rest of the world. Figure 21-1 shows Lance Armstrong, one of the world's top riders.

Figure 21-1:
Former
World
Champion
Lance
Armstrong
of the U.S.

Photo courtesy of Trek.

In Europe and South America, fans watch the spring classics like they were the World Series. And in France, the whole country all but shuts down for three weeks in the summer to watch the annual Tour de France.

Under the larger umbrella of road racing fall a number of sub-genres, each with its own passionate following.

Single-day races

These events, usually around 100 miles, are typically contested either from city to city or over a long course, but either way they make for long days. The most important city-to-city races are the European contests, like Italy's Milan/San Remo and Belgium's Liege/Bastogne/Liege, called the Spring Classics.

Possibly the most famous of the Spring Classics is the grueling Paris-Roubaix. The race is contested over a stretch of wet, slippery cobblestones the size of bread loaves, which can send even top riders tumbling, and everyone who finishes the race does so covered in mud, blood, and tears. It's no surprise that the race's nickname is *L'Enfer du Nord,* or Hell of the North.

The other important single-day races, which consist of several laps of a long course, are the annual World Championships and the Olympics. These events are unique in that racers ride for national teams, instead of the trade teams they represent the rest of the season. These makeshift alliances of erstwhile rivals — not unlike tennis' Davis Cup — often make for great theatre.

Stage racing

This is the most grueling and most glamorous type of road racing, in which riders test not only each other's mettle but their own, knowing that a single moment of weakness can decide a 3,000-mile race. The idea is simple: There's a race within a race (otherwise known as a stage) every day for a week, or even three weeks, and whoever has the lowest cumulative time on the last day wins. The most famous of these races are the Tour de France, the Giro d'Italia (Tour of Italy) and the Vuelta d'España (Tour of Spain).

Most days, not too much happens. On relatively flat stages of 100 miles or more, the pack — or *peloton* — tends to stay together. (See the "Smells like team spirit" sidebar for more on team racing tactics.) A few of the supporting riders may plan a breakaway, but they're usually reeled in by the field, and even when they do manage to stay away, they're usually so far behind in the overall standings that it doesn't affect the final outcome of the race.

And while the sprint finish of a stage is hotly contested, riders in the field generally finish within a few seconds of each other so there's little or no effect on the overall standings.

Stage races are won or lost in the mountains and during time trials. The mountain stages are contested over some of the steepest passes in Europe and feature long, tortuous grades followed by white-knuckle descents in which riders reach speeds over 60 miles an hour. In the mountains, only the strongest climbers can stay at the front, where they can open up a several minute lead on their close competitors and finish an hour or more ahead of the field's stragglers.

Time trial stages also eliminate the teamwork factor. A time trial course is relatively short — between 15 and 40 miles — and riders race one at a time against the clock. Because riders can't depend on help from their teammates, time trials reveal a rider's true strength (or lack thereof). A top rider has the opportunity to gain up to five minutes on his rivals, a margin which can decide the overall outcome of a stage race. That's why time trials are also called *the race of truth*.

The interesting part is that these two decisive types of stages favor different types of riders. Climbers tend to be wiry, almost anorexic, and have great power-to-weight ratio. Top time trialists tend to be much bigger and even more powerful. The greatest stage racers, like Eddy Merckx, Greg LeMond, Bernard Hinault, and Miguel Indurain, were champions because they excelled in both the mountains and in the time trials. And in the cycling-mad parts of the world, this all-around excellence makes them national heroes on par with Michael Jordan or Mark McGwire.

Criteriums

Criteriums are short, fast races around a short, rectangular course, usually in a city square or a park. The pack stays together and racing is elbow-to-elbow, so there are frequent crashes, although they're usually not serious. Criteriums are great for spectators because the riders come past every minute or so. In addition to the big prize at the finish, promoters often announce smaller prizes mid-race called *primes,* for the rider who wins the next lap. Thus the afternoon is filled with a series of exciting sprint finishes.

Track Racing

Track racers are the real speed demons of the bicycle world. They ride bikes that are the hyperactive second cousins of road bikes. Track bikes have a single fixed gear — when the wheels turn, the pedals do too, so there's no coasting — and no brakes. The bikes weigh as little as 16 pounds and the tires are pumped up to as much as 240 pounds per square inch, or three times the pressure of a conventional road bike tire. Track races are held on a banked track around 300 meters long called a *velodrome,* which is often covered in wood planking and resembles a gym floor. While velodromes are common in Europe, there are only a handful in the U.S.

Track racing also has a number of sub-genres, all of them fast.

Sprint racing

Match sprinting is a one-on-one exercise. The field is seeded like a tennis tournament, and riders race one opponent in every round, with the winner advancing and the loser going home.

In each match, two riders, starting at the same time, race two laps around the track. Ironically, the riders often start the race trying to see how *slowly* they can ride. The riders literally stand motionless — it's called a *track stand* — hoping to force the other rider into taking the lead. Why? The trailing rider has a couple of tactical advantages:

Smells like team spirit

When Americans think of a team sport, they normally think about baseball or basketball. But teamwork is every bit as crucial in road racing. Why? Because of wind resistance, a pack of riders can ride faster using less energy than a single rider can alone.

Teams are comprised of a few top riders and a number of *domestiques* — workers whose job is to help the team leaders win. A domestique may do everything from carrying water bottles to giving up his bike to a team leader who's had a mechanical failure.

When a single rider, or more likely a small group of three to ten riders, rides away from the pack, it's called a *breakaway*. In the early stages of a race, the pack often ignores a breakaway — especially if the group consists of unknown riders looking for their moment in the sun in front of the television cameras. Riders in the pack — or *peloton* — make a tacit agreement to let the breakaway riders go and catch up with them later — and they usually do.

But if a breakaway includes any top riders, it becomes a decisive moment in the race. The teammates of the top riders in the breakaway move to the front of the pack and ride relatively slowly to allow the breakaway group to gain time. The teams without riders in the breakaway try to organize a chase group. Thus, especially

in stage races where teams are racing not only for the day's prizes but for time in the overall standings, the peleton can become a very political place, as teams lobby for support from neutral teams to help them block or help them chase a breakaway.

If the pack stays together until the finish, the result is a pack sprint. And again teamwork comes into play. The domestiques lead out their team's sprinters, blocking for them almost the way offensive linemen block for a running back in football. The workers move the sprinters up to the front of the pack while allowing them to sit on their wheels — ride closely behind — to conserve energy and get an aerodynamic slingshot effect as they approach the line. But since as many as a dozen teams may be contesting the sprint, bike racing then becomes a contact sport. Riders will jostle for position, rubbing elbows an even trading punches at over 30 miles an hour.

Here's where teamwork isn't much of a factor: in the mountain stages of a road race, where speeds are low and the field strings out; in track racing, where it's generally one or two riders at a time; or in mountain bike racing, where the narrow trails and lower speeds take the whole issue of aerodynamics out of the picture.

✔ He can see his opponent without having to look over his shoulder.

✔ The lead rider breaks the wind for the trailing, or *drafting*, rider. The drafting rider can then slingshot around in the last turn the same way that stock car racers do.

This combination of brute force — sprinters are typically the beefiest of bike racers — and optimal conditions make for breathtaking speeds. During the last 200 meters of a race, riders can reach speeds of over 40 miles an hour.

Fast faces

Here are thumbnail bios of eight racers you should know.

Greg LeMond, U.S.: He's the first American to win the Tour de France — which he's won three times — and the World Professional Championships — which he captured twice. His story reads a little like a TV movie. In 1987, he went on an off-season hunting trip with his brother in law, who accidentally shot him in the back. LeMond lost so much blood that he was only minutes away from death when he was flown by a helicopter to a nearby hospital. He came back in 1989 to win the closest Tour in history, coming back from 50 seconds down during what was thought to be an all-but-ceremonial final time trial. He retired in 1994 after he was diagnosed with mitochondrial myopathy, a mysterious condition that debilitates muscle cells.

Eddy Merckx: Known as the Cannibal for the way he devoured his competition, this Belgian champion won the Tour de France five times in the 1960s and early 1970s, set the world hour record, and is generally considered the greatest road racer of all time.

Lance Armstrong: A former triathlete, this young Texan was the heir apparent to LeMond, becoming the first American to win a single-day classic and the second to win the World Professional Road Race. Armstrong's rise was cut short in 1996, when he was diagnosed with testicular cancer, but he defied the odds and returned to racing two years later, finishing fourth in the 1998 Worlds.

Miguel Indurain: With unsurpassed power in the time trials and surprising climbing ability, this quiet Spaniard was the best road racer of the 1990s. He won the Tour de France five times in a row, a feat unmatched even by Merckx.

Major Taylor: This African-American track racer was one of the first superstars of American sport. At the turn of the century, when bike races could fill Madison Square Garden, Taylor was as popular as any athlete in the world. Triumphing over Jim Crow-era segregation, Taylor set world records, won world and national titles, and even parlayed his fame into a brief vaudeville career. Unfortunately, his post-retirement life was as tragic as his racing career was triumphant. A series of bad investments, coupled with the sport's waning popularity, left Taylor alone and destitute. He died in the charity ward of a Chicago hospital in 1932, and was buried in an unmarked grave.

Missy Giove: Known as much for her outrageous style as for her blazing speed, Giove was the first poster girl for the adrenalized world of downhill mountain biking. She boldly flaunted her tattoos, body piercing, and her tally of broken bones — 33 and counting. But Giove also has a more sensitive side — she travels with the ashes of her childhood dog Ruffin and wore the freeze-dried remains of her pet piranha around her neck during races. Giove used her fame to fund Team Amazon, which supports up-and-coming female riders who couldn't find other sponsorship.

Paola Pezzo: Pezzo is the dominant female cross country racer of the 1990s and was the winner of the first Olympic mountain biking gold medal. But she's just as famous for her fashion sense as for her results — Italy's blonde bombshell made headlines by unzipping her jersey to reveal her cleavage in Atlanta, and celebrated her Olympic triumph by commissioning a pair of gold lamé shorts.

Shaun Palmer: This heavily tattooed snowboard champion stunned the mountain biking world by becoming one of the world's top male downhillers almost overnight.

Pursuit racing

Picture playing cat-and-mouse on bicycles: two riders on opposite ends of the track. The object is to try to catch the other over the course of 10 laps.

In world-class pursuit races, however, the riders are so equally matched that that almost never happens. In that case, the best time wins. There's also a team pursuit, which pits teams of four riders against each other. Teams ride in a tight formation called a *paceline,* one behind the other, their wheels separated only by inches. One rider rides hard at the front of the field for a few hundred meters, then moves over and slides to the back while the next rider takes a turn breaking the wind.

Keirin

In Japan, track racing is a betting sport. In this distinctive genre of racing, largely confined to that island country, keirin racers take to the track together and are paced by a motorcycle for the first laps of the race: Then it's a free-for-all to the finish line. Riders are kept in seclusion during the racing season, living together in dorms under strict supervision to prevent contact with gamblers and other unseemly types.

Six-day races

At the turn of the century, six day races were wildly popular spectator events both in the U.S. and in Europe. These earlier contests were endurance contests — teams of two riders road around an indoor track all day and all night. Needless to say, the riding was often soporific. A modified version of these multi-day races — riders now contest a series of races over six consecutive evenings with points carried over from night to night — are still a big hit in Europe, with top road riders often collecting significant appearance money on their winter vacations.

Mountain Bike Racing

It's a dirty business, as you might guess from looking at Figure 21-2. But it's also one of the world's fastest growing sports. Mountain bike racing made it into the Olympics in near record time, less than 20 years after the sport's birth. And, as you'd expect in a sport this young, it's still evolving, with new events and variations on old events, still cropping up. It's also racing for the people. Even major professional events include a slate of shorter, easier races for weekend warriors. What follows is a tour of the mountain bike landscape as it stands now.

Figure 21-2:
Mountain
bike racing
on some
rough
terrain.

Cross-country

This is mountain bike racing's main event. Whereas road racing generally pits rider against rider and team against team, mountain bike racing really pits the rider against the course. The races, often held at ski resorts, consist of thigh-burning hills followed by hairy descents and obstacles both natural (like logs and rocks) and man-made (like a flight of stairs) thrown in for good measure. But the heart of the event is a couple hours of leg-sapping, lung-searing riding.

Downhill

This is mountain biking kamikaze style. The object: Start at the top of the mountain, and get down as quickly as possible. It takes the line judgment of a downhill skier, the strength to pump a huge gear, and a high threshold for adrenaline. Top riders can reach speeds of as much as 55 miles an hour during a seven-minute-long run.

These are your legs on drugs

While the annals of bike racing are filled with many heroic feats, not all of them were performed solely on Gatorade and PowerBars. Substance abuse has been a part of the sport almost since its origins, and the results have often been tragic. During the 1967 Tour de France, British rider Tommy Simpson collapsed and later died on the slopes of Mont Ventoux after swallowing a handful of amphetamines and washing them down with cognac.

The success of the 1984 U.S. Olympic cycling team, which won 10 medals including four golds, was tarnished when it was discovered that some members of the team had participated in blood doping, an illegal, but virtually undetectable process in which the racer is transfused with extra red blood cells. One rider from that Olympic team has also admitted to taking anabolic steroids, while in the 1988 Tour de France, Spanish rider Pedro Delgado tested positive for a legal steroid-masking agent during a routine drug test, but won the race anyway after those results were invalidated on a technicality.

Most recently, two top teams were banned from the 1998 Tour de France after team trainers were discovered bringing into the country banned substances, including steroids and EPO, an artificial hormone that causes the body to produce more red blood cells and has been suspected in the deaths of several athletes.

Dual slalom

Borrowing a little from ski racing, this event sees riders carving their bikes around gates on a short steep section of a mountain. This places a premium on balance and bike handling, but falls are still common. ESPN upped the ante and added an on-snow mountain bike slalom to its Winter X-Games lineup.

24-hour races

Sleep, who needs sleep? Passing the bright lights and black coffee, teams of four riders trade laps all night long. The most famous of these increasingly popular races (most of the contestants are just regular riders looking to challenge themselves) are the 24 Hours of Canaan in West Virginia and the 24 Hours of Moab in Utah.

Iditabike

Mush, mush, mush. That's what riders in the Iditabike feel like when they're done. This multi-day Alaskan race follows part of the course of the Iditarod sled dog race. Riders battle not only the extreme cold, but the challenge of riding a bike on everything from glare ice to drifted snow.

Part V
The Part of Tens

The 5th Wave   By Rich Tennant

"There's reflectors and blinking lights, but if you really want to feel safe in traffic, I suggest mounting these signs on your back fender."

In this part . . .

Every ...*For Dummies* book ends with top-ten lists, and this one is no exception. I offer the ten best bike-related Web sites, the ten best places to bike, ten mountain bike slang terms, and much, much more.

Chapter 22

The Ten Best Bike Web Sites

. . . .

*W*hy is it that you can find more cool Web sites for, say, the Bay City Rollers, than you can for the entire sport of cycling? Maybe it's because cyclists are too busy riding to spend much time in cyberspace. And while there is a relative dearth of bike-related sites, and many of them don't quite meet the standard of, say, salon.com, here's a short list of sites that should keep you amused, enlightened, and informed between rides.

Bike Ride Online

www.bikeride.com

A good place to start your cyberhunt. This site consists of hundreds of bike related links ranging from manufacturers' sites to an extensive listing of road and mountain clubs to esoterica like bicycle racing fantasy leagues. ("I'll trade you Barry Bonds and Mark McGwire for Jan Ullrich and Marco Pantani.")

The Science of Cycling

www.exploratorium.edu/cycling

Imagine Bill Nye the Science Guy all decked out in Lycra. That's the vibe of the San Francisco Science Museum's site. It talks in plain English about how bikes work — from why they stay up to how loads are distributed in a wheel — and it's got plenty of pop culture asides to make the subject just plain fun. Any 8-year-old will be fascinated, but there isn't a veteran rider who won't learn something, too. It comes complete with RealAudio/Video clips, including interviews with World Cup mountain biker Ruthie Matthes and jaw-dropping footage of world trials champion Libor Karas climbing cars, leaping gullies, and otherwise defying gravity.

Sheldon Brown.com

www.sheldonbrown.com

The Web is all about one man's opinion. And when that man happens to be an experienced tourist, an expert mechanic, and a world class retrogrouch, like Massachusetts shop owner Sheldon Brown, the results are both idiosyncratic and fascinating. Brown indulges his obsessions with two oddities — fixed-gear bikes and old Raleigh three-speeds—while providing some patently useful stuff, including right-on repair advice, touring tips, and a glossary of bike terms. This site is worth a look, if only for the links to a bad poetry site featuring the work of William McGonagall, widely considered the worst poet in the history of the English language.

MTB Review

www.mtbr.com

Want to get the straight dope on that new Rock Shox fork you're considering? This mountain bike site contains over 35,000 real-rider reviews of 3,100 products, in an easily searchable database. It even includes a Hall of Fame and a Hall of Shame for products that are notable or notorious. This site also features man-in-the-woods trail reviews as well as epic ride stories from folks just like you. MTBR is basically the next best thing to sitting around throwing the bull with your buddies at the end of a ride.

The Bicycle Museum of America

www.bicyclemuseum.com

Darwin was right. Your bike is the product of evolution. From the bone shakers and high wheelers of the 19th century to the cruisers and banana bikes of the 1950s and 1960s, this site, maintained by the Bicycle Museum of America in New Bremen, Ohio, gives a clear picture of the bikes that preceded your 24-speed steed.

International Mountain Bicycling Association

www.imba.com

Rule number one: You can't ride if the trail's closed. That's why every mountain biker should bookmark the IMBA site. It's the clearing house for the latest trail access and advocacy news, as well as a prime resource for trail maintenance tips and responsible riding reminders.

Transportation Alternatives

www.transalt.org

One less car. It's not only an idea whose time has come, but it's also the motto of this New York-based bicycle advocacy group. The Transportation Alternatives site is dedicated to the idea of the bicycle as a viable urban transit option, and it covers that subject inside out. You'll find everything from no-nonsense advice on what to do if you get a ticket or are involved in an accident, to updates on the group's political activities, all aimed at making riding safer and easier.

Rec.Bicycles.FAQ

www.cis.ohio-state.edu/hypertext/faq/usenet/
bicycles-faq/part1/faq.html

Scratching your head over some two-wheeled conundrum? Whether you want to know how to train or how to transport your bike by train, this selection of frequently asked questions from the various rec.bicycle newsgroups probably has the answer. The topics range from the straightforward to the arcane, but the questions are all smart — the dumb ones have already been cyberzapped — and the answers are both authoritative and easily understood.

International Federation of Bicycle Messenger Associations

www.messengers.org

Okay, so you may not want to quit your day job to go head to head with the taxis and buses, but there are few people more passionate about pedaling than bicycle messengers. This very cool site features links to news (did you know that if you ride for a living, you can deduct your larger-than-usual-lunch?) and 'zines that chronicle the spirit of the street. If you're still thinking about ditching your cubicle for a messenger bag, the link to a page of real live x-rays may persuade you otherwise.

The League of American Bicyclists

www.bikeleague.org

The grandaddy of American cycling groups enters the digital age with a solid selection of links — everything from the worthy International Bicycle Fund to the International Police Mountain Bike Association. ("Stop or I'll shift!") Especially useful are the links to member clubs and the how-to notebooks from the organization's Effective Cycling program.

Chapter 23

Ten Places You Ought to Ride at Least Once

• •

*T*he wonderful thing about a bicycle is that you don't have to go to Vail or
Pebble Beach to have fun: The best place to ride is generally out your
front door. But there are a few places that seem to have been made with bikes
in mind, and they're more than worth the schlep.

Moab, Utah

Most places, mountain biking is all about going where the trail takes you. But
the slickrock of this high desert mountain bike mecca provides a riding experience unlike any other. Moab's wide open expanses of rock face give you the
freedom to pick your own line — and contend with the consequences of your
decision. It's a mountain biking experience Sartre would have loved.

Central Park, New York City

Anyplace the average speed of the traffic is below the top speed of a bicycle
is a good bike town. But while on most Manhattan streets, bicyclists are a
stealthy minority, in Central Park the tables are turned. When most of the
park is closed to auto traffic on weekends and afternoons, it becomes a testa-
ment to the two-wheeled lifestyle, as hundreds of riders cruise the park road
on everything from singlespeed delivery bikes to full-zoot dual suspension
mountain mounts.

Alaska

Alaska is not a place for the weak or the unprepared. On most roads, you can
go a day without seeing another vehicle, and quite frankly, you're more likely
to see a grizzly bear than a bike shop. But whether you venture to the northern rainforest of Prince William Sound or the majestic mountains of the

Alaska Range, you'll likely never ride in a place that's more breathtakingly beautiful or stubbornly unspoiled.

Boulder, Colorado

The road biking capital of the United States, Boulder is an endurance junkie's heaven. The foothills of the Rockies and the thin air attracted a number of world class runners in the mid-1970s, and world-class road bikers soon followed. That elite cachet, coupled with a super extensive bike path system to serve all those auto-free University of Colorado students makes Boulder arguably the most bicycle-friendly town in the United States.

Marin County, California

This Northern California nirvana is where the mountain bike revolution started. And you can see why. Marin is home to some of the best singletrack in the nation. But it doesn't come without a price tag. Marin was also home to some of the first and fiercest trail access disputes, and every mile of open trail stands as a monument to the first commandment of responsible mountain biking: Riding isn't a right, it's a privilege.

The French Alps

Bicycle racing fanatics view the mountain passes in the Tour de France the way a baseball fan looks at Fenway Park. But while you can't just waltz up and try to hit one over the Green Monster, you can ride up Alpe d'Huez as far as your legs can take you. And if you go during Tour time, you can get close enough to the action that you can get splashed with the sweat of the world's greatest cyclists.

China

A hundred million bicyclists can't be wrong. Whereas in Europe the bicycle is respected as a sporting icon, in China, a bicycle is as much a part of the landscape as a Ford Taurus is in middle America. But if you're going, do it soon. Beijing's auto population soared from 60 (no, that's not a typo) in the late 1980s to 700,000, and the powers that be are considering the possibility of making the center city a bike-free zone.

The Aran Islands, Ireland

Stare out at the Atlantic from the cliffs of this rugged little island off the west coast of Ireland, and you can understand why people assumed the world was flat. Take a mountain bike to the western part and you'll find a place as rocky and barren as the moon, with nothing but the remains of a 1,000-year-old castle to prove that this place can support life.

Durango, Colorado

This is the last place where you want to challenge some skinny guy to a race to the city line. The informal mountain biking capital of the United States, this central Colorado town is home to dozens of top riders, from John Tomac to Missy Giove, Ned Overend, and Juli Furtado. The reason? Beautiful mountains, a cool little town, prime singletrack — and lots of it.

The White Mountains, New Hampshire

While the Green Mountains of Vermont get more press as a cycling destination, the riding may be even more epic in the Whites. Rolling hills, covered bridges, and foliage that would make Eliot Porter swoon add up to what locals might call wicked fierce good riding. And just as importantly, the state's road crews know what they're doing, so you won't get tossed by hitting a frost heave at 25 mph.

Chapter 24

The Ten Most Extreme Things to Do on a Bike

• •

*B*icycle riders are passionate people. Some might say a little *too* passionate. At least if that passion inspires you to try to ride a bicycle 150 mph (no, that's not a typo), ride a bike across the United States almost nonstop, or follow the trail of the world's most famous dogsled race.

World Hour Record

It's the most basic test of human horsepower. Get on a bike on an enclosed track and ride for an hour and see how far you can go. There's little strategy involved, just pure brute strength and speed. Which is why for more than 100 years, the hour record has been the most coveted record in the sport. Among the holders have been road racing legends like Tour de France winners Fausto Coppi, Jacques Anquetil, Eddy Merckx, and Miguel Indurain. Francesco Moser, who broke the magic 50 km (31 mph) barrier in 1984, ushered in an era of aerodyamic bikes that saw the record jump by almost six kilometers in only a dozen years and prompted the UCI, cycling's international governing body, to place new restrictions on what constitutes a bicycle.

Tour de France

Okay, it seems like a cliché, but the Tour de France is legitimately the toughest event in sports. Picture this. A week and a half of 100-mile-plus days, each with a nice long sprint at the end. Your reward for this? A move to the Alps, with some of the most forbiddingly steep terrain. If you're lucky, you'll only lose half an hour to the leader. If you're not, you'll pass the time limit and you'll end up riding in the broom wagon. Cruel? Oui. After all, the Marquis de Sade was French.

Iditabike

Ah, Alaska in the wintertime. This 320-mile Alaskan race follows part of the route of the fabled sled dog race. But unlike the fabled sled dog race, the entrants provide their own power, chugging along on dual-rim mountain bikes with studded tires. And while frostbite's a concern, the real fear, ironically, is a warm snap that can turn the hard-packed snow into unrideable slush.

Mt. Washington Hillclimb

The bad news: The summit of Mount Washington is the home of what some have called "The worst weather on earth." This site recorded a wind gust of 234 miles an hour, which for more than 60 years stood as the windiest recorded moment in United States history. The worse news: It's a 7.6-mile, 4,727-foot slog to the top, with some sections as steep as 18 percent. Only a love of testing their limits — and a recent first prize of a new sports sedan — keep top riders coming back to New Hampshire every Labor Day.

The Bicycle Land Speed Record

Just how fast can a bike go? Would you believe almost 170 miles per hour? With a racing car breaking the wind at the Bonneville Salt Flats, a bicycle is capable of truly astonishing speeds. In 1995, 50-year-old Fred Rompelberg of the Netherlands set a new bicycle land-speed record of 166.9 mph. In these record attempts, the bike sits in an enclosed fairing behind a racing car. The bike of course is specially designed, with ultra high gearing and reinforced frame to handle the stresses of high speed riding. The rider must be reinforced, in his own way, from the stresses of considering the implications of a 150+ mile an hour fall if he or she should drift out of the cushion of still air created by the lead car.

24 Hours of Canaan

How does that Kinks song go? "All of the day and all of the night?" Well, that's pretty much the idea at this West Virginia race. Four-rider teams start on Saturday afternoon and keep trading places until Sunday afternoon. Good lights and strong coffee are necessities, as are teammates with a good sense of humor.

RAAM

The premise of the Race Across America is simple. Start somewhere in California and point your bike east. Keep riding hard until you hit the Atlantic Ocean. One of the key strategies, in case you hadn't figured it out, is to sleep as little as possible over the race's 10 days. This makes for some interesting riding, with competitors often suffering from hallucinations caused by sleep deprivation, swerving erratically to avoid the phantom riders they're convinced are following them.

ESPN Winter X-Games

Okay, it's made for TV. And yes, the events change quicker than a teenager's infatuations. But that doesn't mean it's not legitimately tough. In its brief history, the Winter X-Games featured truly insane snowbiking events: a straight downhill speed run, a cross-country dual slalom, and most recently, a boardercross-style event in which five riders tackle a hump-filled course all at once.

Trials

Ever get the hankering to ride on a picnic table? Trials riders specialize in defying gravity. Using small fixed-gear bikes that owe as much to BMX as mountain bikes, they bounce, leap, balance, and vault on, over, and around obstacles both natural and man-made.

Human-Powered Vehicle Record

Need proof that the bike is the most efficient machine ever built? When all the rules are thrown out except one — a human being is the only power source — the bicycle is still the vehicle of choice. Riding a Cheetah recumbent with an aerodynamic fairing in September of 1992, Chris Huber covered 200 meters in 6.51 seconds for a speed of 68.72 miles per hour, a mark which has stood for more than six years.

Chapter 25

The Ten Best Mountain Bike Slang Terms

● ●

*M*ountain bikers speak their own language, which is as colorful in its way as the sport itself. Like all languages, it's a hybrid, borrowing and adapting words from skate speak, roadie talk, and everything from Silicon Valley acronyms to bad 1960s television. And if these terms seem to dwell disproportionately on falls and their consequences, it's not an indication of the sport's dangers, but merely a reflection of that all too human tendency to joke about what we're most afraid of.

brain bucket: *n.* A helmet. ("He would have been an HMO's worst nightmare if he didn't have his brain bucket on.")

BSG: *n.* Bike Store Guy. ("Yo, BSG, I need a new tube, a couple of cables, and a Powerbar.")

endo: *v.* To hurl oneself over the handlebars, often resulting in a *soil sample.* A contraction of "end over end." ("If you don't slow down before that dropoff, you'll endo.")

Fred: *n.* In mountain bike parlance, a poseur who has spent too much time shopping for bike stuff and not enough time riding. In road bike parlance, by contrast, the term is used to disparage riders who may be efficient but have no fashion sense whatsoever. According to popular myth, the term was initially coined in homage to a particularly grumpy old touring rider, actually named Fred. Synonym: Barney. Not to be confused with "newbie," which is an affectionate term for a beginner. ("Look at that Fred over there cleaning his saddle when he could be riding.")

HOHA: *n.* A member of the Hateful Old Hikers Association; anyone who would prohibit or unreasonably restrict mountain biking. ("I can't believe it, the HOHAs got South Mountain closed.")

mudectomy: *n.* A post-ride shower. ("I'll be over for dinner right after my mudectomy.")

soil sample: *n.* Meeting the trail face first, usually as the result of an *endo.* Synonym: face plant. ("He took a soil sample, but it was nothing that a little Lava couldn't cure.")

swag (pronounced schwag): *n.* Free stuff, generally from a bike manufacturer, often as part of a sponsorship deal. While the expense of the item factors into its swag value, what's more important is its uniqueness. Derived from an English term for ill-gotten booty and used in reference to pirates, and later, robbers. ("Barrett got some great swag from the shop that's sponsoring her.")

three-hour tour: *n.* A ride that includes a period of lostness, derived from the television show *Gilligan's Island.* ("Then Bob insisted that we had to go left at that fork in the trail, and the ride turned into a three-hour tour.")

yard sale: n. A crash in which one leaves bike parts strewn across the trail. ("You should've seen the yard sale after Wendy slid out on that off-camber switchback.")

Chapter 26
Top Ten Bike Movies

●●

There are a fair number of what you might call "bicycle movies." Some good ones *(Breaking Away)*, some bad ones *(Quicksilver)*, and a few downright silly ones *(Pee Wee's Big Adventure)*. But there are also plenty of classic films that have bicycles in them. Here's a list of films that could find their way onto any critics all-time top-ten list, with a bicycle in a starring role.

Jules et Jim

What does it take to turn a flirty friendship into a passionate love affair? The sight of a beautiful young woman on a bike. The turning point of this Francois Truffaut classic about a doomed love triangle is a point-of-view shot of Jeanne Moreau on two wheels. As Jim catches a glimpse of the bewitching Catherine from behind, his fate is sealed in more ways than one.

HELP!

In a movie that was reportedly filmed though a haze of marijuana smoke, plot continuity is not a big consideration. (Just why *is* Paul McCartney holding a softball glove?) But as they ride in circles in the Bahamas, fleeing from the bad guys who are trying to steal Ringo's ring, with a truly wretched marching band version of "I'm Happy Just to Dance with You" playing in the background, it makes as much sense as anything else in this Richard Lester opus. While not playing for laughs like a skiing scene earlier in the film, the Beatles rode their bikes like guys who spent the last three years of their lives in the back of limos.

The Quiet Man

John Wayne on a bicycle? Yup. And a bicycle built for two to boot. In the middle of an awkward, supervised stroll during their courtship, in John Ford's Irish fable, Wayne and Margaret O'Hara run off and appropriate the vicar's tandem. In the 1950s when the movie was made, their unchaperoned thrill ride was as close to a love scene as the censors would allow. When a thunderstorm interrupts their merriment, they take shelter in a cemetary, a scene that culminates in one of the steamiest, most passionate kisses in screen history.

Do the Right Thing

Sometimes a bike is more than a bike. In an early scene of this Spike Lee agitprop masterpiece, the only white guy on a Bed Stuy block (John Savage), wearing a Larry Bird jersey and pushing his mountain bike back to his brownstone, bumps into Buggin' Out, played by Giancarlo Esposito. A smudge on Buggin's $108 Air Jordans leads to a loud, racially-charged confrontation. "Who told you to buy a brownstone on *my* block, in *my* neighborhood, on *my* side of the street? What you wanna live in a *black* neighborhood for anyway?" shouts Buggin' Out, before finally getting to the point. "Why don't you move back to Massachusetts?" Savage gets the last word: "I was *born* in Brooklyn." But the misunderstandings and mistrust laid out in this brief vignette foretell the larger conflicts that culminate in tragedy later in the film.

2001: A Space Odyssey

In the climax of Stanley Kubrick's epic, the HAL computer is being dismantled by astronaut Dave (of "I'm sorry Dave, I'm afraid I can't do that" fame). As Dave pulls the plug, HAL reverts back to its infancy — a foreshadowing of the birth of man sequence to come — and starts singing the first song it ever learned: "Bicycle Built for Two." And in this moment, HAL seems less like a demonic machine and more like a precocious little kid who suddenly realizes the error of his ways.

The Bicycle Thief (Ladri di Biciclette)

Vittorio De Sica's classic, at one point voted the greatest film of all time by critics polled by *Sight and Sound* magazine, is obstensibly about Antonio, played by Lamberto Maggiorani, and his search for his stolen bicycle, a search made more urgent by the fact that he stands to lose his job if he doesn't recover it. But the larger theme of this neorealist landmark is about the quiet struggles of the working class.

Mr. Smith Goes to Washington

Poor Jefferson Smith. The idealistic young congressman, played by Jimmy Stewart, is about to get railroaded by an unscrupulous colleague. His only hope? The boys in his hometown break the real story of the scandal in Boys Stuff newspaper. "Jeff Tells Truth" blares the headline. How do they distribute this special edition? In typical newsboy fashion, by bicycle. Which leads directly to a typically Capraesque happy ending.

The Wizard of Oz

What's the scariest thing in the Wizard of Oz? The sight of mean Ms. Gulch riding her bike down to Dorothy's farm with a court order to confiscate Toto. But, as luck would have it, Ms. Gulch doesn't observe proper load carrying procedures. Toto jumps out and scrambles back home to Dorothy, who does the only sensible thing, run away from home, setting this classic story in motion.

ET

Bikes are all over this Steven Spielberg blockbuster, for years the highest grossing film of all time. From the first scene when Eliot ventures into the woods to tempt ET with Reese's Pieces, his bike is right by his side. And in the big chase scene, the children, with ET in tow, elude the roadblock set up by the evil government guys with a little anti-gravitational help from their other worldly friend. Don't think that bicycles can fly? If you _believe,_ anything is possible. But it doesn't hurt if you have friends at Industrial Light and Magic.

Butch Cassidy and the Sundance Kid

Talk about the ultimate bicycle sales pitch. Sensing opportunity in a gathered crowd a bicycle salesman touts the wonders of his new two-wheeled contraption. His presentation is cut short by the marshall: "I'm trying to raise a posse here if you don't mind." Later in the film, a bicycle takes center stage in one of the first music videos ever: Paul Newman pedaling with Katharine Ross on the handlebars to the tune "Raindrops Keep Falling on My Head." What did it have to do with the plot? Nothing. But it was pretty to watch.

Appendix A

Glossary

• •

700C: The wheel size used on most road bikes and many hybrids. It's approximately 700 mm (27.6 inches) in diameter.

aero bars: Used primarily by triathletes, these specialized handlebars put the rider in a narrow, aerodynamic position.

aerobic: An exertion level at which the body can take in as much oxygen as it consumes.

aluminum: A strong, lightweight metal used for bicycle frames and components.

anaerobic threshold: The exertion level at which your body begins to use more oxygen than it can take in.

ATB: All-terrain bike. An early, now passé, term for mountain bike.

attack: In racing, a sudden burst of speed designed to build a gap on other riders.

bailout gear: A colloquial term for bicycle's lowest gear, which is often used only as a last resort on a steep hill.

bar ends: Generally found only on mountain bikes, these horn-shaped handlebar extensions bolt to the end of flat bars. Riders use them for extra leverage while climbing or for an alternate hand position on flat ground.

bars: An abbreviation for handlebars.

bead: A reinforcement of metal wire or Kevlar found on the inner edge of a clincher tire, which helps to hold the tire onto the rim.

blow up: A racing term for running out of energy, which results in being forced to slow your pace drastically. *See also* bonk.

bonk: A condition of sudden, extreme fatigue, caused by a drop in blood sugar from not eating.

bottle cage: The plastic or metal device bolted onto the frame to hold a water bottle.

bottom bracket: A spindle and bearings, located at the intersection of the seat tube, downtube and chainstays, which attaches the crankset to the frame.

brake boss: The mount for a long-arm or cantilever brake arm, usually brazed onto the fork or seat stay.

brake hood: The rubber covering for the brake lever on a road bike.

brake lever: A handlebar-mounted device that actuates the brakes by pulling the cable attached to it.

brake pads: The rubber blocks attached to the brake arms that rub on the rim when the brake lever is squeezed. This creates friction that slows or stops the bike. Also called brake shoes or brake blocks.

brakes: The mechanism, consisting on most adult bikes of brake levers, cables, brake arms, and brake pads, that stops or slows a bike.

braze: To join two pieces of steel, such as a bicycle tube, by melting a brass or silver rod which then hardens, solidifying the joint. Most brazed bike frames use lugged construction.

braze-on: A fitting, such as a cable guide or brake boss, that is brazed onto the frame.

breakaway: When a rider or group of riders escapes from the main pack in a bicycle race.

bridge: (v.) To catch a rider or group of riders who have opened a lead in a race. (n.) The small tube that connects the seatstays, which reinforces the bike's rear triangle and provides a place to mount a caliper brake.

bunny hop: Jumping a bike over an obstacle, most commonly done by mountain bikers.

butted tubing: Frame tubes that have a thinner wall in the center and a thicker wall near the ends where the tubes are joined, allowing for lighter weight with no sacrifice of strength.

cadence: The rate at which a rider turns the pedals, expressed in revolutions per minute.

cage: The spring-loaded extension on the rear derailleur that holds the jockey wheels.

caliper brakes: A brake system, found generally on road bikes, that features two overlapping arms that encircle the tire.

Campy: Slang for Campagnolo, an Italian maker of fine bicycle components.

cantiliever brakes: A brake, usually found on hybrids and mountain bikes, that is actuated by the movement of a central cable attached to two pivoting brake arms that pivot on brazed-on brake bosses.

cassette: A collection of cogs designed for use on a freehub.

century: Riding 100 miles in a day.

chain: A collection of links, held together by pins and rollers, that transmits energy from the chain rings to the rear wheel.

chain rings: The toothed rings attached to the crank arms that interlock with the chain, allowing it to transfer pedal energy to the rear wheel. Also called the chainwheel.

chain rivet remover: A small vice-like tool that is used to push the pins in or out of a chain during a repair. Also called a chain tool.

chainstays: The horizontal frame member that runs parallel to the chain and attaches the bottom bracket to the rear dropout.

chain suck: When the chain becomes trapped in the gap between the chain-stay and the chain ring.

chromoly: An abbreviation for chrome molybdenum, a steel alloy used in bicycle frames.

clean: Riding a difficult section of trail on a mountain bike without dismounting or putting a foot down.

cleat: A device on the bottom of a cycling shoe that locks onto the pedal for more efficient pedaling.

clincher: The most common type of tire, which is held onto the rim with a wire or Kevlar bead and houses a separate inner tube.

clipless pedal: A pedal with a locking mechanism that accepts a releasable cleat attached to the bottom of a cycling shoe, allowing the shoe to be secured to the pedal without the use of toe clips.

coaster brakes: An internal braking system found in the rear hub, actuated by pushing the pedals counterclockwise. Coaster brakes are normally found on children's bicycles.

cog: One of the toothed rings on a freewheel.

component: A part on a bike that's not the frame or fork.

component group: A collection of components from a single manufacturer, marketed as a unit.

crank arms: Rotating levers on either side of the bike that attach to the pedals and chain ring at one end and the bottom bracket at the other. Also called cranks.

criterium: A road race contested for a number of laps around a short course, often around several city blocks.

cycle computer: An electronic accessory that measures a bike's speed, distance traveled, and average speed by means of a sensor placed on the wheel.

cyclocross: A variant of road racing contested on a short loop course that includes both paved and unpaved sections and obstacles that require riders to dismount.

dab: To put one's foot down for balance on a difficult section of trail.

derailleur: The mechanism that allows a bike to shift gears by "derailing" the chain from one cog or chain ring to another.

dish: The distance that a rear wheel is offset to make room for the freewheel.

down tube: The frame tube that connects the head tube with the bottom bracket.

draft: To follow another rider closely in an attempt to gain an aerodynamic advantage.

drop handlebars: Handlebars, commonly found on road bikes, that curve downward to provide additional hand positions and put the rider in an aerodynamic position.

dropout: The slotted fitting found at the intersection between the seatstays and the chainstays, into which the rear wheel slides.

dropped: Left behind in a race or on a ride.

echelon: A paceline in which the riders are staggered (instead of directly behind the leader) to compensate for the effects of a crosswind.

fixed-gear: A drive system, usually found on track bikes, in which the pedals turn whenever the rear wheel turns, making coasting impossible.

foldable tire: A tire with a Kevlar bead that allows it to be carried compactly.

fork: The assembly that attaches the front wheel to the frame.

fork crown: The casting that attaches the fork arms to the steerer tube.

fork tips: Slotted fixtures at the end of the fork which hold the axle of the front wheel.

freehub: A hub with an integral freewheel mechanisim.

freewheel: The group of cogs attached to the rear wheel incorporating a ratcheting mechanism that allows the bicycle to coast.

gear inches: A unit of measurement for gear ratios.

grade: A measurement of incline, expressed in terms of percentage. The higher the percentage, the steeper the grade.

granny gear: An extremely low gear used for climbing steep hills or pulling heavy loads.

half century: Riding 50 miles in one day.

hammer: To pedal hard, usually in a big gear, especially on a road bike.

handlebar: The part of the bike that you hold onto, attached to the fork by the stem.

head angle: A measurement of the angle between the top tube and the head tube.

head tube: The short frame tube that is attached to the down tube and the top tube and encircles the steerer tube.

headset: The bearing assembly that attaches the fork to the head tube.

hub: The assembly at the center of the wheel which is attached to the wheel by the spokes and through which the axle passes.

hybrid bike: A bike that shares some components from a mountain bike and some from a road bike.

indexed shifter: A shifter that has a click stop for every gear.

interval: One of a series of periods of intense riding followed by a period of recovery.

jersey: A shirt designed for cycling, often with pockets on the back.

jockey wheel: The small wheel attached to the derailleur cage.

kickstand: A small prop that holds the bike upright while it's parked.

lug: The reinforcing sleeve that is used to join tubes in brazed steel bike frames.

metric century: Riding 100 kilometers (62 miles) in one day.

mountain bike: A bicycle designed for off-road riding.

nipple: A threaded sleeve that attaches the spoke to the rim and allows the spoke to be tensioned.

paceline: A riding formation in which riders take turns pedaling at the front of a group in order to break the wind for the riders following.

pannier: A bag that mounts on a rack and hangs on either side of the rear, and sometimes, front wheel.

pedals: The rotating platforms that attach to the crankarm and are turned by the rider's feet.

peloton: The main pack in a road race.

pinch flat: A puncture caused by pinching the tube between a solid object and the rim, usually caused by an underinflated tire. Also called a snakebite.

presta valve: A thin valve with a locknut used on bicycle tubes.

prime: An intermediate sprint for a prize in a criterium race.

pull: One turn at the front in a paceline.

pump: A device for inflating a tire.

pursuit: A track race in which riders start at opposite ends of the track and try to catch each other, or more often, record a better time than the opponent.

quick-release lever: A cam-operated mechanism that can hold a wheel on securely without bolts and yet can be opened easily without tools.

rear triangle: The portion of the bicycle frame comprised of the seatstays, chainstays, and the seat tube.

rim: The metal hoop on the outside of the wheel on which the tire rests.

rim strip: A thin layer of plastic on the inside of a clincher rim to protect the inner tube from protruding spoke ends.

road bike: A lightweight, high performance bike, usually with dropped handlebars, designed for riding on the road.

road rash: The abrasions that result from a fall on pavement.

rollers: A indoor training device, consisting of three cylinders in a metal frame, in which the bike is unsupported, requiring the rider to balance the bike while pedaling.

sag wagon: A vehicle that accompanies a tour or a race and picks up riders who are unable to continue because of fatigue or mecanical problems.

schrader valve: A type of valve used on both automobile tires and some bicycle inner tubes.

seat tube: The largely vertical frame tube that connects the down tube and the top tube.

seatpost: The tubular post that sits inside the seat tube to which the saddle is secured.

seatstay: The frame tube that connects the seat tube and the chainstay.

sew-up: A specialized road racing tire in which the innertube is sewn inside the tire casing. Also called a tubular.

shifter: The device that pulls or releases the cable to cause the derailleur to shift.

singletrack: A relatively narrow wooded trail used for mountain biking.

slick: A treadless tire.

spin: To pedal in circles, pulling up with one foot while pushing down with the other.

spoke wrench: A small tool that fits on the nipple and is used to tighten a spoke.

steel: An iron alloy used to build bike frames.

steerer tube: The part of the fork that sits inside the head tube and attaches to the headset and the fork.

stem: The fitting that attaches the handlebars to the steerer tube.

technical: Mountain biking terrain made difficult by topography or obstacles.

time trial: A race against the clock.

top tube: The horizontal frame tube that connects the head tube and the seat tube.

touring bike: A bike built for long-distance rides, with a long wheelbase and provisions for mounting racks.

track bike: A light, responsive, fixed-gear bike with no brakes, designed to be raced in a velodrome.

trackstand: Balancing in a stationary positon on the bike, as at a stop light.

trials: A genre of mountain biking that entails surmounting obstacles without dabbing.

true: To take a wobble or a flat spot out of a wheel by adjusting spoke tension.

velodrome: An enclosed, banked bicycle racing track, either indoor or outdoor.

wheelie: Popping the front wheel off the ground to clear an obstacle, or just for fun.

Appendix B
Bicycling Clubs and Resources

• •

Here's a huge list of bicycling clubs and organizations throughout North America.

Road Cycling Clubs

League of American Bicyclists
1612 K Street, NW
Suite 401
Washington DC 20006-2802
Phone: 202-822-1333
Fax: 202-822-1334
www.bikeleague.org

Affiliated Clubs

Alabama

Northeast Alabama Bike Club
205-820-5747

Tandem Club of America
205-991-7766
www.mindspring.com/~strauss/tca.html

Birmingham Bicycle Club
205-733-1488

Baldwin County Tailwinds
334-621-8160

Bicycle Across Magnifient Alabama
(BAMA)
205-881-8032

Spring City Cycling Club
205-881-8032
www.springcity.org

Azalea City Cyclists
334-626-6898

Montgomery Bicycle Club
334-834-8817
garysmith.home.mindspring.com

Circle City Cycling People, Inc.
334-774-4783

Alaska

Audax Club Alaska
907-338-4759

Fairbanks Cycle Club
907-479-2026

Juneau Freewheelers Bicycle Club
907-463-3095
www.ptialaska.net/~mbarrett

Peninsula Bike & Trail Club
907-283-5888

Arizona

Coconino Cycling Club
520-774-4747

Arizona Bicycle Club
602-866-3554
members.aol.com/azbikeclub/

Phoenix Metro Bicycle Club (Phoenix Metro
GABA)
www.sportsfun.com/gaba/

Bicycle Bunch
602-994-3410

California

Delta Pedalers Bicycle Club
510-634-1793
www.ecis.com/~bikeridr/deltaped.html

Victor Valley Bicycle Club
619-261-BIKE

North County Cycling Club
805-466-4369

Auburn Bicycling Club
916-878-1910

Grizzly Peak Cyclists
www.vix.com/gpc/

San Fernando Valley Bike Club
818-705-3166

Chico Velo Cycling Club
800-482-2453

Valley Spokesmen
510-828-5299

Lightning Velo
714-964-2503

Fremont Freewheelers Bicycle Club
408-946-1181
home.earthlink.net/~mpolakoff/

Fresno Cycling Club
209-449-1806

Wandervogel Bike Touring Assn.
P.O. Box 10177
Glendale, CA 91209-3177

Goleta Valley Cycling Club
805-730-1006
www.west.net/nonprof/gvcc

Bicycle Club of Irvine
714-553-6944

Single Cyclists
P.O. Box 656
Kentfield, CA 94914-0656

Over the Bars Mountain Bike Club
P.O. Box 411104
Los Angeles, CA 90041-8104

Colorado

Bicycle Mobile Hams of America
303-494-6559

Colorado Springs Cycling Club
719-594-6354

Denver Bicycle Touring Club
303-756-7240
www.dbtc.org

International Christian Cycling Club
303-787-8672
www.geocities/Colosseum/2847

Team Evergreen Bicycle Club
303-674-6048

West Slope Wheelmen
303-248-6699

Connecticut

Hat City Cyclists
203-778-6382

Pequot Cyclists
860-464-0174

Middlesex Bicycle Club
203-347-0798

Southern Conn. Cycle Club
203-393-0779

Central Connecticut Cycling
860-667-0380

Greater Waterbury Cycling Club
1 Highland Dr.
Prospect, CT 06712-0011

Yankee Pedalers
860-872-1809
members.aol.com/yankpedal/yp.htm

SuperVelo
860-872-7740

Appalachian Mountain Club/CT Chapter
860-236-3925

Sound Cyclists Bicycle Club
203-840-1757
www.soundcyclists.com

Delaware

Biking Blue Hens
302-571-9924

White Clay Bicycle Club
302-529-7929
www.delanet.com/~wcbc

Florida

Florida Bicycle Association, Inc. (FBA)
407-898-4137
www.flbicycle.org/

Georgia

Southern Bicycle League
770-594-8350
BikeSBL.org

Augusta Freewheelers
706-732-0072
www.webscene.com/af

Emerald City Bicycle Club
912-272-6229

Gwinnett Touring Club
Lawrenceville, GA 30246-4365

Coosa Valley Cycling Association
706-291-1501

Coastal Bicycle Touring Club (CBTC)
P.O. Box 14531
Savannah, GA 31410

Hawaii

Big Island Mountain Bike Assn.
808-961-4452

Koolau Pedalers Cycling Club
46426 Hololio St.
Kaneohe, III 90744

Garden Island Bicycle Assn.
808-245-7579

Idaho

Twin Rivers Cyclists, Inc.
509-758-3919

Iowa

Bike Burlington, Inc.
319-753-1625

Riverbend Bicycle Club
P.O. Box 1571
Clinton, IA 52733-1571

Dubuque Bicycle Club
319-582-4381
users.mwci.net/~ploeg/

Bicyclists of Iowa City, Inc (BIC)
319-338-0655
danenet.wicip.org/bcp/bic.html

Keokuk Bike Club
319-524-5686

Iowa Valley BC of Marshalltown
515-752-0896

Siouxland Cyclists, Inc.
P.O. Box 3142
Sioux City, IA 51102-3142

Rainbow Cyclists
P.O. Box 2463
Waterloo, IA 50704-2463

Illinois

Arlington Hts. Bicycle Assn.
708-657-7105

Chicago Area Tandems
708-358-7797

McLean County Wheelers
309-662-0173

Spoon River Wheelmen
309-647-6436

Wheeling Wheelmen Bicycle Club
1507 Keele Clr.
Carpentersville, IL 60110

Prairie Cycle Club
217-333-3163

League of Illinois Bicyclists
708-481-3429
www.LincolnNet.net/LIB/

Chicagoland Bike Federation
312-427-3325

Chicago Cycling Club
773-509-8093
www.suba.com/~ccc

Windy City Cycling Club
5839 N. Magnolia Ave.
Chicago, IL 60660

McHenry County Bicycle Club
815-477-6858
pwp.starnetinc.com/jgehrke/McHenry.htm

Decatur Bicycle Club
www.midwest.net/scribers/mcclure/

Elmhurst Bicycle Club
603-323-4672

Evanston Bicycle Club
708-866-7743

Prairie Pedalers BC
309-289-9292

Folks on Spokes
708-730-5179
www.lib.uchicago.edu/~rd13/fos/

Joliet Bicycle Club
815-436-3539

Lake County Bicycle Club
847-604-0520
www.dls.net/~schaller/bclc.html

Naperville Bicycle Club
708-357-9000, x616

Oak Lawn Bike Psychos
708-599-7515
www.geocities.com/Colosseum/Field/5658/

Oak Park Cycle Club
708-224-8977
homepage.interaccess.com/~opcc

Starved Rock Cycling Association
815-434-6673
www.geocities.com/Colosseum/2947

Illinois Valley Wheelmen
309-685-3921
www.geocities.com/Colosseum/Field/6055

Blackhawk Bicycle & Ski Club
815-397-9667

Fox Valley Bicycle & Ski Club
630-584-7353
www.geocities.com/Colosseum/3073/

Flyer Bicycle Club
630-323-4672

Springfield Bicycle Club
217-544-8410
csc.uis.edu/~edwards/bikeclub.html

Indiana

Bloomington Bicycle Club
www.bloomington.in.us/~bbc/

Driftwood Valley Wheelers
P.O. Box 1552
Columbus, IN 47202-1522

Blazing Saddles Bicycle Club
219-724-3967

Evansville Bicycle Club, Inc.
812-426-1330
www.bicycle.evansville.net

Three Rivers Velo Sport
219-484-2729
www.3rvs.com

Wheel People Bicyclists Assn., Inc.
219-699-6825

Michiana Bicycling Assn.
P.O. Box 182
Granger, IN 46530-0182

Central Indiana Bicycling Assn.
317-327-2453
www.spitfire.net/ciba

Indiana Bicycle Coalition, Inc.
1-800-BIKE-110
317-327-8356

Break-Away Bicycle Club
765-452-7110
members.aol.com/breakkomo/
babc.index.htm

Maple City Bicycling Club
219-362-4200

Delaware Cycling Club (DCC)
765-287-8939

Calumet Crank Club
219-464-4322

Wabash River Cycle Club
www.iquest.net/billcul/wrcchome.html

Kansas

Leavenworth Bicycle Club
913-682-8918

LvnBicycle@aol.com
members.aol.com/LvnBicycle/index.html

Johnson County Bicycle Club
913-962-0876

Kaw Valley Bike Touring Club
913-235-6643

OZ Bicycle Club of Wichita
316-721-5327

Biking Across Kansas
316-684-8184

Kentucky

Bowling Green League of Bicyclists
502-843-8968

Bluegrass Cycling Club
P.O. Box 1397
Lexington, KY 40591-1397

Louisville Bicycle Club
502-491-7120
www.louisvillebicycleclub.org/

Chain Reaction Cycling Club
502-442-4425

Louisiana

Kisatchie Bicycle Club
318-443-8833

Bayou Ramblers
P.O. Box 1233
Bastrop, LA 71221-1233

Baton Rouge Bicycle Club
504-343-7992
www.concentric.net/~gbikes/brbchome.html

Cajun Cyclists
www.packnpaddle.com/cajcycle/
cajcycle.html

Lake City Cyclists
318-478-7707

Crescent City Cyclists
home.gnofn.org/~cyclists/

Shreveport Bicycle Club
P.O. Box 1163
Shreveport, LA 71163

Bayou Country Cyclists
P.O. Box 1022
Thibodaux, LA 70302

Maine

Maine Freewheelers
P.O. Box 2037
Bangor, ME 04402-2037

Merrymeeting Wheelers Bicycle Club
207-725-7314

The County Pedalers
207-764-0393

Maine Wheels Bicycle Club
207-743-2577

Casco Bay Bicycle Club
207-892-8257

Maryland

Annapolis Bicycle Racing Team
410-263-4752

Annapolis Bicycle Club
410-721-9151
www.annapolis.net/abc

Baltimore Bicycling Club
410-792-8308
www.baltobikeclub.org/

Bike & Brunch
301-881-BIKE
members.tripod.com/~bikeandbrunch

Frederick Pedalers
301-698-9090
www.bicycle.naqsi.net

Greenbelt Bicycle Coalition
301-474-6639

Cumberland Valley Cycling Club
301-797-6531
www.pilot.wash.lib.md.us.cvcc.index.html

Oxon Hill Bicycle & Trail Club
www.atlantech.net/ohbike

Salisbury Bicycle Club
members.aol.com/bike4ii/

Patuxent Area Cycling Enthusiasts (PACE)
www.bikepace.com

Massachusetts

Nashoba Valley Pedalers
508-266-1687
www.ultranet.com/~nvp/

Seven Hills Wheelmen
508-756-3148
members.aol.com/shwworc/index.html

North Shore Cyclists
617-229-6009

Cyclonauts Bicycling Club
413-532-0761

Franklin-Hampshire Freewheelers
413-527-5195
freewheelers.org/

Northeast Bicycle Club, Inc.
508-872-4592

Carroll Center Bike Club
617-969-6200

Charles River Wheelmen (CRW)
crw.org.harvard.net

Northeast Sport Cyclists
413-525-3202

Michigan

Ann Arbor Bicycle Touring Society
734-913-9851
www.hvcn.org/info/aabts

Pedal Across Lower Michigan (PALM)
313-665-6327

Tri-City Cyclists
517-892-2100

Ford Cycling Club
313-699-6925

Big Rapids Bicycle Club, Inc.
616-832-2709

Clinton River Riders
810-792-4670
www.msen.com/~duemling/crr/crr.html

Genesee Wanderers Bicycle Club
810-239-BIKE

Rapid Wheelmen
616-452-2453

Harbor Springs Cycling Club
616-347-1266

Kalamazoo Bicycle Club
P.O. Box 50527
Kalamazoo, MI 49005-0527

League of Michigan Bicyclists
www.lmb.org

Tri-County Bicycle Assn.
www.voyager.net/TCBA

Muskegon Bicycle Club
616-722-0522

Cycling Saddlemen Bike Club
313-941-2688

Slow Spokes of Macomb, Inc.
313-879-7660

Wheel People of St. Joseph County
616-651-5088

Three Oaks Spokes Bicycle Club
616-756-3361

Cherry Capital Cycling Club
616-941-BIKE

Downriver Cycling Club
P.O. Box 811
Trenton, MI 48183-0811

Ford Cycling Club
313-699-6925

Minnesota

Bloomington Bicycle Club
c/o Dale Shepard
5124 W. 105th St.
Bloomington, MN 55437-2835

Wood City Wheelers
218-879-3079

Itasca Cycling Club
218-245-1901

Northwest Airlines Cycling Club
612-431-3246
www.NWACC-bike.org

Central Minnesota Bicycle Club
320-654-8041

Pedal & Wheels Bicycle Club
320-352-6422

Missouri

Jackson County Wheelmen
816-229-6485

Velo Girardeau
P.O. Box 974
Cape Girardeau, MO 63702-0974

Missouri Bicycle Federation
www.toto.net/kcbc/mbf/

Kansas City Bicycle Club
816-436-5606

Kirksville Bicycle Club
816-665-5016

Folks on Spokes Cycling Club
734 Strafford Ridge Drive
Manchester, MO 63021

Blood, Sweat, & Gears
816-886-8372
Lesa Banks
pobox.com/~bs.g

MDC Bicycle Club
314-946-2882

Skinker Debaliviere Youth CC
314-862-5122

Hostelling International
7187 Manchester Rd.
St. Louis, MO 63143-244

St. Joseph Bicycle Club
2811 Duncan
St. Joseph, MO 64507

Springbike Bicycle Club
417-886-8901
members.aol.com/springbike

Montana

Montana Tour Group
406-652-5523

Missoulians on Bicycles
TOSRV-WEST
Missoula, MT 59807

Nebraska

Mid-America Bicycle Club
308-234-3822

Great Plains Bicycling Club
402-441-9636

Omaha Pedalers Bicycle Club
402-331-9209

Nevada

Las Vegas Valley Bicycle Club
702-645-2434

The Procrastinating Pedalers of Reno
702-329-4302
www.wwwebcrafters.com/pp

New Hampshire

Granite State Wheelmen
www.geocities.com/Colosseum/Loge/9605/

New Jersey

East Coast Bicycle Club of Ocean County
www.baumann.org/ecbc

Central Jersey Bicycle Club, Inc.
732-225-HUBS

The Wayfarers
201-796-9344

New Jersey Tandem Club
732-566-9536

Western Jersey Wheelmen
908-832-7161
www.bike.princeton.edu/wjw

Morris Area Freewheelers Bicycle Club
users.aol.com/atbbiker/fwnews/maf.html

Shore Cycle Club
609-652-0880
pages.prodigy.com/kchf06a/scc.htm

The Chain Gang
610-837-4884

Princeton Freewheelers, Inc.
609-921-6685

Jersey Shore Touring Society
732-747-8206
www.erols.com/jsts/

South Jersey Wheelmen
609-848-6123

Bicycle Touring Club of North Jersey
home.att.net/~btcnj

New Mexico

New Mexico Touring Society
505-298-0085

Santa Fe Century Committee
505-982-1282

New York

518-437-9579
www.albany.net/~kormisto/index.htm

New York Bicycling Coalition
P.O. Box 7335
Albany, NY 12224-0335

Southern Tier Bicycle Club, Inc.
pages.prodigy.net/ira/stbc.htm

Niagara Frontier Bicycle Club, Inc.
716-741-4144

Canton Bicycle Club Inc.
315-379-0014
www.northnet.org/bikenny

Cruise Brothers Bike Club, Inc.
516-541-1707

Long Island Bicycle Club
516-379-4484
www.bicyclelongisland.org/libc/

Huntington Bicycle Club
516-499-7994
www.bicyclelongisland.org/hbc/

Finger Lakes Cycling Club
1431 Mecklenburg Rd.
Ithaca, NY 14850-9301

Big Wheels Bicycle Club
716-625-8308

Massapequa Park Bicycle Club
www.li.net/~msmingel/mpbc.html

Catskill Wheelmen
914-794-3000 ext. 3560

Black Rock Mountain Bike Club
P.O. Box 203
Mountainville, NY 10953

Fast & Fabulous Cyclists
P.O. Box 87, Ansonia Station
New York, NY 10023

Five Borough Bicycle Club
212-932-2300, x115
www.panix.com/fivebbc

Mid-Hudson Bicycle Club
www.mhv.net/~mhbc.htm

Rochester Bicycling Club
716-723-2953
www.win.net/~rbcbbs

Suffolk Bicycle Riders, Assn.
516-842-4699
www.bicyclelongisland.org/sbra/

Staten Island Bicycling Club
P.O. Box 141016
Staten Island, NY 10314-1016

Onondaga Cycling Club
www.cny.com/OCC/

Orange County Bicycle Club
914-986-2659

Country Cycle Club, Inc.
914-723-5362
www.mvisibility.com/ccc

Concerned Long Island Mountain Bikers
(C.L.I.M.B.)
516-271-6527

North Carolina

Blue Ridge Bicycle Club
704-258-1820

Tarheel Cyclists
704-559-8076

Carolina Tarwheels
P.O. Box 111
Durham, NC 27702-0111

River City Cycling Club
919-338-1698

The Smoky Mountain Cycling Club
www.main.nc.us/SMCC

Richmond County Bike Club
910-582-6747

Incredible Challengers
704-726-0616

North Carolina Bicycle Club
P.O. Box 10346
Raleigh, NC 27605-0346

Roanoke Valley Bike Club
919-535-3634

Tar River Riders Cycling Club
919-446-5186

Sandhills Cycle Club
919-692-4494

Mount Jefferson Century Flyers
919-426-4483

Cape Fear Cyclists
P.O. Box 3644
Wilmington, NC 28406-0644

Law Enforcement Cycling Association
910-760-0311

Ohio

Ohio Bicycle Federation
www.coil.com/~bt364

Akron Bicycle Club, Inc.
c/o Robert Iden
20251 Annetta Ave.
Akron, OH 44313

Lorain Wheelmen
216-988-5016

Western Reserve Wheelers
216-291-3960

Black Swamp Bicycling Society
419-353-3518

Stark County Bicycle Club
330-877-1301
members.aol.com/starkscbc/scbc/index.htm

Lake Erie Wheelers
216-779-8392
www.geocities.com/yosemite/trails/2665

Cleveland Touring Club
216-383-7100

Kicking Asphalt
P.O. Box 24622
Columbus, OH 43224

Dayton Cycling Club
dmapub.dma.org/dcc

Delaware Cycling Club
c/o Ed Richardson
771 Bunty Station Rd.
Delaware, OH 43015

Hancock Handlebars
419-423-2760

Great Miami Bicycle Club
P.O. Box 684
Hamilton, OH 45012-0684

Mid-Ohio Bikers
330-884-0277

Lima Road Runners-A.Y.H.
419-222-7301

Hocking Hills Bicycle Club
614-385-7744

Mid-Ohio Bikers
419-884-0277

Heart of Ohio Tailwinds Bicycle Club
home1.gte.net/danshel/index.html

Folks on Spokes
330-833-9357

Sandusky Bicycle Club
419-625-3445

Seneca Sprockets Bicycle Club
419-447-8492

Toledo Area Bicyclists
419-385-7584

Toledo Area Council, A.Y.H./HI
419-841-4510

Westerville Bicycle Club
614-470-0640
www.macconnect/~bikepeddler/

Out-Spokin' Wheelmen
216-792-0822

Oklahoma

Wichita Mountains Bike Club
405-355-1808

Oklahoma Bicycle Society
405-942-4592
www.icon.net/~jwente

Tulsa Bicycle Club
918-241-2453

Tulsa Wheelmen
918-371-0967

Siskiyou Wheelmen
541-482-8704
home.cdsnet.net/~pauld/wheelmen/
wheelmen.htm

Oregon

Klah Klahnee Cycling Club
930 NW Newport Ave.
Bend, OR 97701-1616

Central Oregon Wheelers Bicycle Club
P.O. Box 8269
Bend, OR 97708

Mid-Valley Bicycle Club
www.mvbc.com

Greater Eugene Area Riders
503-342-5719

Santiam Slow Spokes
c/o Lebanon Community Hospital
P. O. Box 739
Lebanon, OR 97355

Redmond BC of Central Oregon
541-923-5395

Salem Bicycle Club
503-588-8613
www.teleport.com/nonprofit/sbc/

Pennsylvania

Lehigh Wheelmen Assn., Inc.
610-967-2653
www.enter.net/~lehighwheelmen

Anthracite Bicycling Club
717-788-2965

Tandems of York Society
members.aol.com/ToysofYork/home.htm

The Wayfarers
717-275-1707

Harrisburg Bicycle Club
717-975-9879
members.aol.com\mfm2783\hbc2.html

Lackawanna Bicycle Club
717-347-7620

Hanover Cyclers
717-633-7273
www.bicycleclubs.com/hanovercyclers/

Suburban Cyclists Unlimited
215-628-8636

Lancaster Bicycle Club
717-396-9299
www.concentric.net/~Outspokn/
lbcmain.html

Endless Mountains Cycling Club
717-265-9208

Two-Tired Bicycle Club
3447 Wilmington Rd., Ste. C
New Castle, PA 16105

Valley Forge Bicycle Club
215-233-4183

Bicycle Club of Philadelphia
215-735-2453
www.libertynet.org/~bikeclub

Cycling Enthusiasts of Delaware Valley
215-338-9159

Western Pennsylvania Wheelmen
trfn.clpgh.org/wpw/

Berks County Bicycle Club
215-370-5092

Brandywine Bicycle Club
P.O. Box 3162
West Chester, PA 19381-3162

Lebanon Valley Bicycle Club
RR 1 Box 153
Womelsdorf, PA 19567

The Delaware Valley Bicycle Club
www.netreach.net/people/elzchris/dvbc/
home-page.htm

Wyoming Valley Bicycle Club
717-675-4866

Rhode Island

Narragansett Bay Wheelmen
401-246-2753
www.aljian.com/nbw/

South Carolina

Aiken Bicycle Club
803-649-1780

Electric City Cycling Club
864-972-0184
www.clemson.edu/~sjm/eccc

Coastal Cyclists
803-873-8779
www.awod.com/gallery/probono/ccy

Carolina Cyclers
803-791-4495
www.city-online.com/people/ronw/ccyclers/

Freewheelers of Spartanburg, Inc.
864-578-1527
members.aol.com/freewhspa/welcome.html

Tennessee

Chattanooga Bicycle Club
615-344-0710

Kennessee Bicycle Club
615-648-2095

Columbia Bicycle Club
615-380-9173

Harpeth Bicycle Club
615-661-4940

Tri Cities Road Club
bergg.etsu.edu/tcrc/tcrc.htm

Kingsport Bicycle Assn.
423-239-4406
members.tripod.com/~KBA

Memphis Hightailers
615-755-0091

Murfreesboro Bicycle Club
615-893-3357

Nashville Bicycle Club
615-356-4074

Highland Rimmers Bicycle Club
edge.net/~scoulter/bikeclub.htm

Texas

Austin Cycling Assn.
512-477-0776

Greater Dallas Bicyclists
rampages.onramp.net/~msargent/gdb/

Fort Worth Bicycling Assn.
817-377-BIKE

Lone Star Cyclists
214-264-1132

Northwest Cycling Club
713-466-1240

Houston Bike Club
713-935-2810

Space City Cycling Club
P.O. Box 591101
Houston, TX 77259-1101

Kerrville Bicycle Club
210-257-6723

Longview Bicycle Club
P.O. Box 6694
Longview, TX 75608-6694
903-984-0400

Williamson County Cycling Club
512-255-1701

Crossroads Cycling Club
512-576-9502

Waco Wild West Century, Inc.
817-772-7150

Wichita Falls Bicycling Club
P.O. Box 2096
Witchita Falls, TX 76307-2096

Williamson County Cycling Club
512-255-1701

San Angelo Bicycle Assn.
P.O. Box 60942
San Angelo, TX 76906-0942

San Antonio Wheelmen
210-221-6500

Texarkana Bicycle Club
903-792-3829

Crossroads Cycling Club
512-576-9502

Waco Wild West Century, Inc.
817-772-7150

Wichita Falls Bicycling Club
P.O. Box 2096
Witchita Falls, TX 76307-2096

Vermont

Green Mountain Bicycle Club
802-529-0595

Virginia

Nelson Bicycle Alliance
540-456-6746

New River Valley Bicycle Club
P.O. Box 488
Blacksburg, VA 24063

A.P. Hill/Rappahannock B.C.
804-633-6500

Mid-Atlantic Off Road Enthusiasts
14846 Basingstoke Loop
Centerville, VA 22020-3104

Eastern Shore of Virginia Bike Club
5248 Willow Oaks Rd.
P.O. Box 882
Eastville, VA 23347

Fredericksburg Cyclists
540-371-0398
www.illuminet.net/~fcyclist/

Shenandoah Valley Bicycle Club
P.O. Box 1014
Harrisonburg, VA 22801-1014

Wheel Power Christian Cyclists
804-385-7213

Potomac Pedalers Touring Club, Inc. (PPTC)
cyberider.us.net/bikes/PPTC.html

Peninsula Bicycling Assn.
757-875-1594

Tidewater Bicycle Assn.
804-490-1831

Reston Bicycle Club
703-391-9051
blueridge.databolts.ibm.com/bikes/clubs/
Reston/

Richmond Area Bicycling Assn.
804-270-9506

Blue Ridge Bicycle Club, Inc.
540-343-7632

Eastern Tandem Rally, Inc.
703-978-7937

Williamsburg Area Bicyclists
757-722-3194

Winchester Wheelmen
540-662-1510

The Single Track Society of Virginia LLC
540-662-7654

Eastern Shore Bike Club of Virginia
www.esva.net/~cbes

Washington

Northwest Bicycle Touring Society
206-941-5870

Green River Bicycle Club
206-848-1801

Mount Baker Bicycle Club
206-734-2422

Klein Club
360-262-3305

B.I.K.E.S.
206-339-7655

Wheelsport Cycling Team
206-852-4946

Capital Bicycling Club
360-956-3321

Olympic Peninsula Bicyclists
360-683-1253

Cascade Bicycle Club
206-522-3222
cascade.org.

Backcountry Bicycle Trails Club
206-283-2995

Highline Bicycle Club
206-244-8414

Seattle International Randonneurs
www.cnw.com/~jmwagner/SIR/
SIR-FrontPage.htm

Seattle Bicycle Club
206-298-3722
www.seattlebike.org

West Sound Cycling Club
360-779-6676

Spokane Bicycle Club
509-325-1171
home.att.net/~loyd.phillips

Wheatland Wheelers Bike Club
509-529-0595

West Virginia

Harrison County Bicycle Club
304-366-5613

Blennerhassett Bicycle Club
304-422-7808

Mountain State Wheelers
304-344-5886

Wisconsin

Fox Valley Wheelmen
P.O. Box 4034
Appleton, WI 54915-0034

Southwest Chain Gang
608-935-7433

Tour de Fort Bicycle Club
414-674-9621

Bay Shore Bicycle Club
414-468-5986

Bombay Bicycle Club of Madison, Inc.
danenet.wicip.org/bcp/

Lakeshore Pedalero
414-682-1041

Spokes & Folks
906-864-2984

Cream City Cycle Club
414-427-0251

Spring City Spinners
414-297-9135

Wausau Wheelers Bicycle Club
715-358-9338
www.apexcomm.net/~blackc/wwbc.html

Mountain Biking

**International Mountain Bicycling
Association (IMBA)**
P.O. Box 7578
Boulder, CO 80306
1121 Broadway; Suite 202
Boulder, CO 80302
Phone: 303-545-9011
Fax: 303-545-9026
www.imba.com/imba.form.html

Affiliated Clubs

Alaska

Arctic Bicycle Club
P.O. Box 244302
Anchorage, AK 99524

Alabama

Birmingham Urban Mountain Pedalers
(BUMP)
205-879-8373

Arkansas

Arkansas Mountain Bike Association
501-394-5856
www.Mena-ark.com/arkmtbike

Ozark Off Road Cyclist
501-582-3472

Arizona

C.R.U.S.T.
602-779-5969, 602-779-6048

Gila Trails Association
c/o KMOG
Box 44A
Payson AZ, 85541

Mountain Bike Association of Arizona
(MBAA),
602-320-0287, 602-275-7393

Pima Trails Association
520-577-7919

Red Mountain Cycling Club
602-940-0434

Red Rock Pathways
520-284-4202

Sedona Bicycle Club
520-284-4203

Sedona Bike & Bean
520-282-3515
www.bike-bean.com

Southern Arizona Mountain Bike Assoc.
(SAMBA)
520-882-0965

Verde Valley Mountain Bicyclists
520-634-7113

Way Out West MTB
520-825-4590
www.azstarnet.com/~wayout/wow.html

California

12th Council District TMF
818-882-5522

Badwater Bicycle Club
619-255-8204, 619-256-7162

Berkeley Bicycle Club
510-527-3222

Bicycle Trails Council Marin (BTCM)
415-456-7512
www.btcmarin.org

Bicycle Trails Council of the East Bay
(BTCEB)
415-775-2135

Bicyclists of Nevada County (BONC)
916-477-6422, 916-273-8427

Big Bear Bikes Racing Club
909-866-2224, 909-584-9183, 909-866-7352

California Associations of Bicycling Org.
415-828-5299

Campus Life Rock Riders
805-544-3000, 805-534-9884

Central Coast Off-Road Cyclists (CCORC)
805-756-6428

Chico Velo Club
916-343-VELO

Chino Hills State Park Bicy. Assist. Unit
714-632-838, 714-525-3020

Cielo Velo Bicycle Club
805-898-9956
cv.navisoft.com

Coachella Valley Cycling Association
619-360-0761, 619-320-7135

Coast Range Riders Bicycle Club
510-222-8004, 510-222-8015

Concerned Central Coast Mountain Bikers
805-528-0430, 805-756-1284

Concerned Cyclists of Crystal Cove
714-222-3334

Concerned Off Road Bicyclists' Assoc.
(CORBA)
818-773-3555
www.usc.edu/go/corba/

Cyclonauts
238-6144, 238-7968

Different Spokes/San Francisco
415-681-5720, 415-282-1647

Donner Ski Ranch
916-426-3635, 916-426-9350

Eagle Cycling Club
707-253-7000, 707-253-7000

FATRAC
916-339-2833
www.jps.net/fatrac/index.htm

Forest Knolls Freewheelers
415-488-1750

Grapevine Mountain Bike Association
805-724-9066
www. haskins.net/grapevine

Grizzly Peak Cyclists, Inc.
P.O. Box 9308
Berkeley, CA 94709

Lassen Velo
916-251-8260, 916-257-5023

Mammoth Area Mountain Bike Organization
(MAMBO)
619-934-3708

MCART
408-649-8006

McDonnell Douglas Mountain Bike Club
818-303-9445, 818-303-9792

Monterrey Mountain Bike Association
(MoMBA)
408-484-9000, 408-372-5532

Mountain Bike Club
1321 West Willow
Lompoc, CA, 93436

Mountain Bikers of Santa Cruz
408-462-0967

Mt. Wilson Bicycling Assn.
818-795-3836

North County Cycle Club
619-758-8057, 619-489-1482, 619-758-8059

Orange County Trails Coalition (OCTC)
714-890-3925, 310-430-7884

Over the Bars Mountain Bike Club
818-504-9512

Pasadena Mountain Bike Club
818-799-8785

Redwood Empire Trails Assistance Group
(RETAG)
707-538-1829
www.sonic.net/~greenman/

Real Riders-Mountain Bike Club
805-438-4375, 805-238-4343

Responsible Organized Mountain Pedalers
(ROMP)
www-leland.stanford.edu/~scoop/romp/

Sacramento Rough Riders
916-978-4833, 916-485-5782, 916-978-5348

San Diego County Bicycle Coalition
619-258-9140
www.sdmba.com

San Diego County Trails Council, Inc.
619-563-5025, 619-561-7755

San Diego Mountain Biking Association
(SDMBA)
www.sdmba.com

San Luis Obispo Bicycle Club, Inc.
805-543-5973

Santa Barbara Mountain Bike Trail
Volunteers
805-683-0371

SHARE Mountain Bike Club
714-759-8485
members.aol.com/sharemtb

Single Cyclists
415-459-BIKE

South Bay Mountain Biking Club-SBMBC
310-379-7058
www.usinter.net/SBMBC

South Bay Wheelmen Inc.
310-372-3537

Southern Sierra Fat Tire Association
805-632-BUGS, 805-322-8829
members.aol.com/ssfta

Sport Chalet Bicycle Club
818-566-6670, 818-365-6600

Stockton Bicycle Club
P.O. Box 4702
Stockton, CA 95204

Tahoe Area Mountain Bike Association
(TAMBA)
916-541-7505

Team Wrong Way
510-551-8785
www.hooked.net/~ginmtb/

Trips for Kids
415-381-2941, 415-332-8082
www.webcom.com/tfk

U of CA at Santa Barbara
805-961-4430, 805-563-2623

UCLA Cycling Club
310-458-5996

Ukiah Wheelers
707-462-6204

WOMBATS
415-459-0980

Yosemite Fat Tire Association
209-683-3379
www.sierranet.net/fat-tire

Colorado

Aspen Cycling Club
970-925-7334

Bicycle Colorado (a statewide coalition)
719-530-0051

Boulder Off-Road Alliance
www.boa-mtb.org

Summit Fat Tire Society
970-949-8057

Clear Creek Bicycle Club
303-567-4666, 303-569-2729

Colorado Plateau Mountain Bike Assoc.
(COPMOBA)
303-241-9561, 303-242-2636
www.rmwest.com/copmoba

Crested Butte Mountain Biking Assn.
303-349-5517 or 303-349-6817

Diamond Peaks Mountain Bike Patrol
Ft. Collins, CO 80526
970-226-4126

Dogs at Large Velo
719-380-9592, 719-380-9592, 719-596-1484

Front Range Mountain Bike Assoc.
boulder.earthnet.net:80/~erickson/frmba.html

Medicine Wheel
719-634-5566, 719-522-9083, 714-634-4003
www.qrz.com/medicine.html

Mountain/Road Biking Assn. Rocky Flats
(MRBARF)
303-966-5135, 303-422-2792

Routt County Riders
303-879-8300, 303-879-5470

Team Babes on Bikes
1608 Remington St
Fort Collins, CO 80525

Team Evergreen
303-793-2755, 303-770-1134

Trail Conservation Services (TCS)
303-977-5328, 303-470-5672

Trail Mix
303-258-3435

Trails 2000
970-259-4682

Winter Park King of the Rockies
970-726-5741, 970-887-2519

Connecticut

Central Connecticut Cycling Club
860-667-3428

Connecticut Bicycle Coalition
860-527-5200
www.ctbike/org

Cycle Fitness Cycling Club
203-261-8683

Mattabassett Cycle Club
203-346-7498

Connecticut NEMBA
members.aol.com/joeorto/index.html
www.nemba.orgu6

West River Riders
203-453-2513

Delaware

White Clay Bicycle Club (WCBC)
302-774-0146, 302-994-9161

Florida

Chipola Bicycle Association
904-482-8592, 904-482-8592

Florida Freewheelers, Inc.
407-894-8082, 407-894-8082

Metro Dade Off Road Bicycle Club
305-945-3425, 305-829-1351

North Florida Bicycle Club
904-721-5780
personal.jax.bellsouth.net/jax/c/t/ctburns/
nfbc/

Ocala Mountain Bike Association
352-854-7810
members.aol.com/FlaMap/bargeC.html

South Florida Trail Blazers
305-420-2434, 407-434-3523, 305-420-2032

South West Association of Mountain
Peddlers (SWAMP)
813-978-7471, 813-988-6435

Suwannee Bicycle Association
904-828-1886, 904-695-9791
www.cycling.org/freeweb/sbalo.gulfnet.com/
non-profit/suwanneebike

The Unknowns
407-732-5947

University of Florida Mountain Bike Club
904-374-9149, 904-378-4806

Georgia

Augusta Freewheelers
706-732-0072
www.webscene.com/af

Georgia Cycling Club
706-549-BIKE

Southern Off Road Bicycle Association
(SORBA)
www.sorba.org

Hawaii

Hawaii Bicycling League
P.O. Box 4403
Honolulu, HI 96812-4403

Kauai Bicycle Club
808-826-6040

Maui Mountain Bike Club
808-572-8840, 808-572-8840

Mauka Bike Club
808-732-8950

Idaho

Moscow Area Mountain Bike Association
208-882-9366

South West Idaho Mountain Biking
Assoc. (SWIMBA)
members.aol.com/jjlehn/SWIMBA/index.htm

Illinois

Bicycle Club of Lake County
P.O. Box 521
Libertyville, IL 60048

Blackhawk Bicycle & Ski Club
P.O. Box 6443
Rockford, IL 61125

Friends of Off-Road Cycling (FORC)
309-786-7979
home.revealed.net/forc

Folks on Spokes
708-730-5179
www.lib.uchicago.edu/~rd13/lib/

Peoria Bicycle Club
309-346-3965, 309-578-3605

Recreation for Individuals Dedicated to the
Environment (RIDE)
800-458-2358
www.bike-ride.com

Trail Users Rights Foundation (TURF)
708-496-4619, 708-535-6315, 708-496-4888
members.aol.com/turfinfo

Wheel Fast Racing 2308 Flambeau Drive
630-717-5341
www.dupagecyclery.com

Indiana

Bloomington Bicycle Club
812-339-1722

Central Indiana Bicycle Assoc.
317-862-5859

Fat Trackin Homies
317-848-9300

Three Rivers Velo Sport, Inc.
www.3rvs.com

Iowa

Iowa City Off Road Riders (ICORR)
319-626-2261
soli.inav.net/~icorr

Kansas

Kaw Valley Bicycle Touring Club
913-234-8683
www.inlandnet.net/~lrhodes/kvbc.

Kentucky

Bowling Green Bicycle Club
502-843-8968

Kentucky Mountain Bike Assoc.
502-569-7676
www.louisville.edu/~lnweed01/

MTB @ Cycling.Org
606-269-2982

Northern KY Mountain Bike Assoc.
606-581-3960

Purchase Area Mountain Bike Assoc.
502-554-0671, 502-898-4085
www.apex.net/users/weyers;

Louisiana

Baton Rouge Area Mountain Bike Assoc.
(BRAMBA)
800-527-3854, 504-344-7211

Kisatchie Bicycle Club
P.O. Box 8625
Alexandria, LA 71306

Shreveport Bicycle Club
318-688-8505, 318-632-6402

Maine

Camden Hills Off Road Bicycling Assoc.
(Fiddlehead Cycling Club)
207-236-2383, 207-236-4592

Mount Desert Island (MDI) Bicycle
Association
207-288-3886, 207-288-3028

Seacoast NEMBA
603-332-0979

Team Allspeed
207-878-8741
www.allspeed.com

YMCA Mountain Bike Program
207-775-4252, 207-775-4329

Maryland

CAPYBARA Mountain Bike Club of Central
Maryland
410-674-3467
www.digizen.net/member/capybara/

Maryland Association of Mountain Bike
Operators (MAMBO)
410-902-1295
www.bikemobile.com/mambo/

St. Mary's Mountain Biking Club
301-862-0209, 301-862-0308

Massachusetts

New England Mountain Biking Association:
NEMBA (headquarters)
800-576-3622

New England Mountain Bike Assn. (NEMBA),
617-497-6891, 617-776-4686
www.nemba.org

Berkshire Chapter NEMBA
413-298-0073

Blackstone Valley NEMBA
508-887-2028

Cape Cod & Islands NEMBA
508-888-3861

Greater Boston NEMBA
978-263-0459

Merrimack Valley NEMBA
978-452-1590
www.movement4health.com/merrimack/

North Shore Mass. NEMBA
978-774-0906

Shay's NEMBA
413-772-0496

Southeast Massachusetts NEMBA
508-643-2453

Somerset Area Mountain Bike Assoc.
508-673-8195

Vineyard Off Road Bicycle Assoc.
508-693-4905, 508-693-4905

Wachusett NEMBA
978-425-2067

Michigan

Michigan Mountain Biking Association
(MMBA)
www.mmba.org

MMBA's Mountain Kids program:
home.earthlink.net/~dutchrider/MK/
mountnkids.html

Western Michigan Michigan Biking
Association Info
www.Concentric.net/~Khorton/Index.html

Minnesota

Minnesota Off Road Cyclists
612-895-1744

Winona Area Mountain Bikers (WAMB)
507-452-4228, 507-452-4211

Northwest Airlines Cycling Club, Inc.
www.nwacc-bike.org
www.isd.net/jpugh/schedule.html

Missouri

Earth Riders Mountain Bicycle Club
913-362-1818 x303, 816-523-6483
www.qni.com/~acstokes/earthriders/
erbc.html

Cyclists of Greater St. Louis (COGS)
314-353-2461

Mountain Trail Builders of Missouri
314-966-0903, 888-802-8111
members.aol.com/trailtraks

Montana

Low Impact Mountain Bicyclists (LIMB)
406-329-3814

Beartooth Fat Tire Society
P.O. Box 84
Red Lodge, MT 59068

Plains Crazy Road & Trail Club
406-365-5931

Nebraska

UNO Cycling Club
402-554-2539, 402-551-5382

New Hampshire

Biking Expedition
603-428-7500, 603-428-7500

Seacoast Chapter, New England Mountain
Bike Association
603-742-9462
24.1.69.170/snemba

New Hampshire Mountain Bicycling Assoc.
603-236-4666, 603-968-7840, 603-236-4174

White Mountains NEMBA
603-356-023

White Mountain Wheel People
603-383-4660

Nevada

Eureka Silver State Cyclists
702-237-5401

Reno Wheelmen
702-359-3303, 702-747-3843

Las Vegas Valley Bicycle
702-361-4319

New Jersey

Chain Gang / Team Reaction
908-638-4488

East Coast Bicycle Club of Ocean City
908-929-2999, 908-269-9702

G.S. Park Ridge
201-391-5269

Jersey Rock 'N' Road
201-293-3619, 201-293-7743

Jersey Shore Touring Society
732-747-820
www.erols.com/jsts/

Morris Area Freewheelers
973-236-1092, 973-538-0200

New Jersey Cycling Conservation Club
908-972-8822, 908-842-8727

Ramapo Valley Cycling Club, Inc.
201-831-6199, 201-839-4304

Wheelsport Cycle Club
201-529-1467

Wrecking Crew
908-431-5610

New Mexico

New Mexico Mountain Bike Adventures
505-473-1374, 505-264-5888

Ruidoso Cycling Club
505-258-3224

Sangre De Cristo Cycling Club
505-466-7434

Tuff Riders Mountain Bike Club
505-672-9025

Velo De Animas
505-328-0214, 505-326-3727

New York

CNY DIRT
315-699-8635, 315-458-5260
www.thebook.com/dirt

Concerned Long Island Mountain Bicyclists
(CLIMB)
516-351-0909, 516-271-6527

Croton Mountain Biking Center
914-271-6661

Cortlandt Area Bicycle Network
914-271-2640, 914-271-6661

Eastern New York Fat Tire Club
914-896-9067, 914-228-1206

Fats in the Cats Bicycle Club
914-331-9800, 914-338-3552, 914-331-2554

Finger Lakes Cycling Club
602-273-0779

G.S. Tiburon
914-352-0305

Gunks Off Road Patrol (GORP)
914-691-3684, 914-691-3684

Millbrook School Bike Club
914-677-6253

Onondaga Cycling Club
P.O. Box 6307
Teall Station
Syracuse, NY 13210

Rochester Bicycling Club
716-723-2953
www.win.net/~rbcbbs/

Saratoga Freewheelers Bicycle Club
518-583-7706, 518-587-5856

Spokes-N-Wheels Mountain Bike Team
716-477-1540, 716-288-7349

Westchester Velo Cycling Club
914-682-4909

Western New York M.B. Assoc. (WNYMBA)
716-655-3364
www.wnymba.org

Xtreme Cycling Club
315-638-2161, 315-652-5858

North Carolina

Blue Ridge Bicycle Club
704-684-1085, 704-684-1560

Gaston County Cyclists
704-875-4586, 704-825-7982

Greensboro Fat Tire Society
910-668-7113

High Country Mountain Bike Assoc.
(HCMBA) 704-295-9815

Nantahala Bike Club
704-488-2175 x188, 704-488-9735

North Carolina Fats Mountain Bike Club
919-269-7566

North Raleigh Mountain Biking Assoc.
919-781-5400, 919-846-8198

Smokey Mountain Cycling Club
704-369-3835, 800-614-8838
www.main.nc.us/SMCC/

Tarheel Cyclists
704-588-2716, 704-545-3930

Ohio

Central Ohio Mountain Bike Organization
(COMBO)
614-457-2136

Cincinnati Off Road Alliance (CORA)
513-558-2861

Dayton Cycling Club
513-848-8466, 513-698-6081
www.dma.org

Northeastern Ohio M.B. Assoc. (NOMBA)
216-987-5459, 216-734-2704

Ohio University MTB Club
614-594-7669, 614-594-7669

Queen City Wheels
513-351-5020

Oklahoma

Oklahoma Earthbike Fellowship
www.telepath.com/mudpup/contents.htm

Oregon

Bicycle Federation of Oregon
660 High Street NE #150
Salem, OR 97301

Central Oregon Trail Alliance (COTA)
541-385-1985

Merry Cranksters
www.engr.orst.edu/~reed/bike/cranksters/
index.html

Club Bump
541-572-2745

Disciples of Dirt
503-343-8877, 541-343-0314
www.themudzone.com/work/dod.html

Knobby By Nature
541-476-3830, 503-474-5093

Portland United Mountain Pedalers (PUMP)
503-222-3821, 503-281-9800
www.rdrop.com/users/terryh/pump.html

Pennsylvania

Global Experience
215-491-2459, 215-491-9882

Lackawanna Bicycle Club
717-347-7620, 717-344-6602

Montgomery County MBA
215-287-7870, 215-287-5819

Pennsylvania Bicycle Club
215-871-1100, 215-643-2329

Pennsylvania Trail Hands (PATH)
717-626-0552, 610-701-7353, 610-701-7401

Pittsburgh Off Road Cyclists (PORC)
412-492-9909, 412-492-9910

Rocky's Bicycle Shop
717-265-9208

The Garnished Ace Society
610-760-9635

Wyoming Valley Bicycle Club
717-675-4866

York Area Mountain Bike Association
717-852-9553, 717-792-2831

Rhode Island

Eastern Fat Tire Association (EFTA)
401-377-2231, 401-364-0786,

Rhode Island NEMBA
401-397-8127

Rhode Island Fat Tire Assoc. (EFTA)
401-596-6700, 401-364-0786

South Carolina

Greenville Spinners Bicycle Club
803-458-5976, 803-322-7423

Rock Hill Bicycle Club
803-684-7215

South Dakota

Black Hills Mountain Bike Association
605-342-0982, 605-787-5645

Custer Bicycle Club
605-390-7731, 605-673-4764, 605-673-4764

Tennessec

Appalachian Mountain Bike Club
423-397-4510, 423-675-BIKE
www.serversolutions.com/ambc

Big South Fork Bicycle Club
615-569-8652, 615-569-9186

Chattanooga Bicycle Club
706-820-1157

Kennessee Bicycle Club, Inc.
P.O. Box 30731
Clarksville, TN 37040-0013

Mountain Trails Bicycle Club
615-794-3313, 615-292-8691
www.tallent.com/mtbc

R.A.T.T. Mountain. Bike Club
423-932-4294

Sumner County Cycle Club
615-672-4565, 615-672-4565

Texas

Austin Ridge Riders
512-445-4459, 512-280-2316
www.io.com/austinridgeriders

Central Texas Trailblazers
817-771-1172, 817-939-3170

Dallas Off-Road Bicycle Assn (DORBA)
214-556-0640, 214-424-1066
www.dorba.org

Desert Ratz MB Club
915-755-7656

Hill Country Cyclist
210-341-0899, 210-249-8978

Houston Area M.B. Riders Assoc. (HAMBRA)
713-963-5227, 713-488-0207
www.neosoft.com/~fletch/hambra.htm,

San Angelo Bicycling Association
915-658-6571 x189, 915-947-2675

South Texas Off Road Mountain-Bikers
210-826-7564

The Unknowns
512-445-4459

Utah

Campus Bike Club
801-942-3498, 801-943-5616

So. UT Trail Users Riders & Equestrians
801-772-3745, 800-4-SLIKROK

Utah Mountain Bike Association
801-531-7703, 801-237-5910

Wasatch Walkabout Touring
801-322-1166, 801-322-5771

Vermont

Brattleboro Velo Club
802-257-5185, 802-257-4137

Killington-Pico Cycling Club
802-746-8076

Mountain Bikers of Vermont
800-628-4040, 802-244-5067

Vermont NEMBA
802-824-3642

Virginia

Central Virginia Mountain Bike Assoc.
804-237-1000

Eastern Virginia Mountain Bike Assoc.
804-827-1045

Iron Mountain Trail Club
540-475-6108

Mid-Atlantic Off-Road Enthusiasts (MORE)
703-502-0359
apollo.gmu.edu\~chain\more

Mountain Bike – Virginia
804-222-8006, 804-782-7903

Potomac Pedalers Touring Club
703-442-8780, 202-363-8687

Virginia Creeper Trail Club
540-475-6108
www.naxs.com/people/thorsch

Washington

Backcountry Bicycle Trails Club (BBTC)
206-286-2744

Bainbridge Island Mountain Bikers Organized
206-842-9779

Greatful Tread
509-575-5408, 509-575-3061

Methow Valley Sport Trail Association
509-996-3287, 509-996-2451

San Juan United Mountian Pedalers
360-468-3519
www.intergrade.com/s-jump

Singletrack Mind Cycling Club
206-565-5124, 206-566-0359
members.aol.com/STMClub/stmclub.html

Tacoma Wheelmen's Bicycle Club
206-759-2800

Whatcom Independent Mountain Pedalers
(WHIMP)
206-671-4107

West Virginia

Gear Pushers Bicycle Club
304-363-2058, 304-366-7760

Mountain State Wheelers Bicycle Club
P.O. Box 8161
South Charleston, WV 25303-0161

Mountaineer Off Road Bicycling Assoc.
(MORBA)
304-624-0671, 304-842-2077

Pocahontas County Tourism Commission
304-799-4636, 800-336-7009

Riders of the Gorge
304-787-3221, 304-438-6728

West Virginia Mountain Bicycling Assoc.
(WVMBA)
304-296-4925, 304-296-4142

Wisconsin

Baka Mountain Bike Club
414-235-6673, 414-727-4878

Bay Shore Bicycle Club
414-336-7410

Bleu Moon Mountain Bike Society
P.O. Box 67
Baraboo, WI 53913

Chequamegon Area Mountain Bike Assoc.
800-533-7454, 715-798-3833
cable4fun.com/camba.htm

Mad Trail FORCS
608-255-8494

Neillsville Area Trail Association
715-743-3323, 715-743-4937

Spoke in the Mud
P.O. Box 40
Lake Geneva, WI 53147

Wisconsin Off-Road Bicycling Association
(WORBA)
www.worba.org

Wyoming

Friends of Pathways
307-733-4534

Laramie Bicycling Association
307-766-2239, 307-745-9382

Rawlins Bicycle Club
307-324-6200, 307-324-6729

Alberta, Canada

Calgary Mountain Bike Alliance
403-220-1868
members.home.net/cmba/

Alberta Bicycle Association
403-453-8518, 403-288-0680

Trail Riders Access Club of Edmonton
403-963-8514, 403-435-1407

British Columbia, Canada

Cycling B.C.
604-737-3034, 604-737-1403

Prince George Cycling Club
604-963-7626

Sea to Sky Trail Society
604-892-5467, 604-892-9266

Simon's Cycles
604-339-6683, 604-339-6766

South Island Mountain Bike Society
604-727-6655, 604-474-3112

Ontario, Canada

Ontario Cycling Assn.
416-495-4141, 416-495-4038

Quebec, Canada

Capital Off Road Bicycle Association
819-685-0304

Laurentian Mountain Bike Centre
819-322-6853

Safety Organizations

SNELL
916-331-5073
www.smf.org/

Bicycle Helmet Safety Institute
www.bhsi.org

Bicycle Charity Rides

AIDS Rides
212-242-7433
www.aidsride.org/

American Diabetes Association
1-800-342-2383
www.diabetes.org/tour98/

Leukemia Society
1-800-486-8417
www.lsa-teamintraining.org/

National Multiple Sclerosis Society
800-Fight-MS (800-344-4867)
www.ms150.org/

Index

•*Numbers*•

24-hour races, 263

• *A* •

ABS brakes, 30
accessories
  basic description of, 57–68
  for kids' bikes, 194
  shopping for, 55, 194
accidents, 100, 200
"active rest," 135
acute injuries, 117, 121–122
aero bars, 45, 123
aerobic exercise, 112, 113
aero-bikes, 29
aerodynamics, 9, 29
  handlebars and, 20, 45, 76
  recumbent bicycles and, 37
AIDS ride, 207
air molecules, 13
air-oil cartridges, 24
airport transfers, 209
Alabama, 201
Alaska, 263, 271–273
alertness, 98
Allen (hex) wrenches, 72, 73,
    143–144, 147
altimeters, 63
aluminum, 11–13, 151
  frames, 10, 11, 29, 31
  rims, 12–13
  seat posts, 19
  stems, 20
amber-tinted sunglasses, 79

American Diabetes Association, 207
American Lung Association, 207
anabolic steroids, 263
anaerobic zone, 131, 132
animals, 106–108, 220
ankle joint, 83–84
ANSI, 58
antibiotic ointment, 121
antibiotics, 234
Aran Islands, Ireland, 273
argon, 11
Armstrong, Lance, 256, 260
arteriosclerosis, 123
ATM cards, 79
attentiveness, 210
attitudes, 241
Auto-D system, 35
automobiles, 97–106
axles, 96

• *B* •

backcountry rides, 217
balaclavas, 67
balance, 198
bananas, 90, 115
bandages, 121
bar ends, 44–45, 76
basketball, 112, 135
baskets, 33, 61
batteries, 37, 61, 242
bearings
  basic description of, 160–161
  on kids' bikes, 193
  sealed, 26
bells, 61–62

bicycle messengers, 270
Bicycle Museum of American Web
    site, 268
bicycle paths, 109
bicycle tours, 208–209
Bike Ride Online Web site, 257
binder bolts, 22, 97
biomechanics, 72
Blackburn, 61
blood vessels, 58, 122
BMC bikes, 214
BMX bikes, 26, 37
bolt-on tandems, 191–192
"bonking," 116
bottom bracket, 21–22, 40, 42
Boulder, Colorado, 272
bowling, 113
boxing, 113
brain damage, 58
brake(s)
  ABS, 30
  adjusting, 163–174
  basic description of, 20, 164
  cables, 96, 148–149, 166–168
  caliper, 20, 30, 164, 174
  cantilever, 20, 22, 164, 174
  checking, before going on a ride, 96
  levers, 22, 28, 42, 166
  locking up, 89
  long-arm, 20, 27, 32, 164
  on kids' bikes, 193
  pads, 165–166, 168
  problems, fixing common, 164–168
  tandem, 36
  techniques for using, 88–89, 94,
      229, 243
  that squeal, 168
  troubleshooting, 164–166
  V-brakes, 174
brand names, 50–51

brazing, 11
breakaways, 259
Breeze, Joe, 214
Brown, Sheldon, 268
Bruce Gordon (company), 61
budgets, 49–50, 55
bungee cords, 242
bunny hops, 218
buying
  basic description of, 49–56
  at bicycle stores, 53–54
  bike frames, 11–12
  bikes for kids, 192–195
  brand names and, 50–51
  comparing bikes, 52–53
  during the off season, 54
  two-bucks-a-ride rule for, 49–50
  on weekends, 54

• C •

cable(s)
  brake, 96, 148–149, 166–168
  cutters, 145
  derailleur, 154–157
  guidance, 148–149
  housing, 148
  locks, 62
cabs, money for, 79, 147
calculators, 72
California, 23, 201, 214, 272
caliper brakes, 20, 30, 164, 174
calories
  burning, 34, 112
  in specific foods, 115
Camelbak, 64
Campagnolo, Tullio, 158
Campagnolo Company, 21
camping equipment, 242–243
cancellation policies, 209

cancer, 114
Cannondale, 25, 51
cantilever brakes, 20, 22, 164, 174
carbohydrates, 114, 115, 116
carbon fiber, 10–11, 29, 51
cardiovascular fitness, 126
cars, 97–106
cartridge bearings, 160
cause and effect, 199
Central Park, New York City, 271
centrifugal force, 87–88, 197
century rides, 206
chain(s)
  broken, 182–183
  guards, 33, 35
  link fences, 253
  locks, 62
  lube, 146
  removing/replacing wheels and,
    175, 176
  replacing, 160
  ring, 15, 21–22, 27, 32
  rivet tools, 145, 147, 182
  stays, 22, 24
  taking care of, 159–160
  thrown, 182–183
chamois, 66
charity rides, 206–207
checklists
  post-crash, 185
  pre-ride, 96–97
child carriers, 190–191
children
  buying bikes for, 192–195
  as passengers, 190–191
  riding with, 189–202
  teaching, to ride a bike, 195–199
  watching out for, when riding, 107
China, 272
chronic fatigue, 135

city bike(s)
  basic description of, 33–36
  components, 36
  frames, 34–35
  history of, 33
  pedals, 47
  purpose of, 33–34
  wheels, 35–36
climbing hills
  basic description of, 91–94
  on mountain bikes, 227–229
  out-of-the-saddle, 228
  seated, 227–228
clipless pedals, 20, 47, 67–68, 84, 86
clock position, 82
clothing
  basic description of, 65–67
  for bike tours, 241–242
  color of, 78
  for commuting to work, 249–250
  fleece, 66, 242
  foul weather gear, 67
  importance of warm, 77–78
  jerseys, 65–66, 67, 77–78
  for kids, 190–191
  layering, 77–78, 250
  rain shells, 67
  reflective vests, 60
  shorts, 28, 66–67, 120, 242
  tights, 66, 78
club rides, 205–206
CO2 tire inflators, 65
codependency, 203
cogs, 15
Colorado, 272, 273
commissions, on sales, 54
common cold, 114, 135
commuting, with your bike, 245–254
compass, 242

components
  basic description of, 19–22
  city bike, 36
  hybrid bike, 32–33
  manufacturers of, 51
  mountain bike, 27
  road bike, 30
  shopping for, 52, 53
  weight of, 52
composite materials, 10, 29
compression, 122
cone wrenches, 146
Connecticut, 201
connective tissues, 135
contact, points of, 44–45
conventional stems, 74–75
cool downs, 131, 132
cornering technique, 87–88, 243
courtesy, 102–103
crank
  arm, 21
  extractors, 146
  set, 15, 21, 40, 154
credit cards, 79
criterium races, 258
cross-country
  racing, 262
  rides, 215–216
  skiing, 112, 135
cruiser bikes, 33, 44–45
CSA Auto Bike, 35
Cunningham, Charlie, 213
curbs, 35
custom-made bikes, 43
cycle computers, 63
cyclecross bikes, 31, 135, 214
cycling clubs, 205–206
cycling gloves, 66, 67, 91
cyclometers, 63, 126, 127

• *D* •

decisiveness, 98
deer ticks, 234

DEET, 234
Delaware, 201
Department of Transportation, 200
derailleur(s)
  basic description of, 15, 22
  cables, 154–157
  bent, 183–184
  fixing, 155–157
  parts of, 154–155
  shifters and, 20
  upgraded, 21, 51
descent techniques, 94, 229–230
diabetes, 114, 123
diaries, training, 126, 127
doctors, 118
dogs, 106–108. *See also* animals
Donovan, Leigh, 216, 229, 230
down tube, 8, 22
downhill
  bikes, 26
  racing, 262
  rides, 216–217, 229–230
drafting, 259
drivetrain. *See also* gears
  basic description of, 14–16, 153–162
  checking, after a crash, 185
  city bike, 35
drop handlebars, 20, 28, 45
dropouts, 96, 174
drug tests, 263
dual slalom racing, 263
duct tape, 151, 179, 242
Dunlap, Alison, 218, 226, 227
Durango, Colorado, 273

• *E* •

echelons, 211
ecology, 37
electric bikes, 37
electrolytes, 117
elevation, 122
emergency supplies, 233

encouragement, 196
endurance, 128–129
energy drinks, 64
English races, 33
enlightenment, 107–109
EPO hormone, 263
erectile dysfunction, 123
ESPN, 263
etiquette, cycling, 209–210
exercise, 112–114. *See also* fitness
expansion joints, 106
experimentation, 196
Exploratorium Web site, 267
eyelets, brazed-on, 35

• *F* •

fallbacks, 93–94
fantasy, 200
FAQs (Frequently Asked Questions), 269
Farmer, David, 218
fashion, 18
Fat Chance mountain bikes, 63
FDA (Food and Drug Administration), 234
feet, proper alignment of, 83–84
fenders, 33, 35, 64, 247
fiberglass, 10
fig bars, 115
fighter jets, 10
Fisher, Gary, 214
fitness. *See also* training
  basic description of, 111–124
  losing weight and, 113–114
  for mountain bike riding, 218
  programs, 126–128
fitting bicycles
  basic description of, 39–48
  cycling injuries and, 119–120, 123
  inseam measurements for, 39–40,
    41, 72
  saddle position and, 42–43, 72–77,
    119–120, 123
  sizing kids' bikes, 195

flashlights, 242
flat bars, 20
fleece clothing, 66, 242
flexibility, 237, 250
Florida, 201
foam padding, 46
food, 114–116
  after rides, 116
  before rides, 113–114
  during rides, 115–116
fork(s), 8, 22
  checking, after a crash, 185
  clearance around, 24
  crown, 97
  overhauling, 25
  suspension, 24–25, 175, 225
foul weather gear, 67
frame(s)
  angles, 8–9, 30, 35, 42, 52
  basic description of, 8–9
  checking, after a crash, 185
  choosing, 12, 40–41
  city bike, 34–35
  custom, 43
  determining the quality of, 12
  failures, 97
  fitting, 40–41, 72–77
  geometry, 8–9, 30, 35, 42, 52
  hybrid bike, 31–32
  mountain bike, 24–26
  reinforcement of, with lugs, 9
  road bike, 27, 29
  sizes, 40–41
  weight of, 52–53
frame pumps, 147
France, 256
freeride bikes, 26
freewheel(s), 15, 21, 154
  basic description of, 158
  cassette removers, 146
  dished wheels and, 181
  removing/replacing wheels and,
    175, 176

French Alps, 272
Freon, 62
friction shifting, 30
Furtado, Juli, 218

• G •

garage sales, 34
garbage bags, 242
gardening, 113, 135
Gatorade, 263
gauze, 121
gear(s). *See also* drivetrain
  history of, 158
  how they work, 154–155
  ratios, 21
  selecting the right, 82, 84–85, 87, 91–94
  ultra-low, 30
gel saddle pads, 65
genetics, 132
Georgia, 201
Giove, Missy, 260
girl's bicycles, 42
Giro d'Italia (Tour of Italy), 257
gloves, 66, 67, 91
goals, setting, 93, 196, 206
Goldilocks test, 55
golf, 113
grease, 146
Grip Shift shifting system, 21
ground clearance, 24
guarantees, 53

• H •

halogen lights, 61
hamstring stretches, 118
hand positions, 44–45
hand signals, 210. *See also* signals
handlebar(s)
  adjusting, 74–77
  bags, 239

basic description of, 20
checking, after a crash, 185
checking, before going on a ride, 97
drop, 20, 28, 45
flat-bar, 44
grips, 33
mountain bike, 26
-mounted baskets, 61
-mounted lights, 60–61
positioning, 76, 120
road bike, 27
selecting, 44–45
tandem, 36
tilt, 76
turning techniques and, 87–88
upper body position and, 91
head injuries, 58
head tube, 8, 22, 185
headsets, 20, 75
headwinds, 85, 130
health insurance, 79
heart disease, 123
heart rate(s)
  maximum (MHR), 128, 130–132
  monitors, 126, 127, 128
  resting, 135
helmet(s)
  basic description of, 57–58
  covers, 67
  for kids, 192, 194, 200, 201
  laws, 201
  -mounted lights, 60–61
  shopping for, 58–59
  sizing, 58–59
  straps, 59
Hemingway, Ernest, 235
hex (Allen) wrenches, 72, 73,
    143–144, 147
high blood pressure, 123
hill climbing
  basic description of, 91–94
  on mountain bikes, 227–229

out-of-the-saddle, 228
seated, 227–228
Hinault, Bernard, 258
hormones, 263
horns, 61–62, 194
horseback riders, 220
hubs, 13, 21–22
  city bike, 34
  internally geared, 159
  for kids' bikes, 193
  three-speed, 34
humor, 241
hybrid bike(s)
  basic description of, 30–33
  components, 32–33
  frames, 31–32, 40
  handlebars for, 45
  history of, 31
hydration, 64–65, 116–117. *See also*
  water

• I •

IBMA (International Mountain Bicycling
  Association), 219, 221, 269
ibuprofen, 242
ice, 122
Iditabike, 263
Iditarod sled dog race, 263
impotence, 122–123
index shifting, 30
Indurain, Miguel, 258, 260
inert gases, 11
inflammation, treating, 122
injuries
  acute injuries, 117, 121–122
  knee injuries, 73, 119–120
  overuse injuries, 117–119
  preventing, 117–122
  repetitive stress injuries, 91
  wrist injuries, 91, 120

inner tubes, 55, 147, 170–171, 177–179
inseam measurements, 39–40, 41, 72
insect repellant, 234
insurance, 79, 209
International Bicycle Fund, 270
International Federation of Bicycle
  Messenger Associations Web
  site, 270
International Police Mountain Bike
  Association, 270
Ireland, 273
Italy, 21, 256, 257

• J •

Japan, 21, 51, 261
jerseys, 65–66, 67, 77–78
Johnson, Steve, 118, 121–122, 132, 134
jumping rope, 113

• K •

keirin races, 261
Kelly, Charlie, 214
Kevlar, 10
kickstands, 35, 65
kids
  buying bikes for, 192–195
  as passengers, 190–191
  riding with, 189–201
  teaching, to ride a bike, 195–199
  watching out for, when riding, 107
knee(s)
  injuries, 73, 119–120
  position of, over the pedal, 73–74, 75
  protecting, with tights, 78, 121
Kneivel, Evel, 216
knobs, 26–27
Kryptonite locks, 62. *See also* locks

• L •

lactic acid, 123, 131
layering, 77–78, 250
League of American Bicyclists Web
    site, 270
LED-based lights, 60
left-hand turns, 101–102
leg(s). *See also* knees
    shock absorption and, 224–225
    warmers, 78, 121
LeMond, Greg, 45, 258, 260
lifetime maintenance packages, 54
lightheadedness, 116
lights, 60–61
limit screws, 156–157
locks, 34, 62–63, 194, 251–253
lower back, 28
LSD (long, steady distance) rides,
    129–134
lubrication, 149, 167
lugs, 9
lungs, 131
Lycra gloves, 67. *See also* gloves
Lyme disease, 234

• M •

magazines, cycling, 52, 209
"magical thinking," 236–237
marathon runners, 117
Marin County (California), 23, 214, 272
Maryland, 201
Massachusetts, 201
massage, 123, 134
matches, 242
Matthes, Ruthie, 218, 267
mechanical engineering, 8
mechanics, how to think like, 179
Merckx, Eddy, 66, 125, 216, 258, 260
mesh gloves, 67. *See also* gloves

metabolism, 114
metal grates, 106
metric
    hex wrenches, 143–144
    open-end wrenches, 144
    socket sets, 144
MHR (maximum heart rate), 128,
    130–132
microprocessors, 63
mirrors, 64
money, bringing along, 147
Morrissey, Steve, 165, 179
motorcycles, 261
mountain bike(s)
    basic description of, 22–27, 213–222
    components, 11, 27
    cost of, 24–25
    frames, 24–25, 40
    history of, 23, 214
    lights, 60–61
    racing, 261–263
    riding techniques, 223–234
    saddles, 46
    seat height and, 73
    seat posts, 19, 73
    shoes, 68
    shorts, 66
    specialized, 26
    stems, 20
    tires, 13, 26–27, 169, 170, 238
    weight of, 51
    wheels, 13, 26–27
MS-150 rides, 207
MTB Review Web site, 268
Murphy's Law, 179
muscles
    buildup of lactic acid in, 123, 131
    fast-twitch/slow-twitch, 132
    stretching, 118

• N •

nausea, 116
neck pain, 120
needle and thread, 242
New Hampshire, 273
New Jersey, 201, 218–219
New York, 201, 271
newsgroups, 269
Newton, Isaac, 13
"no hands" riding, 90
noises, strange, 161, 168
non-sealed bearings, 160–161
Nye, Bill, 245, 267

• O •

obstacles, overcoming, 231
odometer, 29
off season
  buying a bike during, 54
  training during, 135–37
Olympics, 132, 170, 257, 261, 263
Oregon, 201
orthotics, 110
osteoporosis, 114
overtraining, 117–119, 135
overuse injuries, 117–119
oxygen consumption, 131

• P •

pacelines, riding in, 211
paint schemes, 33
Palmer, Shaun, 216, 260
panic, 233
panniers, 61, 239–240
Paris-Roubaix race, 257
parking
  meters, 252, 253
  your bike, 251–252
patellar/femoral pain, 119

pavement, slippery, 104–106
pedal(s). *See also* pedaling
  alignment of the feet over, 83–84, 119
  basic description of, 20
  city bike, 33
  clipless, 20, 47, 67–68, 84, 86
  rubber, 33
  selecting, 46–47
  wrenches, 146
pedaling. *See also* pedals
  basic description of, 82–87
  cadence, 84–87, 92–93, 119, 130
  drivetrain and, 15
  "effortless," 84
  frame fit and, 42–43
  out-of-the-saddle, 93
  positions, 82–87, 93
pedestrians, 107
peloton, 257, 259
Pennsylvania, 201
perineum, 122
peripheral vision, 199
Pezzo, Paola, 260
Pfeiffer, Michelle, 153
phone calls, 79
physics, 8, 86
pillowcases, 243
pliers, 144
poison ivy, 234
poison oak, 234
police whistle, 62
polymer bumpers, 24
polypropylene, 242
posture, 9, 31, 82–87, 198
potholes, 35, 104–105, 181
power
  building, 129–131, 133–134
  intervals, 130–131
PowerBars, 90, 115, 165, 179, 263
practice, 226–227
preparedness, 98, 238–239

pre-ride checklists, 96–97
Presta valves, 177
price/weight equation, 51–52
primes, 258
product managers, 51
progress, charting your, 134
psi (pounds per square inch), 169
psychology, 236–237
pulleys, 154–155
pulse, taking your, 126
pumps, 144–145, 147, 178
pursuit racing, 261

• *Q* •

quadricep stretches, 118
quick-release mechanisms, 22, 96,
     174, 176
quill, 75

• *R* •

racing
  basic description of, 29, 255–264
  cross-country racing, 215–216
  mountain bike racing, 261–263
  pursuit racing, 261
  road racing, 256–257
  single-day races, 256–257
  six-day races, 261
  sprint racing, 258–260
  stage racing, 257–258
  track racing, 258–261
racks, 33, 35, 61
rain shells, 67
Raleigh Sport, 34
range-of-motion exercises, 122
rattrap pedals, 46–47
realism, 236–237
rear suspension, 25
rec.bicycle newsgroups, 269

rechargeable batteries, 61
recovery, 134–135
recumbent bicycles, 37, 123
red blood cells, 263
reflective vests, 60
reflectors, on pedals, 46
repair
  shops, 53
  stands, 146
repetitive stress injuries, 91
rescuers, 233
resolutions, 246
responsibility, 194
resting
  heart rate, 135
  metabolism, 114
return policies, 53
Rhode Island, 201
RICE regime, 121, 122
"righty tighty" rule, 148
rims, 12–14. *See also* wheels
  basic description of, 22
  brakes and, 165, 166–167
riser bars, 20
road(s)
  rash, 121
  slippery, 104–106
road bike(s)
  basic description of, 27–30
  components, 30
  drop bars for, 20
  frame sizes for, 40
  history of, 28
  shoes, 68
  specialized, 29
  tires, 169
road racing, 256–257. *See also* racing
rollers, 137–138
rolling resistance, 14
rpm (revolutions per minute), 85, 130
rubber-treaded pedals, 47

rules
  for cycling etiquette, 210
  for riding on trails, 219–220
  for tightening/loosening bolts, 148
running, 107, 112, 117, 132

• S •

saddle(s)
  bags, 239
  basic description of, 19
  city bike, 33
  cycling injuries and, 120
  distribution of weight on, 43
  gel pads for, 65
  on kids' bikes, 193
  position/height, 42–43, 72–77,
      119–120, 123
  selecting, 46, 65, 123
safety. *See also* helmets
  basic description of, 95–110
  checking wheels, 176
  checklists, 96–97
  issues for kids, 189–202
  on mountain bike trails, 232–234
  pedals and, 46–47
  tips for riding in traffic, 97–106
sag wagons, 208
salespersons, 53–54
Schuler, Tom, 253
Schwinn, 23, 28, 51, 214
Science of Cycling Web site, 267
screwdrivers, 143
sealants, 179
search and rescue teams, 233
seat binder bolt, 42
seat post(s), 22, 42
  adjusting, 72–73
  basic description of, 19
  height mark, 73
  suspension, 33
  tandem, 36

seat tube, 8, 22, 40
seatstay, 22, 24
sensors, 63
sewer grates, 105
shake test, for helmets, 59
Sheldon Brown Web site, 268
shifters, 20, 30, 32, 35, 158
Shimano, 21, 35, 51
shock absorption, 35, 224–225
shoes, 28, 67–68, 119
shopping
  basic description of, 49–56
  at bicycle stores, 53–54
  bike frames, 11–12
  bikes for kids, 192–195
  brand names and, 50–51
  comparing bikes, 52–53
  during the off season, 54
  two-bucks-a-ride rule for, 49–50
  on weekends, 54
shorts, 28, 66–67, 120, 242
signals, 101–102, 109, 210
signposts, 253
simplicity, 247
Simpson, Tommy, 263
single-day races, 256–257
single-speed mountain bikes, 26
six-day races, 261
sizing bicycles
  basic description of, 39–48
  cycling injuries and, 119–120, 123
  frame size and, 31, 24, 40
  inseam measurements for, 39–40,
      41, 72
  saddle position and, 42–43, 72–77,
      119–120, 123
  sizing kids' bikes, 195
  standover clearance and, 31, 24, 40
skating, in-line, 107, 113
ski bindings, 67
slalom racing, 263

sleeping, 113
slippery pavement, 104–106
Snell Memorial Foundation, 58
social cycling
  basic description of, 203–212
  through bicycling vacations, 208–209
  through charity rides, 206–207
  through cycling clubs, 205–206
socket sets, 144
Soviet Union, 10
space blankets, 233
Specialized, 33, 51
speed, 216–217, 259
  building, through training, 129, 131–132
  intervals, 131–132
  limits, 100
  tracking, 63, 194
speedometers, 194
spinning, 85–87, 93
spokes, 13, 22, 171–172, 180–181
sponges, 243
Spring Classics, 256–257
sprint racing, 258–260
sprinting, 132, 257–260
stage racing, 257–258
stainless steel, 13
standover clearance, 31, 24, 40
stationary bikes, 72, 85, 86, 136
steel, 9, 11, 29, 31
stems 20, 74–76
steroids, 263
stickers, 194
streamers, 194
stretching, 118, 119, 135
strollers, bike-mounted, 191–192
studio cycling bikes, 138
styrofoam shells, for helmets, 59
sunglasses, 66, 78–79
sunscreen, 79, 242
survival strategies, 109

suspension
  forks, 24–25, 175, 225
  seatposts, 36
sweat, 250–251
swelling, treating, 122
swimming, 112, 128
Swiss Army knife, 242
synergy, 126

• *T* •

tacoed wheels, 13
tail winds, 85
tailor-made bikes, 43
Taiwan, 21, 51
tandems, 36, 191–192
tax deductions, 207
taxis, carrying money for, 79, 147
Taylor, Major, 260
team spirit, 259
telephone numbers, 79
television, watching, 113
Tennessee, 201
tennis, 113, 257
tent stakes, 242
Terry, Georgena, 42
test rides, 55–56
third hands, 146
threadless stem systems, 75, 76
thumb shifters, 22
tick-borne diseases, 234
tights, 66, 78
TIG-welded frames, 11, 217
time trials, 45, 257
tire(s). *See also* rims; wheels
  basic description of, 13–14, 169–171
  for bike tours, 238–239
  fixing flat, 177–179
  levers, 145, 178
  mountain bike, 13, 26–27, 169, 170, 238

patch kits, 145
pressure, 14, 96–97, 147, 169–171, 178
road bike, 27, 30
tandem, 36
titanium, 10–11, 29, 51
toe clips, 47, 86
Tomac, John, 218
tool(s), 141–152, 233
    Allen (hex) wrenches, 72, 73,
        143–144, 147
    basic tool chest, 142–146
    for bike tours, 242
    chain rivet tools, 145, 147, 182
    cone wrenches, 146
    for kids' bikes, 194
    kits, 65, 146–148, 242
    open-end wrenches, 144
    pedal wrenches, 146
    for on the road, 146–148
    rules for using, 150–151
    screwdrivers, 143
    socket sets, 144
    third hands, 146
top tube, 8, 22
    girl's bicycles and, 42
    standover clearance and, 40, 42
Tour de Cure, 207
Tour de France, 28, 45, 66, 117, 253
    drug tests during, 263
    entering, 255
    importance of, 256
    mountain passes in, 272
    as a stage race, 257
touring
    basic description of, 29, 235–244
    bike handling techniques for, 243–244
    gear for, 238–240
    packing for, 241–243
    partners, 239–240
    preparing for, 236–239

track bikes, 29, 63, 170
track racing, 258–261
track stands, 258
traction, 13, 169
traffic, 97–106
    riding with kids in, 201
    school quiz, 99–100
trail(s)
    access, 218–221
    maintenance, 220–221
    safety, guide to, 232–234
trailers, for kids, 191–192
train tracks, 105
training. *See also* fitness
    basic description of, 125–138
    building blocks, 128–129
    charting your progress, 134
    diaries, 126, 127
    for mountain bike riding, 218
    off season, 135–37
    rides, three kinds of, 129–132
    stands, 136
    wheels, 194–195
    workout plans, 132–135
Transportation, Department of, 200
Transportation Alternatives Web
        site, 269
travel agents, 236
treadmill stress tests, 128
Trek, 51
triangulation, principle of, 8, 42
triathlons, 29, 45
TriFlo, 149
trigonometry, 8
trucks, 104. *See also* automobiles
truth, race of, 257
tubing, weight of, 51
tunnel vision, 199
turn signals, 101–102
turning technique, 87–88

twist shifters, 27
24-hour races, 263
two-bucks-a-ride rule, 49–50
two-speed bikes, 158

• U •

U-locks, 62–63
upper body position, 91
upswept handlebars, 44–45
urologists, 122
USA Cycling, 118, 121–122, 134, 165
Utah, 271
utility poles, 253

• V •

vacations, 208–209
vaccines, 234
velodromes, 258
Vuelta d'Espana (Tour of Spain), 257

• W •

walking, 112, 135, 246
warm-ups, 118
warning devices, 61–62
water
  bottle cages, 64
  consumption, 64–65, 116–117
  crossings, 230–231
  filtration systems, 242
  -proof rain shells, 67
  purification tablets, 242
Web sites, 267–270
weekends, buying a bike on, 54
weight
  of bikes, 51–52
  of components, 51
  body, 43–44, 113–114, 169
  of frames, 51
  of wheels, 51

welding, 11, 193, 217
West Virginia, 201
wet surfaces, 221
wheel(s). *See also* rims
  24-inch, 42
  aligning, 174
  basic description of, 12–14
  checking, after a crash, 185–186
  checking, before going on a ride, 96
  city bike, 35–36
  composite, 29
  dished, 171
  hybrid bike, 31
  mountain bike, 26–27
  overlapping, 210
  removing/replacing, 173–176
  road bike, 30
  spokes, 13, 22, 171–172, 180–181
  "tacoed," 184–185
  trueness of, 90, 171–172, 185
  weight of, 52
wheelies, 218, 231–232
White Mountains, 273
Whitehead, Cindy, 227, 231
wind-chill factor, 77
Winter X-Games, 263
wool, 242
work, riding to, 245–254
workout plans, 132–135
World Championships, 257
wrenches, 143–144, 146–148
wrist injuries, 91, 120

• X •

X-Games, 26, 263
xylocain ointment, 122

• Y •

Yellow Pages, 53
yielding, 109

• Z •

Zen, 17, 80, 81, 117, 225
zip ties, 151, 242
Ziploc bags, 242

Notes

YOUR ONLINE RESOURCE

WWW.DUMMIES.COM

Discover *Dummies*™ Online!

The *Dummies* Web Site is your fun and friendly online resource for the latest information about *...For Dummies*® books on all your favorite topics. From cars to computers, wine to Windows, and investing to the Internet, we've got a shelf full of *...For Dummies* books waiting for you!

Ten Fun and Useful Things You Can Do at www.dummies.com

1. Register this book and win!
2. Find and buy the *...For Dummies* books you want online.
3. Get ten great *Dummies Tips*™ every week.
4. Chat with your favorite *...For Dummies* authors.
5. Subscribe free to *The Dummies Dispatch*™ newsletter.
6. Enter our sweepstakes and win cool stuff.
7. Send a free cartoon postcard to a friend.
8. Download free software.
9. Sample a book before you buy.
10. Talk to us. Make comments, ask questions, and get answers!

Jump online to these ten fun and useful things at
http://www.dummies.com/10useful

SURF THE NET

WWW.DUMMIES.COM

For other technology titles from IDG Books Worldwide, go to
www.idgbooks.com

Not online yet? It's easy to get started with *The Internet For Dummies*®, 5th Edition, or *Dummies 101*®: *The Internet For Windows*® *98*, available at local retailers everywhere.

IDG BOOKS WORLDWIDE

Find other *...For Dummies* books on these topics:

Business • Careers • Databases • Food & Beverages • Games • Gardening • Graphics • Hardware
Health & Fitness • Internet and the World Wide Web • Networking • Office Suites
Operating Systems • Personal Finance • Pets • Programming • Recreation • Sports
Spreadsheets • Teacher Resources • Test Prep • Word Processing

IDG BOOKS WORLDWIDE
BOOK REGISTRATION

We want to hear from you!

Register This Book and Win!

Visit **http://my2cents.dummies.com** to register this book and tell us how you liked it!

- ✔ Get entered in our monthly prize giveaway.

- ✔ Give us feedback about this book — tell us what you like best, what you like least, or maybe what you'd like to ask the author and us to change!

- ✔ Let us know any other ...*For Dummies*® topics that interest you.

Your feedback helps us determine what books to publish, tells us what coverage to add as we revise our books, and lets us know whether we're meeting your needs as a ...*For Dummies* reader. You're our most valuable resource, and what you have to say is important to us!

Not on the Web yet? It's easy to get started with *Dummies 101*®*: The Internet For Windows*® *98* or *The Internet For Dummies*®, 5th Edition, at local retailers everywhere.

Or let us know what you think by sending us a letter at the following address:

...*For Dummies* Book Registration
Dummies Press
7260 Shadeland Station, Suite 100
Indianapolis, IN 46256-3917
Fax 317-596-5498

BESTSELLING BOOK SERIES